D1794501

New Handbook of Basic Writing Skills

Harcourt College Publishers

Where Learning Comes to Life

TECHNOLOGY

Technology is changing the learning experience, by increasing the power of your textbook and other learning materials; by allowing you to access more information, more quickly; and by bringing a wider array of choices in your course and content information sources.

Harcourt College Publishers has developed the most comprehensive Web sites, e-books, and electronic learning materials on the market to help you use technology to achieve your goals.

PARTNERS IN LEARNING

Harcourt partners with other companies to make technology work for you and to supply the learning resources you want and need. More importantly, Harcourt and its partners provide avenues to help you reduce your research time of numerous information sources.

Harcourt College Publishers and its partners offer increased opportunities to enhance your learning resources and address your learning style. With quick access to chapter-specific Web sites and e-books . . . from interactive study materials to quizzing, testing, and career advice . . . Harcourt and its partners bring learning to life.

Harcourt's partnership with Digital:Convergence™ brings :CRQ™ technology and the :CueCat™ reader to you and allows Harcourt to provide you with a complete and dynamic list of resources designed to help you achieve your learning goals. You can download the free :CRQ software from www.crq.com. Visit any of the 7,100 RadioShack stores nationwide to obtain a free :CueCat reader. Just swipe the cue with the :CueCat reader to view a list of Harcourt's partners and Harcourt's print and electronic learning solutions.

http://www.harcourtcollege.com/partners

FIFTH EDITION

New Handbook of Basic Writing Skills

Cora L. Robey

Cheryl K. Jackson

Carolyn M. Melchor

Helen M. Maloney

Tidewater Community College
Portsmouth Campus

Harcourt College Publishers

Fort Worth   Philadelphia   San Diego   New York   Orlando   Austin   San Antonio
Toronto   Montreal   London   Sydney   Tokyo

Publisher	Earl McPeek
Acquisitions Editor	Stephen Dalphin
Marketing Strategist	Katrina Byrd
Project Manager	Angela Williams Urquhart

ISBN: 0-15-507071-1

Library of Congress Catalog Card Number: 2001024692

Address for Domestic Orders
Harcourt College Publishers
6277 Sea Harbor Drive, Orlando, FL 32887-6777
800-782-4479

Address for International Orders
International Customer Service
Harcourt College Publishers
6277 Sea Harbor Drive, Orlando, FL 32887-6777
407-345-3800
(fax) 407-345-4060
(e-mail) hbintl@harcourt.com

Address for Editorial Correspondence
Harcourt College Publishers
301 Commerce Street, Suite 3700, Fort Worth, TX 76102

Web Site Address
http://www.harcourtcollege.com

Harcourt College Publishers will provide complimentary supplements or supplement packages to those adopters qualified under our adoption policy. Please contact your sales representative to learn how you qualify. If as an adopter or potential user you receive supplements you do not need, please return them to your sales representative or send them to:
Attn: Returns Department, Troy Warehouse, 465 South Lincoln Drive, Troy, MO 63379.

Printed in the United States of America

1 2 3 4 5 6 7 8 9 0   0 1 6   9 8 7 6 5 4 3 2 1

Harcourt College Publishers

TO THE INSTRUCTOR

The Handbook of Basic Writing Skills was originally written in response to a need for a reference and writing aid that could be readily understood by all students, regardless of their backgrounds in English. *The New Handbook of Basic Writing Skills,* Fifth Edition, is like the earlier editions in that it uses clear and simple language in its examples and explanations and contains an abundance of exercises. It offers assistance in all the areas covered by the traditional handbooks and gives special emphasis to the problems that trouble beginning writers—particularly fragments, run-together sentences, subject–verb agreement, noun and verb endings, possessive forms, and sentence logic. It helps the student through each step from constructing a sentence to organizing and writing a full-length paper. It also offers assistance in writing a mini-research paper.

There are twenty-eight chapters in *The New Handbook of Basic Writing Skills.* You can refer students to the appropriate section of the *Handbook* for virtually any error found in a student paper. The first eight chapters cover such basic writing concerns as fragments, run-together sentences, agreement, and verbs; Chapters 9–12 address other important elements of sentence structure. Chapters 13–19 cover punctuation, focusing on questions inexperienced writers are most likely to ask. Chapters 20–23 represent a simple approach to diction. (Chapter 20 offers help on using the dictionary for usage and spelling.) Chapters 24–26 deal with the writing process and offer specific advice on writing paragraphs and full-length papers. (You might want to use these chapters for beginning the teaching of rhetoric.) Chapter 26 includes basic instructions and outlines, as well as sample papers for many types of assignments. Chapter 27 helps the student who needs to use some outside sources in writing a mini-research paper; it also has a section on business writing. Chapter 28, along with an ESL index, is a handy reference for students for whom English is a second language.

The exercises in the *Handbook* are aimed particularly at areas in which students need practice. Not all exercises will be helpful to all students, of course, so you might choose to use some exercises as general class exercises while assigning certain others—especially in Chapters 1–8—to students with particular writing problems, on an individual basis. The examples used in the explanations and in the exercises are mainly student sentences; they are, therefore, interesting to the students and are close to the style students use in their own writing.

Although *The New Handbook of Basic Writing Skills* has the strengths of the earlier editions, it is intended to be even more responsive to the needs of students. The Fifth Edition includes the following features:

1. Chapters 1, 2, and 3 focus on sentence completion. Chapter 1 stresses sentence identification, Chapter 2 helps students recognize and eliminate fragments, and Chapter 3 deals with run-together sentences, including comma splices. Several exercises have been added to these chapters to give students more practice in sentence completion.
2. Chapter 12 includes more suggestions and practice combining sentences.
3. The rhetoric section now contains more details on the stages of the writing process. There are organizational charts and strategies, more emphasis on prewriting, and detailed guidelines for editing and proofreading in Chapter 24.
4. Chapter 25 emphasizes paragraph unity, coherence and development and offers patterns and models.
5. Chapter 26 has charts showing organizational similarities between paragraphs and full-length essays and has added an improved section on writing introductions and conclusions.

6. Chapter 27 now has information on the use of the Internet for on-line research and contains more on note-taking and avoiding plagiarism in the preparation of a mini research paper.

7. The business writing section of Chapter 27 reflects current trends and includes advancements and expectations in technology and a new e-mail section.

8. Chapter 28 is a new addition for writers for whom English is a second language. There is also an ESL index, which lists all sections of the handbook that may be of particular help to ESL students.

Throughout the book, such labels as RIGHT and WRONG identify example sentences. These labels are designed to help students recognize Standard American English. We are not commenting in any way on the acceptability of the language that students use in their own informal speech.

An Instructor's Manual is also available and includes diagnostic tests and answers to all exercises in the *Handbook*.

Special thanks go to the many people who helped us in the preparation of the manuscript for the fifth edition. We would like to thank our colleagues Priscilla Haley and Orlando Stone at Tidewater Community College, Portsmouth Campus, who suggested specific improvements for this edition, and the staff at Harcourt College Publishers: Stephen Dalphin and Angela Urquhart. We would also like to thank the reviewers, who read and helped improve the manuscript.

Cora L. Robey
Cheryl K. Jackson
Carolyn M. Melchor
Helen M. Maloney

TO THE STUDENT

This handbook is designed to help you express your ideas correctly and clearly in writing. When you talk with your friends, you may use informal language or even leave out words and still be understood; but when you write for college classes or in your work, you need to be careful in your selection and use of words.

Since what you say and the way you say it must be understood by both you and the person who reads what you have written, certain forms have been accepted as usual, or standard, ways to write what you want to write. In this book you will see examples with labels such as RIGHT and WRONG to help you recognize and use these standard forms.

Each section of the book covers a different area of writing skills. Your instructor will usually let you know, by chapter number, what chapters you need to refer to in order to correct errors in your papers. You do not have to start at the beginning of the book unless directed to do so. By doing the exercises in each chapter, you will have a chance to practice what you have learned.

If you are confused about how to organize your paper, which form of a word to use, or how to say clearly what you mean to say, you may want to look at a particular chapter for help while you are writing a paper. Chapters 1–23 help you construct sentences and choose correct words. Chapters 24–27 tell how to plan, write, revise, and edit your paragraphs and full-length papers, with and without outside sources, and to master the basics of acceptable business writing. Chapter 28 may be of help if English is your second language.

Learn to use this handbook both as a reference book while you are writing and to correct your finished work. Let it help you prevent errors as you fulfill your writing assignments.

Brief Contents

Contents

New Handbook
of Basic
Writing Skills

Chapter 1

SENTENCE MAKEUP

___

Review some basic facts about sentences.

___

1*a*
What is a sentence?

You probably think about a sentence in one of five ways. Let us look at these ways one by one.

1*a*-1
In appearance, a sentence is a group of words beginning with a capital letter and ending with a period, a question mark, or an exclamation point.

The most common type of sentence makes a statement. It begins with a capital letter and ends with a period.

> Some mothers never learn from experience.
> The Beatles changed the course of modern music.

Sometimes a sentence asks a question. It begins with a capital letter and ends with a question mark.

> Do mothers ever learn from experience?
> Did the Beatles change the course of modern music?

A sentence showing strong feeling or surprise begins with a capital letter and ends with an exclamation point.

> It's a miracle!
> Show me a 1964 Oldsmobile, and I'll show you a great car!

A command begins with a capital letter and ends with either a period or an exclamation point.

> Show me a 1964 Oldsmobile, please.
> Hold your horses!

1a-2
A sentence contains a subject and a verb.

Throughout this book we will be using these two words: *subject* and *verb*.

1. The *subject* of the sentence is the who or what word
    the who (or person) doing something
    or the what (or thing) that is happening.

    A *simple subject* is one word.

    WHO WORD   Lily listens to others.
    WHAT WORD   My garage is always littered with hubcaps.

    A subject may also have two or more words, joined by *and*, *but*, *or*, or *nor*.

    > Fathers and sons frequently don't get along.

A subject with some words that describe or identify it can be called a *complete subject*.

> My uncle Juan has eaten too much lunch.
> Some of my money is gone.

2. The *verb* tells what the subject is doing or what is happening to the subject.

    A subject may have a one-word verb.

    > Few domestic geese fly.

A subject may also have a linking verb like *is*, *are*, *look*, *seem*, *feel*, or *taste*. A linking verb tells about the condition or location of the subject.

Sarah <u>looks</u> comfortable.

The hammer <u>is</u> in my toolbox.

A subject may have a verb of more than one word.

She <u>is waiting</u> patiently.

A subject may have more than one verb.

Alice just <u>sits</u> and <u>reads</u> after dinner.

There are usually more words than a subject and a verb in a sentence, but the subject and verb are the only two words necessary to make a sentence.

SENTENCE   Frank <u>cried</u>.

SENTENCE   After many days of waiting and wondering about Al Gore's choice for vice president, <u>we</u> finally <u>heard</u> the name Joe Lieberman.

1a-3
A sentence is made up of words that we call parts of speech.

Listed below are the most common parts of speech:

NOUN: the name of a person, place, thing, or idea

<u>Maria</u> has a <u>bloodhound</u> guarding her <u>castle</u> in bad <u>weather</u>.
The noisy <u>crowd</u> in the <u>park</u> demanded <u>justice</u>.

PRONOUN: a word that takes the place of a noun

(the lotion)   (the people's)
<u>I</u> use hand lotion because <u>it</u> is good for people <u>whose</u> hands are red.

VERB: a word that expresses action or state of being

ACTION VERBS   BEING VERBS
run, sit, stood, listened, repeats   is, are, was, were, will be, has been

The verb tells what the subject is doing.

(action)   (state of being)
When Helen <u>works</u>, she <u>is</u> always happy.

ADJECTIVE: a word that describes a noun or pronoun

> As a *happy* child, I enjoyed washing *dirty* dishes. *Crazy* me!

The article (*a, an,* or *the*) is a type of adjective since it comes before and describes or limits a noun.

> A carrot and *an* apple are sitting on *the* table.

ADVERB: a word that describes a verb, an adjective, or another adverb

> Millicent dresses *elegantly*, but her *radiantly* beautiful sister dresses *very conservatively*.

An adverb tells how, when, or where.

> (how) (when)   (where)
> José dances *divinely, often,* and *everywhere*.

More detailed definitions of adjectives and adverbs are in Chapter 4.

PREPOSITION: a word generally used to show how a noun or pronoun is related to another word in the sentence

COMMON PREPOSITIONS

about	as	during	near	through
above	at	except	of	throughout
across	before	for	on	to
after	behind	from	out	toward
against	below	in	outside	under
along	between	inside	over	up
among	by	into	since	upon
around	down	like	though	with
				without

> My brother lives *with* me *on* Hennepin Avenue *in* Minneapolis.

CONJUNCTION: a word used to connect words or parts of sentences.

1. *Coordinating conjunctions (and, but, or, nor, for, so, yet)* join words, clauses, or other groups of words.

    > You *or* I will visit Al now *and* then.

2. *Subordinating conjunctions* join clauses (groups of words containing subjects and verbs) to make one idea dependent on another.

COMMON SUBORDINATING CONJUNCTIONS

after	as though	since	when
although	because	though	whenever
as	before	unless	while
as of	if	until	

I will see you *when* and *if* you arrive.
Jane rested *because* she was tired.

INTERJECTION: a word that shows emotion

Oh! What a wonderful surprise!

EXERCISE 1

For every underlined word in the following paragraph write the appropriate part of speech (noun, pronoun, verb, adjective, adverb, preposition, or conjunction) in the blank at the right.

Jogging is my favorite outdoor activity. I   1. _____

like it not only because jogging keeps me in   _____

good physical condition, but also because as I   2. _____

jog, I become familiar with my neighborhood   3. _____

and can now see the whole scene. I notice the   4. _____

effects of the changing seasons on the houses   5. _____

and yards that I pass. I see many of the same   6. _____

people and dogs every day. This helps me to   7. _____

know the people of my neighborhood, so that I   _____

feel more a part of it. In addition my muscles are   8. _____

firm. I sleep better and I have lost fifteen pounds   9. _____

already. The benefits of jogging are so many   10. _____

that I look forward eagerly to my daily routine.   11. _____

1a-4
A sentence is made up of groups of words called phrases and clauses.

Phrases

A *phrase* is a group of words that has no subject or verb. Three common phrases are the following:

1. *Prepositional phrase*: a group of words starting with a preposition and containing a noun or pronoun

   We decided to call *at the last minute.*
   Don't worry *about me.*

2. *Participial phrase*: a group of words containing a present or past participle, which is an adjective formed from a verb. Present participles end in *-ing*; past participles of regular verbs end in *-ed*.

   Brushing her beautiful hair, Gwendolen gazed at herself admiringly.
   Exhausted from studying, I left the campus for a rest.

3. *Infinitive phrase*: a group of words beginning with an infinitive, which is a verb form with no ending (*-s,-ed*, or other), usually introduced by *to*.

   I once tried *to interview a famous actress.*

Clauses

A *clause* is a group of words with a subject and a verb. A clause is either main (independent) or dependent. A *main clause* is really a sentence; it can stand by itself.

   I am here.
   Sea water is very salty.

A *dependent clause* (subordinate clause) cannot stand by itself; it needs, or depends on, a main clause.

1. A dependent clause can be introduced by a subordinating conjunction (*because, before, after, while, if, although,* and so on).

DEPENDENT CLAUSES		MAIN CLAUSES
If you need me,	←	you can call me.
Although it looks good to drink,	←	sea water is very salty.

2. A relative clause is a dependent clause which needs, or depends on, a main clause. It is usually introduced by the pronoun *who*, *which*, or *that*.

MAIN CLAUSES		DEPENDENT (RELATIVE) CLAUSES
John Glenn is an astronaut	←	*who* became a senator.
Sea water is a liquid	←	*that* is very salty.

For more information on clauses and phrases, see 2a-e.

EXERCISE 2

Identify each of the seven items listed below as a phrase or a clause.

1. near the end of the year
2. if I wanted to do it
3. unless you call
4. to turn in an application
5. looking into the mirror admiringly
6. we sang
7. who found my note

1a-5

A sentence expresses a complete thought.

A sentence must contain a main (or independent) clause. That main clause may express a complete thought by itself.

> We must mention the victories of Susan Butcher.

Or it may be in a sentence with one or more dependent clauses.

> (dependent clause)
> *When we think of successful competitors in formerly male-dominated*
> (main clause)
> *fields*, we must mention the victories of Susan Butcher,
> (dependent clause)
> *who has won the Iditarod sled dog race four times.*

Only a main clause can express a complete thought.

You have just looked at five ways of thinking about a sentence. If you keep all five in mind, it may be easier to decide whether your

own sentences are complete and to avoid running sentences together. If you have problems with sentence completion or with run-
together sentences, see Chapters 2 and 3 for more help.

EXERCISE 3

The following paragraph is not separated into sentences. Correct it
by starting each sentence with a capital letter and ending each with
a period. There are ten sentences.

My dog loves to go to the vet I have to take him there often just
to see a girl dog he likes I really do think that he is in love with her
all during the week he just lies around and looks crazy because he
misses her he will not eat anything that I feed him he looks at me as
if he wants me to go get his friend one Saturday I left the house to
go to the vet without him when I returned, there was King just
barking his heart out when he saw that I had brought his friend to
him, he went wild now I have two of the sorriest dogs in the world.

1b
Recognize the subject and verb.

Before you can really understand and correct most writing problems, you must be able to identify the subject and verb of a sentence. In a very short sentence, this is no problem.

Subject—the person   →   Frank cried.   ←   Verb—the word
    you are   telling what the
    writing about   subject is doing

Often, even in a longer sentence, the subject and verb come first.

Judgment is a necessity in surfing.
I wanted a job working in a bank.
We have enjoyed painting in our spare time.
Stews are cooked slowly.

Not every sentence begins with a subject and a verb, however. Here
are some suggestions that may help you find these two basic parts
of the sentence.

1b-1
Locate the verb first.

When trying to locate the simple subject of a sentence, you may discover that it is easier to find the verb first. The verb is the word that tells you what the subject is doing or what is happening to the subject. Then you can ask yourself *who* is doing something or *what* is happening. That *who* or *what* word is the subject.

> **My sister usually stays home on week nights.** [*Stays* is the verb. Who stays home on week nights? *My sister* is then the subject because she is the one who stays home.]
> **Parenting these days is a very big responsibility.** [*Is* is the verb. What is a big responsibility? *Parenting* is the subject because it is the responsibility.]

EXERCISE 4

Underline the verb in each of the following sentences.

1. Some friend's boat always sits in my parents' yard.
2. Almost every customer in this restaurant asks the waiter for bluefish.
3. None of my friends now live in the Detroit area.
4. Listening to guitar music is my favorite way to relax.
5. A machine useful for cutting all kinds of wood is called a lathe.

1b-2
Remember that words may come between the subject and its verb.

Very often a word like *one*, *all*, *each*, *any*, *some*, *many*, or *none* is the simple subject.

> **One of the men works on Sunday.** [Who works on Sunday?]
> **Some of your advice is helpful.** [What is helpful?]

The subject of the first sentence is *one*. (Only one of the men works on Sunday.) The subject of the second sentence is *some*. (Only some of the advice is helpful.) Do not let phrases beginning with *of* mislead you when they come between the simple subject and its verb.

The children of today will be our salvation. [*Children*, not *today*, is the subject; *children* will be our salvation.]

Some of the players are doing different things. [*Some*, not *players*, is the subject. *Some*, not *all*, of the players are doing different things.]

Here are some other examples.

All of the patients in the hospital want a doctor to show a personal interest in them.

None of the women has a different idea on the subject.

After such a narrow escape, John never went swimming in rough surf again.

EXERCISE 5

In the following sentences, the verb is underlined twice. Underline the simple subject once.

EXAMPLE One of the students in this class registered last week.

1. The sight of my old glasses under the recliner really surprised me.
2. Many of the sailors on the *America* surely miss home at this very minute.
3. Some of the most enthusiastic supporters of John McCain did not vote in the presidential election.
4. All of the money went to my sister.
5. One of the banks makes loans for automobiles.

1b-3

Remember that the verb sometimes comes *before* the subject.

You usually expect the subject to come before its verb in a sentence, but that is not always the case. In a *there is* (*are*), *here is* (*are*), or *where is* (*are*) sentence, the verb comes before the subject.

There are mosquitoes all over the place.

Here is the best reason for buying a new car.

Where are my old friends?

There, here, and *where* are not subjects. The simple subjects of the sentences above are *mosquitoes, reason,* and *friends. There, here,* and *where* only introduce the subject.

Be sure that when you use *there* to introduce the subject, you do not confuse *there* with *it. It* refers to something definite.

It is too early to visit your sister. [It (the time) is too early.]

Do not use *it* in place of *there* to introduce the subject of a sentence.

WRONG   It is only five of us at home now.
RIGHT   There are only five of us at home now.

The verb may come before its subject in sentences other than those beginning with *there is* (*are*), *here is* (*are*), and *where is* (*are*).

Next to his desk are four filing cabinets. [The subject is *cabinets*;

the cabinets are near the desk.]

On the wall hang the racks that hold the cue sticks. [The subject

is racks; the racks hang on the wall.]

Is anyone coming today? [The subject is *anyone*; in a question,

the verb has to appear before its subject.]

1b-4
Remember that the subject of a command or request is *you*.

In a command or a request the subject is not written out in the sentence. Since you are talking to someone when you command or request something, the subject is *you* (understood).

SUBJECT	VERB
(You)	Leave my house immediately!
(You)	Please wear hiking boots if you are going into those woods.

EXERCISE 6

In the following sentences, each verb is underlined twice. Underline each subject once. If a subject is understood, write *you* next to the sentence.

EXAMPLE   The man threw the Frisbee over the woman's head.

1. All along the stairs were my brother's toys.

2. In the room there are three chairs, a sofa, a loveseat, and a cedar chest.
3. Please walk the dog on the other side of the street.
4. Here comes the package I have been expecting.
5. Do your plants get enough sun in the morning?
6. The house on that side of the road belongs to my aunt.
7. Nonviolent protest marches were organized by Martin Luther King, Jr.
8. Develop your paragraph by adding specific examples.

1b-5
Recognize the subject and verb of the *main* clause.

A main (independent) clause has a subject and verb and can stand by itself. Since a sentence may have more than one clause, it is important to recognize the subject and verb of the *main* clause so that you can tell when you are writing complete sentences. The following is a main clause. It is also a sentence, since it needs nothing else to express a complete thought.

> (subject)(verb)
> Farid waited for me.

The following are dependent clauses. Even though each has a subject and a verb, it needs a main clause, so they are not sentences.

> although he was impatient
>
> who is very impatient

The following are complete sentences which include the dependent clauses given above. The subject and verb of the main clause are underlined.

> Farid waited for me although he was impatient.
>
> Farid, who is very impatient, waited for me.

If you need help in deciding whether you have written a dependent clause or a main clause (sentence), see **2b**.

EXERCISE 7

Each of the following sentences has more than one subject and more than one verb. Underline the simple subject of the main clause once and its verb twice.

EXAMPLES After the bell rang, the <u>students</u> <u>wasted</u> no time in leaving the room.

An <u>announcer</u> who forgets his lines <u>needs</u> to practice before his broadcasts.

1. Since the poll was taken close to the election, the results are surely reliable.
2. If this talk of a recession doesn't stop, interest rates will go higher than they are right now.
3. Oil companies that do not recognize that they have a responsibility to prevent oil spills endanger our environment in a very real way.
4. The umbrella that you needed this afternoon seems to be hanging in your closet.
5. My research paper required more reliable sources before my instructor would accept it.
6. Because highways are so crowded, many people now form car pools to get to work.

 CHECKLIST: Locating the Subject and Verb

In locating the subject and verb, remember that

1. It is helpful to find the verb first.

2. Words may separate a subject from its verb—particularly a simple subject like *one*, *all*, *each*, and *some*. (<u>Some</u> of the girls <u>look</u> worried.)

3. In a *there is* (*are*), *here is* (*are*), or *where is* (*are*) sentence, the verb comes before its subject. (There <u>is</u> no <u>reason</u> for your decision.)

4. In questions and some other sentences the verb sometimes comes before its subject. (<u>Are</u> <u>you</u> happy?)

5. In a command or request the subject (*you*) is understood. ([<u>You</u>] <u>close</u> the door.)

6. A sentence may have more than one subject and verb, but it must have at least one subject and one verb in a main clause. (After I arrive, <u>I</u> <u>will call</u> you.)

EXERCISE 8

Identify the main clause in each sentence. Then underline the simple subject of each main clause once and the verb that goes with it twice. Do not underline the subject and verb of any dependent clause. When the subject is understood, write *you* next to the sentence.

EXAMPLES   When I finally met my roommate, I really got a shock.

Go home immediately. (You)

1. When Uncle Jerry goes fishing, he fishes from sunup to sundown.
2. In the summer of 1865, Mr. Costello bought a small dry-goods business.
3. Of all the activities that help me stay in shape, my favorite activity is running.
4. Shawn stepped on the accelerator again and finally started his car.
5. According to the newspaper reports, all of the candidates supported routine drug testing of railroad employees.
6. All across the hardening cement are the unmistakable pawprints of my curious cat, Tagi.
7. In case of an emergency, have several fuses in the house.
8. One of our airplanes has disappeared.
9. Mr. Vernon, who considered work in his garden more a labor of love than a weekly duty, grew some of the most marvelous vegetables that I have ever seen.
10. For information on the essentials of automotive maintenance, people often sign up for some courses at a nearby community college.
11. Here in the newspaper, after the news, the comics, and all of the classified ads, is the notice of that great sale.
12. After all the kind words of encouragement and the frequently given, but not unwelcome, words of advice, I never dreamed of such an outcome.

EXERCISE 9

Write five sentences of your own. At least two of them should have a main clause and a dependent clause. (In each main clause, underline the subject once and the verb twice.)

1c
Write correct negative sentences.

1c-1
The most common negative sentence uses one negative word, such as *no, not, never, nothing, nowhere,* or *hardly.*

In addition to telling the reader what is happening to the subject, a sentence can also tell what is not happening.

> There are *no* drill bits in that drawer.
> Midnight is *not* a good time to study.
> You can *never* cheat an honest person.
> I have *nothing* to do today.

Sometimes a contraction is used instead of the word *not.*

> Midnight is not a good time   OR   Midnight *isn't* a good time
>   to study.   to study.
> You cannot cheat an honest   OR   You *can't* cheat an honest
>   person.   person.
> I do not have anything to do   OR   I *don't* have anything to do
>   today.   today.

Remember to use an apostrophe before the *t* in a contraction, since the *o* of *not* is omitted (*isn't, don't, hasn't, didn't*).

NOTE: *Ain't* is not a correct contraction for *am not, is not, are not, has not,* or *have not.*

>   WRONG   That ain't any way to run a railroad.
>   RIGHT   *That's* no way to run a railroad.

1c-2
Do not use more than one negative word to say that something is not true.

English is unlike most other languages in its negative sentences. In Spanish, for example, the more negative words you use, the more you deny that something is true.

> No vi a *nadie* ni oí *nada* en *ninguna* parte.
> I didn't see no one nor hear nothing nowhere.

In your papers, however, remember not to use two negative words such as *no, no one, not, never, nothing, nowhere,* or *hardly* when you want to say that something is not so.

Wrong	If something went wrong, neither one of them would think nothing about it.
Right	If something went wrong, *neither* one of them would think *anything* about it.
Wrong	I did things for them that no other person would never have done.
Right	I did things for them that *no* other person would *ever* have done.
Wrong	I can't hardly hear.
Right	I *can* hardly hear.

**REMINDER:**   Avoiding Two Negatives

---

To avoid using two negative words, remember that you can usually do one of the following:

1.   Eliminate one of the negative words.

Wrong	There are not hardly any peaches left.
Right	There are *hardly* any peaches left.

2.   Substitute *ever* for *never.*

Wrong	They're not never here.
Right	They're not *ever* here.

3.   Substitute *any* for *no* or *none.*

Wrong	I can't find him nowhere.
Right	I can't find him *anywhere.*
Wrong	I don't see none on the shelf.
Right	I don't see *any* on the shelf.

Note: The only time you do use two negative words to say that something is not true is when you use the pair *neither . . . nor.*

Neither my English teacher *nor* I can understand why I continue to make verb errors.

EXERCISE 10

Correct the following sentences by changing any incorrect negative words.

EXAMPLE   I don't have no more money.

I don't have *any* more money.

1. Joey feels so bad he can't hardly hold his head up.
2. I love my job and wouldn't trade it for nothing.
3. No wonder they didn't know how to act at her house; they've never been nowhere outside of New Jersey.
4. Didn't nobody figure out the ending to that story?
5. A Rottweiler will often let an unfamiliar person enter the house, but he won't let nobody leave.

Chapter 2

INCOMPLETE SENTENCES

Be sure that your sentences are complete.

A complete sentence has a subject (the person or thing you are writing about) and a main verb (the word that describes what the subject is doing or what is happening to the subject). Remember that when you write a complete sentence, you are saying something about the subject and you finish saying it. When you write a fragment you do not finish your statement.

FRAGMENT	As a sales representative. [What are you saying about a sales representative?]
SENTENCE	Karen works as a sales representative.
FRAGMENT	And depends on her commission on sales. [Who depends on her commission on sales?]
SENTENCE	Karen works as a sales representative and depends on her commission on sales.
FRAGMENT	Because Karen depends on her commission from sales. [What happens because Karen depends on her commission from sales?]
SENTENCE	Because Karen depends on her commission from sales, it is hard for her to plan her expenses.

Usually a sentence can be completed in two ways:

1. You can rewrite the fragment completely.

FRAGMENT   Fear that I would be unable to do the work.
COMPLETE   I was afraid that I would be unable to do the work.

2. You can join the fragment to the complete sentence before or after it.

FRAGMENT   Fear that I would be unable to do the work.
COMPLETE   One of my biggest problems was fear of returning to school, fear that I would be unable to do the work.

It is often better to join a fragment to the sentence either before or after it. This is because a fragment is usually just a group of words that was left out of the sentence next to it. If you find a fragment in your paper, look to see if you really meant to join it to a sentence next to it.

2a
Correct a phrase fragment.

Remember that a group of words that does not have a subject and a verb is not a sentence; it is a *phrase fragment*. Whenever possible, join these words to the sentence next to them.

FRAGMENT	JOIN	COMPLETE
Without thinking about the danger.	People going downhill sometimes coast and ride their brakes. ← Without thinking about the danger.	People going downhill sometimes coast and ride their brakes without thinking about the danger.

2a-1
Join a prepositional phrase fragment to the sentence next to it.

A prepositional phrase is a group of words that starts with a preposition (*to, for, without,* and so on) and contains a noun or pronoun. Some of the common prepositions used in such a phrase are listed on page 6.

When you separate a prepositional phrase like *for a whole hour* from the rest of a sentence, you are writing a fragment.

FRAGMENT	JOIN	COMPLETE
For a whole hour	Bill did go to work on Friday. For a whole hour.	Bill did go to work on Friday for a whole hour.

2a-2

Join an *-ing* fragment to the sentence next to it, or change the *-ing* word to a verb that tells what the subject is doing.

FRAGMENT	JOIN	COMPLETE
Checking myself, proofreading, and correcting errors.	I have to write my paper very slowly. ← Checking myself, proofreading, and correcting errors.	I have to write my paper very slowly, checking myself, proofreading, and correcting errors.
Having no income of his own.	Having no income of his own. ← George is always borrowing from his brother.	Having no income of his own, George is always borrowing from his brother. or Since George *has* no income of his own, he is always borrowing from his brother.

EXERCISE 1

Complete all of the following sentences by joining the fragments to the sentences. Do not join two sentences that are already complete. (A sentence is complete when it contains a subject and a main verb.) Do not add any words to the sentences.

EXAMPLE For the entire week. I sat waiting for the telephone to ring.

> *For the entire week, I sat waiting for the telephone to ring.*

1. Don't waste time moving the person to a better place. Loosening the clothing or draining water from the lungs. Begin emergency treatment. As soon as possible.

2. How can the authorities make schools safer by searching students? Or by turning schools into jails?

3. Students often rush home from school and go straight to work. They leave no time for studying.

4. My Siberian husky feeds on the attention of others. Always getting just what she wants.

5. You may find that a wave snatcher forces you to move to a slower place to surf. Slower meaning you will have to wait longer for sets of waves to come in.

6. My little nephew was lying quietly in his crib. His eyes following the mobile hanging above him. His perfect little hands reaching as high as he could get them.

EXERCISE 2

Correct the fragments in the following paragraph.

Chinese Shar-Peis are size-six dogs. Sporting around in size-twelve suits. With their wrinkled appearance. They make you want to grab an iron and an ironing board. When you take one of them for a walk, people are always stopping you. Inquiring about the appearance or history of the dog. Winning the hearts of hermits, the lives of workaholics, and the love of dog haters. Shar-Peis are almost perfect dogs. They travel well and are easy to get along with. Putting up with children better than most parents.

2b
Correct a clause fragment.

A group of words with a subject and verb is not always a sentence; sometimes it is a *clause fragment.*

2b-1
After, although, because, etc., often signal dependent clauses.

Words like *after, although, as, as if, as though, because, before, if, since, though, unless, until, when, whenever*, and *while* (subordinating conjunctions) often signal dependent clauses. They help you recognize that something needs to be explained before the sentence is complete.

DEPENDENT CLAUSE   Because this is a job she can never quit.
FRAGMENT   [What is true because this is a job she
            can never quit?]

SENTENCE   The hardest decision a woman will have
            to make is whether she is ready to be a
            mother because this is a job she can
            never quit.

DEPENDENT CLAUSE   Whereas country music is made with real
            instruments like drums, guitars, and
            bells. [What is being compared with
            country music?]

SENTENCE   Rap beats are made electronically on a
            keyboard, whereas country music is
            made with real instruments like drums,
            guitars, and bells.

EXERCISE 3

Write three sentences, beginning each one with a different subordinating conjunction. Each sentence will have a dependent clause
and a main clause. Put commas between clauses. Then write three
sentences, beginning each with a main clause and ending each
with a dependent clause. There is no comma needed between
clauses.

EXAMPLES If you hurry, you won't be late.
          You won't be late if you hurry.

2b-2

**Who, whose, whom, which, and that often signal relative
(dependent) clauses.**

When you use such clauses, make sure that your sentences are complete. A relative clause has a verb and a subject, but it needs a main
clause to complete its meaning.

RELATIVE CLAUSE   Who are searching for their biological
FRAGMENT   parents
SENTENCE   Montel Williams's guests are sometimes
            adults who are searching for their biologi-
            cal parents.

RELATIVE CLAUSE FRAGMENT	A profession that makes me feel useful to others.
COMPLETE SENTENCE	Nursing is a wonderful profession, a profession that makes me feel useful to others.
RELATIVE CLAUSE FRAGMENT	Whose car wouldn't start yesterday.
COMPLETE SENTENCE	There is the man whose car wouldn't start yesterday.

EXERCISE 4

Combine each pair of sentences below to make one sentence. Turn one into a relative clause, using *who, which*, or *that*.

EXAMPLE On Broadway are many old theatres. They are still standing after many years.

On Broadway are many old theatres that are still

standing after many years.

1. Mrs. Reece is a busy teacher. She is always flying all around the room knocking books and papers off desks.
2. Oysters serve as food for starfish. They get the oyster meat by wrapping their tentacles around the shell and prying it open.
3. As a child he heard stories from his grandfather. The stories were accounts of the history of his people.
4. Black females on TV shows used to be housekeepers or nannies. They only did domestic chores.
5. Recently I visited Myrtle Beach. It is near a beautiful wildlife refuge.

EXERCISE 5

Identify all complete sentences.

1. Before I thought, I spoke.
2. Remember, if this is your first try, pick something that is simple to make.
3. The letters, which the letter carrier delivered yesterday, are sitting on your desk.

4. While, on the other hand, I need pressure to force me to cope with my everyday problems.
5. Blizzards that leave our highways ice covered and unusable for days.
6. Television shows that deal with the conservation of our natural resources.
7. If you know in advance the subject matter of the test and the time allowed to take the test.

EXERCISE 6

Turn all of the fragments into complete sentences. Write *S* to the left of any numbered item that is already a sentence.

1. Although there are many jacks-of-all-trades who can produce quantity and not quality. We have a need for craftsmanship.
2. Obnoxious students sit as far back in the classroom as possible. So that their rude comments cannot be heard.
3. There are many steps. That lead up to the house.
4. If you didn't know better, you'd think she was a doctor.
5. When I picked up the telephone and the medical secretary gave me the decision of the board.
6. The "head bobber" is a student. Who can't stay awake during a class lecture.
7. This is the best dinner that I have ever eaten.

EXERCISE 7

Write five sentences of your own, using the fragments given. At least two of your sentences should have the fragment at the end.
EXAMPLES   *If I can,* I will help you.
            I will help you *if I can.*

1. When I find the job of my dreams.
2. Whether you live in the city or in the country.
3. Which is located near our college.
4. Who made me feel welcome.
5. Unless I win the lottery.

2c
Correct a verb fragment.

A *verb fragment* has no subject. You may find that you write verb fragments when you are using the same subject with more than one verb.

WRONG   The lecturer was very uptight. And kept a straight face the entire hour.

RIGHT   The lecturer was very uptight and kept a straight face the entire hour

One good way to correct a verb fragment is to join the fragment to the sentence that comes before it.

FRAGMENT	JOIN	COMPLETE
And in many cases share the bills.	Roommates share their food and time. ← And in many cases share the bills.	Roommates share their food and time and in many cases share the bills.

EXERCISE 8

Each of the following fragments lacks a subject. Add something to the beginning of each fragment to make it a sentence.
EXAMPLE But knew it was not for her.

> *Anne heard the telephone ring but knew it was not for her.*

1. And decided to take it home.
2. But is often sick the next morning.
3. And hoped no one would hear me.
4. Or may not even have a license to drive.

2d
Correct a noun fragment.

A *noun fragment* is a group of words that contains a noun but no verb. Often you accidentally write a noun fragment when you are saying more than one thing about the subject. By mistake, you separate the noun fragment from the sentence itself.

SENTENCE   There are three types of drivers I meet on the road.
FRAGMENT   The fast driver, the slow driver, and the good driver.

You can rewrite the sentence, adding the information in the fragment.

SENTENCE   The three types of drivers I meet on the road are the fast driver, the slow driver, and the good driver.

You can also use punctuation to join the fragment to the sentence. Try placing a comma or a colon (:) instead of a period after the sentence and joining the noun fragment to the sentence.

SENTENCE   There are three types of drivers I meet on the road: the fast driver, the slow driver, and the good driver.

Here are some other noun fragments corrected by punctuation:

SENTENCE   He was from a military family.
FRAGMENT   The second son of a naval officer.
CORRECTION   He was from a military family, the second son of a naval officer.

SENTENCE   I have all I ever wanted.
FRAGMENT   Money, friends, and a nice apartment.
CORRECTION   I have all I ever wanted: money, friends, and a nice apartment.

If the noun fragment comes before the sentence, you can rewrite the sentence, adding the information in the fragment.

FRAGMENT   A phone call from his father.
SENTENCE   That was something Paul was dreading.
CORRECTION   A phone call from his father was something Paul was dreading.

You can instead use a comma or a dash and join the fragment to the sentence.

SENTENCE   A phone call from his father—that was something Paul was dreading.

NOTE: For more information on the dash and the colon, see Chapter 17.

EXERCISE 9

Write *S* next to each complete sentence. Correct all fragments.

1.   The Eastern Shore has many historic places. Coast Guard stations and houses that are over a century old.

2. My little girl asks me questions that surprise me. Questions like "How did the world begin?"
3. The coming of Michael Jackson to the Frank D. Lawrence Stadium. That was a big event. People waited in long lines for tickets.
4. The beautiful decorations that brought happiness to so many. They have been put away for the winter.
5. There are three kinds of sleepers who annoy me. The easy-to-wake sleeper, the hard-to-wake sleeper, and the sleeper who snores.

2e
Correct an infinitive fragment.

An *infinitive* is a verb form with no ending (*-s*, *-ed*, or other), usually introduced by *to* (*to laugh, to work*). An infinitive is not a verb itself, but it usually appears with a verb.

> (verb infinitive)
> My uncle loves *to talk.*

An infinitive should not be left out of the sentence that comes before it.

> FRAGMENT   To let the past be the past.
> SENTENCE   I am ready to move forward, to let the past be the past.

 CHECKLIST: Checking for Fragments
To check your papers for fragments, ask yourself the following questions:

1. Does every sentence have a subject and verb in a main clause?

2. Does every sentence with a dependent clause (introduced by *because*, *when*, *after*, and so on) also have a main clause?

3. Does every relative clause (introduced by *who*, *which*, or *that*) also have a main clause?

EXERCISE 10

Correct all fragments. Write *C* next to each item that is already correct.

1. A thong should never be worn on the beach. Unless the wearer has something else on. Like a shirt or some shorts.
2. I came. I saw. I conquered.
3. Now that VCRs are so common. There aren't many people. Who stay up to watch late movies.
4. The perfect party must be held at a prime location. Anywhere with lots of space for people to move about.
5. By 2005. If people don't have a college degree, they won't be able to find jobs. That's why I'm going to college. Aren't you worried about your sister? Who didn't even finish high school?
6. There are long lines at ticket counters. People hurrying as if it were their last day on earth.
7. Hoping for the best but expecting the worst. Janet answered the telephone.
8. Frank has his own dance studio. And teaches all kinds of people. Who have never really learned to dance.

EXERCISE 11

Edit the following paragraphs for fragments.

(a) My brother's room could be called the D-zone. Dirty, dingy, and disgusting. As you enter his room, you will find a pile of dirty clothes. That reek of sweat from last summer's football games. You can also smell the moldy cereal bowls, stale pizza, and old waffles with syrup on his bookcase. He claims that these breakfast and dinner treats have their own blue trim. Which matches his curtains. Only my sister and I have been brave enough. To make it to his closet. Inside his closet you will find clumps of hair from three years ago. When he decided he wanted a buzz cut. On the top shelf is a small green box. Which contains my brother's pet goldfish from second grade. I have heard of boys being pack-rats, but his room is ridiculous. There is no telling. What else is in his room. I am just too afraid to find out.

(b) Oprah Winfrey's talk show caters to different types of audiences. It doesn't have any one format. One day it is about battered housewives. Who have overcome hurdles. Another day the news media, cooking, or fashions. And once a month book club luncheons. That introduce people to authors. No matter what people's interests are. They will find something to enjoy.

EXERCISE 12

Correct all fragments. Write *C* next to each item that is already correct.

1. Jean was caught at her favorite vice. Sleeping in class.
2. Make sure you have the necessary tools. A crowbar and a jack.
3. Down comes that dreaded snow.
4. While Rome burned, Nero fiddled.
5. Have you been married long? Sometimes it seems long.
6. Whenever you are playing poker. It is important to know when to pass a hand. And just as important to know when to bluff.
7. A skillet should be made of good quality iron. To retain heat properly.
8. Being a "playa" is not for everyone. Especially someone who is a sensitive, kind-hearted person.

EXERCISE 13

Correct all fragments by adding or removing words. Be able to explain why each group of words is a fragment.

1. and swore he would never get married again _____

2. knowing he might change his mind later_____

3. which caused him much anxiety _____

4. since Justin is only three years old _____

5. a science course and two semesters of physical education _____

EXERCISE 14

Newspaper headlines are often fragments because they are titles. Turn each of these headlines into a complete sentence. You may add any words or information necessary.

1. Tennessee Tigers in, Jaguars out?
2. When the cure for the mother poses a threat to the child
3. Republicans questioning House version of welfare bill
4. Thousands of veterans on parade
5. One teacher who continues to learn
6. Where whooping cranes winter
7. Value of homeless study questioned
8. No headway on budget
9. Tips to improve air quality
10. Coping with canceled flights

Chapter 3

RUN-TOGETHER SENTENCES AND COMMA SPLICES

Separate your run-together sentences;
avoid comma splices.

Each of the following groups of words actually contains two sentences.

I bought a used boat this past summer from a friend at work it needed several repairs.

Years have passed since I was last here now the windows are covered with boards.

The score was eight to nine, the Mets were ahead.

In the first two examples, you can see that the writers did not show that there were two complete thoughts and ran two sentences together. In the third example the writer created a comma splice by using only a comma to separate two complete thoughts. Chapters **1** and **2** help you recognize when sentences are complete. This chapter describes some common ways of separating sentences and avoiding comma splices.

32

3a
Separate sentences by using a period.

Notice that there are two complete sentences or main clauses in the
wrong example below. In the first sentence, *I* is the subject and *bought*
is the verb. In the second sentence, *it* is the subject and *needed* is the
verb. You can separate the sentences by placing a period after *work* and
starting *it* with a capital letter; then the sentences will be correct.

> WRONG   I bought a used boat this past summer from a friend at
> work it needed several repairs.

> RIGHT   I bought a used boat this past summer from a friend at
> work. It needed several repairs.

For help in recognizing sentences or main clauses, look back at
sections **1a** and **1b**.

3b
Separate sentences by using a semicolon.

A semicolon (;) is like a period in that it can be used to separate two
complete sentences, but when you use a semicolon, the sentences
should be closely related. In the example below, the subject of the
first sentence is *years* and the verb is *have passed*. In the second sentence, the subject is *windows* and the verb is *are covered*. Since the
thoughts in the sentences are closely related, the sentences can be
separated with a semicolon instead of a period. Notice that the
word following the semicolon does *not* begin with a capital letter.

> WRONG   Years have passed since I was last here now the win-
> dows are covered with boards.

> RIGHT   Years have passed since I was last here; now the
> windows are covered with boards.

Semicolons are often used to separate sentences when the second sentence is introduced by a transitional word or expression.
Some common ones are

also	however	nevertheless
as a result	in addition	on the other hand
besides	in fact	still
for example	instead	then
furthermore	meanwhile	therefore

These expressions are often called *conjunctive adverbs.* A comma usually follows the transitional word or expression.

Anna was very intelligent; however, people didn't always realize it.

 Caution: Be sure that you do *not* use a semicolon to separate a main clause from a dependent clause (introduced by a subordinating conjunction such as *before, after, because, although,* or *if*).

WRONG   **Anna was very intelligent although she didn't show it.**

For more information on the uses of the semicolon, see Chapter **14**.

EXERCISE 1

Each item below contains two complete thoughts. Show the separation clearly by using periods or semicolons where needed. Remove commas and semicolons and add capital letters where necessary to mark complete sentences.

1. My life can go along smoothly as if it were on cruise control then something happens to send it into a downward spiral.
2. Most cars that drag race cannot pass inspection for street driving, they are too noisy.
3. Face it no player wants a ball hog on his team.
4. Lucy's voice is as loud as a bullhorn's, in fact, I can hear her before I see her.
5. Laura likes shopping, but it's not at the mall, it's at the Goodwill store.
6. Over the past several years colleges have become concerned about hazing problems ours is no exception.
7. If you want to be late to class, ignore the alarm when it goes off just hit the snooze button and go back to sleep.
8. Abortion may not be the right thing for everyone, this is a difficult decision for many women.
9. There are three important differences between rap and country music, they are the beats, the messages, and the people who listen.
10. When I am on the road; look out, you never know what I will do next.

3c
Correct run-together sentences by using a comma and a coordinating conjunction such as *and*, but, or, nor, for, so, *or* yet.

You may want to use a comma to connect two sentences. Remember that this method is only correct when you also use a coordinating conjunction after the comma. A *coordinating conjunction* is a word that joins two equal elements: two words, two phrases, two clauses, or two sentences. You can use a coordinating conjunction to separate two main clauses or sentences. The following are some common coordinating conjunctions:

and	nor	so
but	for	yet
or		

WRONG	The score was eight to nine the Mets were ahead.
RIGHT	The score was eight to nine, *and* the Mets were ahead.
WRONG	I want to go home I have to stay at school.
RIGHT	I want to go home, *but* I have to stay at school.

Notice that all of these sentences are really two main clauses; each could stand by itself. If a comma is used between the two main clauses or sentences, a coordinating conjunction like *and* or *but* must also be used. When only a comma is used, the error is called a *comma splice*. (See **3e**.)

EXERCISE 2

Each of the following is the beginning of a sentence that contains one main clause and a coordinating conjunction (*and, but, or, nor, for, so,* or *yet*). Add another main clause to complete each sentence. Be sure each clause contains a subject and a verb.

EXAMPLE The prisoner arose and faced the jury, and *the whole courtroom awaited the verdict.*

1. The police had been watching my neighbor's house for an hour, and _____

2. I tried to warn my sister that her green shoes did not match her purple dress, but _____

3. When we get home, either there will still be water in the tea kettle you left on the hot burner, or _____

4. Try to get to bed early tonight, so _____

5. I know in my heart that you are right, yet _____

3d
Correct run-together sentences by making one of them a dependent clause.

Usually the best way to correct run-together sentences is by turning one of them into a dependent clause. This way is best because it shows a relationship between the two sentences.

INCORRECT (RUN-TOGETHER)   The bus was late Peter missed his train connection.

This run-together sentence can be corrected with a period, a semicolon, or a comma and a coordinating conjunction (*and, but,* and so on).

CORRECT BUT WEAK   The bus was late, and Peter missed his train connection.

The relationship between the two complete thoughts would be clearer, however, if you put one of them in a dependent clause. Then the reader could easily see that one event led to the other.

CORRECT AND IMPROVED   Because his bus was late, Peter missed his train connection.

A dependent clause is introduced by a subordinating conjunction. The following are some common subordinating conjunctions:

after	as though	since	when
although	because	though	whenever
as	before	unless	while
as of	if	until	

When you are turning one sentence into a dependent clause, use the subordinating conjunction that makes the relationship between the two sentences clear. If you need more help recognizing dependent clauses, see **1a-4**.

3d-1

To make the time of an event clear, use *before*, *after*, *as*, *when*, and *while* in the dependent clause.

BEFORE   Steve and Pete ran along the street and reached the building *before* the man saw them.

AFTER   He picked up the ball *after* it fell from the table.

WHEN   The car turned over *when* another car hit it.

3d-2

To show the cause of something, use *because* or *since* in the dependent clause.

BECAUSE   The rubber raft sank *because* it hit a sharp rock.

SINCE   I am finishing school *since* without an education I cannot reach my goal.

 Caution: If the dependent clause comes first in the sentence, use a comma after it. If it comes after the main clause, you do not need a comma.

> After you get here, we will have lunch.
> We will have lunch after you get here.

For more examples, see **13b**.

 CHECKLIST: Correcting Run-Together Sentences
Remember how conjunctions are used in correcting run-together sentences.

1. Coordinating conjunctions (*and*, *but*, *or*, *nor*, *for*, *so*, and *yet*) after commas join main clauses or sentences.

    Carolyn was happy, *but* she managed to conceal it.

2. Transitional words or conjunctive adverbs (*also*, *besides, furthermore*, *however*, *meanwhile*, *nevertheless*, *still*, *then*, *therefore*, and so on) separate main clauses or sentences. They can be used after a semicolon, or they can begin sentences.

    Carolyn was happy. *However*, she managed to conceal it.
    Carolyn was happy; *however*, she managed to conceal it.

3. Subordinating conjunctions (*after, although, as, because, before, if, since, unless, until, when, whether, while,* and so on) introduce dependent clauses. When the main clause comes first, there is usually no punctuation between clauses.

    Carolyn was happy *although* she managed to conceal it.

Let your conjunctions and transitional words help you decide whether you really have run two sentences together.

EXERCISE 3

In each of the following sentences identify any subordinating conjunction or transitional word. Then write *M* above each main (independent) clause or sentence. Write *D* above each dependent clause.

EXAMPLE Some people are going to gamble whether it is legal or not.

1. If a four-wheel-drive vehicle is driven as roughly as the one in that commercial, it will probably fall apart.
2. The initial cost of a solar conversion plant might be high, but the long-range benefit would make it well worth that cost.
3. Long naps are helpful if one has time for them; however, just a five-minute rest will do wonders to keep a person going until the day is over.
4. There are many professions to pursue; therefore, choose one that will give you pleasure and a feeling of accomplishment.
5. The day students are majoring in cafeteria; the night students are deep in slumber.

EXERCISE 4

Divide the following paragraphs into sentences, using periods, semicolons, and commas.

(a) When I was a child and not as tall as a sewing machine, I watched my mother daily as she sewed as I grew older, I dreamed more and more about being a seamstress one day at the age of nine, I sat at the machine and pedaled it electric machines were not available for sewing in those days to hear the machine and to see it operate really fascinated me then I gathered pieces of scrap material, and my mother helped me cut out small things the first dress I made was for a doll in a few years I knew how to select material, cut it out by using a pattern, and, in a few hours, produce a garment that was ready to wear now I sew my clothes instead of buying them being a seamstress is my favorite pastime, and I am delighted and proud that I learned to sew.

(b) Having more than one of the same kind of pet is hard enough, but when you have three different kinds of pets, there is a lot of work to be done. For example, I have a dog, four turtles, and a bird, all six of them need love and attention. I play with my dog, take him for walks, brush him, bathe him, and feed him, I also feed and bathe my turtles, you can't really play with turtles. I teach my bird to talk and let it fly around the house, my bird speaks better English than most of my friends. I don't always have enough time to take good care of my pets then I get my mom to take care of them for me.

3e
Avoid the comma splice. Do not use the comma alone to separate sentences.

Using only a comma between sentences is called *comma splice* or *comma fault*. When you signal a new thought, you need to do so in a definite way; a comma alone is not enough to give this signal.

WRONG	Mary left her new coat on the bus last week, she is now more careful about her possessions.
RIGHT	Mary left her new coat on the bus last week. She is now more careful about her possessions.
RIGHT	Mary left her new coat on the bus last week; she is now more careful about her possessions.
RIGHT	Mary left her new coat on the bus last week, so she is now more careful about her possessions.

▽ **Caution:** Remember that a command is a sentence—even though the subject is not written out in the sentence. Do not use a comma to separate commands.

WRONG	Jack up the car carefully, remove the lug wrench from the trunk.
RIGHT	Jack up the car carefully. Remove the lug wrench from the trunk.

EXERCISE 5 ▰▰▰▰▰▰

Decide whether any comma in each of the following sentences produces a comma splice. If it does, correct the sentence by using a period, a semicolon, or a main clause and a dependent clause. Add capitalization if necessary.

EXAMPLE At a concert you should enjoy the music⸍ᴰ Don't be impatient with people who visit with friends⸍ just relax and have a good time.

1. The Salvation Army cares about the less fortunate, it is really great during the Christmas season.
2. Try skydiving, you might enjoy it!
3. Many things hang on the wall of my grandmother's attic, they include old portraits and wind chimes, I am surprised every time I visit her at what she has collected over the years.
4. When I call, I give the name of my company and identify myself by name.
5. Be careful next time you are having a private conversation, make sure nobody is listening.

EXERCISE 6 ▰▰▰▰▰▰

Correct all comma splices in the following paragraphs, using any of the methods suggested in this chapter.

(a) If you are sick of your job, just plain tired of your boss, and annoyed by the menial work that you do, I would like to give you some suggestions on how to get yourself fired. The first step on the road to unemployment is the easiest—come in late, this move should gain you at least a reprimand from management, next you should ignore your work and gossip with your co-workers. If these steps don't work, insulting your boss should do the trick. You should now be walking the streets, but if you still find yourself at the same job, there is only one remaining step, take the coward's way out and just quit!

(b) Ever since Stone Cold Steve Austin came along, my cousin Eddie has been a big wrestling fan. For Eddie's birthday my mother bought him some toy wrestling figures, she also got him a Steve Austin T-shirt and videotape. In his spare time Eddie watches *Monday Night Raw* or *Sunday Night Heat*, if wrestling isn't on TV, he will practice wrestling moves on the pillows in his mom's room.

The thing that he does most often is walk around the house pretending he is a wrestler. His friend Clay, also a wrestling fan, comes to play with him almost every day, while Clay is there, he and Eddie practice wrestling moves on one another and quote some of Steve Austin's favorite sayings. Maybe one day Eddie will get a new interest, I know his family certainly hopes so.

 ## CHECKLIST: Avoiding Run-Together Sentences and Comma Splices

For avoiding run-together sentences and comma splices in your papers, ask yourself these questions:

1. Am I certain that each sentence is complete (that each has a main clause with a subject and a verb)?

2. Did I separate the sentences using one of these methods:
   a. a period
   b. a semicolon
   c. a comma and a coordinating conjunction (*and, but*, etc.)
   d. a main clause and a dependent clause (beginning with a subordinating conjunction—*after, because*, etc.)?

3. Am I certain I did not use a comma alone to divide two complete thoughts?

EXERCISE 7

Separate all run-together sentences and comma splices by using any of the methods described in this chapter. If an item is already correct, write *S* to the left of it.

1. On weekends she opens her beauty shop, she has many of the people in the neighborhood as customers, even those who used to cut their own hair.

2. My brother, who is a postal clerk, has two sons one is a professional basketball player, and the other is in college but has not yet made a career decision.

3. Some people think they are sisters they look very much alike, especially when they are dressed alike.

4. Dustin is a serious student, he comes to class on time and always sits in the front of the room, pays attention to the lecture, and asks questions.

5. Over the past five months it has rained for more than sixty days in the Tidewater area. That is twenty more days than Noah had to worry about.

EXERCISE 8

Correct any of the following sentences that are run together or have comma splices. Use periods, semicolons, or commas with coordinating conjunctions.

1. A drum brake is a mechanism used to slow or stop a vehicle, it is found on most cars or trucks.
2. I often wait until I am in the car to brush my hair, therefore, I have to finish the job while driving.
3. It is hard to believe that the garbage collectors could leave so much of our trash they are continually doing this.
4. When the light was green, I pressed the gas pedal then I had to brake because another driver was pulling in front of me.
5. Don't expect that you will never make a mistake, everyone is wrong occasionally.
6. Bus drivers need to stop students from disturbing others on the bus when people ride the bus every day, they expect to have a comfortable ride. Some students stand in the front of the bus this situation could lead to an accident.
7. A San Francisco trolley sign said, "Please hold on sudden stops are necessary."
8. Some people seem to attract misfortune, my friend Gwen is an example, when trouble comes, she never seems to move out of the way.
9. My favorite style of swimming is the breast stroke I like to make my arms spread out and scoop in the water with great force.
10. Island foods are fun to prepare, I love stir-fried foods, not only are they healthful, but they taste wonderful.

EXERCISE 9

Correct any run-together sentences or comma splices in the following paragraphs.

(a) Two types of used car salesmen I try to avoid are the smilers and the talkers, the smiler watches me from his office as I check out his inventory. He waits for about five minutes, then he springs from his office, smiling as he comes toward me. After he has greeted me, he keeps the same idiotic grin on his face, this makes me feel that he thinks I am easy prey. This type of salesman turns me off very quickly, then there is the talker, he knows everything about everything. As he approaches me, he starts to tell me everything about the car starting from the day it was made. He knows how the car got all its dents. He even knows how each stain on the seat got there, sometimes I wonder how one person can know so much about a used car. The smilers and the talkers make shopping for a used car a real headache, I hope I can avoid both types in the future.

(b) To get Henry started in the morning, first wipe his windshield then pat him on the trunk, don't rush him. If you try anything rough such as kicking him in the shin (bumper) he will fight back. After these initial steps and a few kind words of appreciation; get into the car and turn the key in the ignition. After Henry has whined a little; he will probably allow you to back him out of the driveway don't go far, though, without buying him some breakfast at the gas station, remember, if you don't take good care of Henry, he will never even get going, much less do his maximum of 30 miles an hour.

(c) There are three types of patients that are almost always in a dentist's office, they are the unconcerned mother, the complaining teenager, and the "lifestory lifer." The unconcerned mother allows her children to jump all over the chairs while she is reading a magazine just when the other patients think she is going to say something to her children, she turns a page and continues reading. The complaining teenager is another type of patient. She announces to everyone that she had to break some important plans to be there, she always wants to be seen first, no matter how many people are there. Finally, there is the "lifestory lifer," in just fifteen minutes he manages to describe to everyone in the room his children, his job, and his medical and dental problems without ever taking a breath, he is able to talk for as long as there is anyone in the waiting room. These three types of patients can be annoying, but just think, it is only one day of horror for a lifetime of pearly whites.

Chapter 4
ADJECTIVES AND ADVERBS

Recognize adjectives and adverbs,
and use them correctly.

When you write a sentence, you are telling about someone doing something or about something happening. You might write:

> The woman screamed.
> OR
> The clock fell.

As you know, not many sentences are so short. You will usually want to say something more about the woman or the clock. One of the ways you can do that is to use words that describe. You can say:

> The *tall* woman screamed.
> The *tall, mysterious* woman screamed.
> One *tall, mysterious, dark-haired* woman screamed.

You can say:

> The *large* clock fell.
> The *large cuckoo* clock fell.
> The *large, white, antique cuckoo* clock fell.

Adjectives

The words *one, tall, mysterious, dark-haired, large, white, antique,* and *cuckoo* describe persons and things and are called *adjectives.* Adjectives usually tell what kind or which one or how many or how much:

> the *tall* woman
> the *antique* clock
> *one* woman

The italicized words below all tell what kind, which one, how many, or how much about the things they describe.

WHAT KIND	a *good* day
	an *interesting* story
WHICH ONE	*first* mile
	tallest tree
HOW MANY	*four* movies
	few friends
HOW MUCH	*great* success
	little food

Adjectives usually come before the nouns they describe.

> We have an *enthusiastic* teacher.

Adjectives can appear after forms of *to be* (*is, are, was, were,* and so on).

> Our teacher is *enthusiastic.*

Adverbs

In addition to describing people and things, you will want to use words that say something about how, when, and where something is happening. These words are called *adverbs.* You might write:

HOW	The woman enters *suddenly.*
WHEN	The woman enters *early.*
WHERE	The woman enters *below.*
HOW	The clock fell *noisily.*
WHEN	The clock fell *yesterday.*
WHERE	The clock fell *there.*

Adverbs describe verbs, adjectives, or other adverbs.

VERB   I will act *quickly*.

ADJECTIVE   Was it *very* hot? It was *too* hot.

It is *strangely* quiet.

ADVERB   She works *really* hard.

Notice that adverbs, which are words that tell how, when, and where, often end in -*ly* (sudden*ly*, occasional*ly*, sharp*ly*, rude*ly*, happi*ly*).

EXERCISE 1

In the following sentences underline all the adjectives and circle all the adverbs.

1. Parents usually treat adopted children as lovingly as they do their own children.
2. Police cars monitor automobiles electronically to detect speeding.
3. The sleepy students entered the room slowly.
4. My older brother has always done his job well.
5. The crackling fire soon cheered us up.

4a
Use adverbs, not adjectives, to tell how, when, and where something happens.

Remember to use adverbs, not adjectives, when you are describing verbs, adjectives, or other adverbs.

WRONG   The accident happened quick.

RIGHT   The accident happened *quickly*.

[*Quickly* is an adverb that describes the verb *happened*.]

WRONG   He is breathing normal.

RIGHT   He is breathing *normally*.

[*Normally* is an adverb that describes the verb *breathing*.]

WRONG   Rodney talks proper when he is around teachers.

RIGHT   Rodney talks *properly* when he is around teachers.

Caution: Do not forget that adverbs describe adjectives as well as verbs and adverbs. Words describing adjectives like *good, easy,* and *young* should have *-ly* or other appropriate adverb endings.

WRONG   I feel *real* good today.

RIGHT   I feel *really* good today.

EXERCISE 2

Correct any errors in the use of adjectives and adverbs in the following sentences. Write a *C* next to any sentence in which there is no error.

1. I am a fast learner, so I caught on to surfing real quick.
2. My employer told me to finish the job as fast as I could and to stop for the day.
3. Almost anyone works bad when he is in a terrible big hurry.
4. I can finish this ice cream easily before it melts.
5. If you drive too slow, you may not be safe on the roads.
6. Keeping a house real clean, cooking, and raising children constitute a full-time job.
7. Talk soft because my sister is not sleeping very sound.
8. It is a real problem getting a good job if you write bad.
9. In order to clean windows properly, you will need paper towels, window cleaner, rags, and some windows.
10. Swimming does not come easy to everyone.

4b
Recognize participles used as adjectives.

4b-1
Use participles ending in *-ed* and *-ing* correctly.

Many adjectives end in *-ed* or *-ing*. These adjectives come from regular verbs. Since they are participles used as adjectives, they use the participle endings. The regular past participle ending is *-ed*.

-ed FORM USED AS A VERB	-ed FORM USED AS AN ADJECTIVE
The gun is not *loaded*.	Don't carry a *loaded* gun.

The present participle ending is *-ing*.

-ing FORM USED AS A VERB	-ing FORM USED AS AN ADJECTIVE
The girls are *working* hard.	They are *working* girls.

Here are some participles used as adjectives.

Xeroxed copies are available. [copies that have been xeroxed]
This is an *aged* cheese. [a cheese that has been aged]
Don't open any *closed* doors. [doors that have been closed]
My *sewing* box is on the desk. [a box used in sewing]
We have no more *washing* powder. [powder used for washing]
She saw a *purring* cat. [a cat that was purring]

Do not omit the *-d* or *-ed* participle ending.

WRONG	a love one
RIGHT	a loved one
WRONG	a load gun
RIGHT	a loaded gun
WRONG	a toss salad and a bake potato
RIGHT	a tossed salad and a baked potato

Do not omit the *-ing* participle ending.

WRONG	a gather storm
RIGHT	a gathering storm
WRONG	a work girl
RIGHT	a working girl

When verbs like *love, load, toss, bake, change, gather*, and *work* are used as adjectives, remember to add *-ed* or *-ing* to them.

EXERCISE 3

Read the examples below. Then make a participle from each of the following verbs, and use it in a sentence.

EXAMPLES *burn*

   The burned child dreads the fire.

   wish

   I need a wishing well to make my front yard complete

1. help _____
2. admire _____
3. work _____
4. short _____
5. finish _____

EXERCISE 4

Change the verb to the left of each sentence into a participle, if necessary, and complete each of the sentences below.
EXAMPLE (terrify) People are afraid of your _terrifying_____
temper.

(age)   1. Health spas are becoming popular with middle _____ men and women.
(age)   2. The _____ process cannot be stopped, but it can be made less painful.
(injure) 3. Who is the _____ party in the accident case?
(cover) 4. Everyone had to bring a _____ dish to the barbecue.
(cook)   5. Low _____ temperature tenderizes meat.
(use)   6. Be on your guard when buying a _____ car.
(starch) 7. Who doesn't dislike _____ collars?
(ice)   8. I really like _____ tea when I am hot.

EXERCISE 5

Correct any -ed adjective errors in the following paragraph.

My dog Lady is the most spirit dog I have ever known. She never seems tire herself although she exhausts everyone around her. When there are unuse boxes or bags within her reach, you can be assure that she will attack them playfully. She will attack shoes, pocketbooks, toys, or any other unattend items. That's why many of my pocketbooks and my husband's shoes look chew. I hope she calms down before everything in our house is completely ruin.

4b-2
Learn irregular past participles used as adjectives.

Not all verbs are regular. Some are irregular; that is, their past and past participle forms do not always end in -*ed*. Irregular verbs have special past participle forms. When these forms are used as adjectives, they, of course, are irregular too.

> My coat was *torn*.   I have a *torn* coat.
> My fingers were *frozen*.   I had *frozen* fingers.

These are some common past participles used as adjectives.

a *beaten* egg	a home*grown* vegetable
a *broken* glass	the best-*laid* plans
a *chosen* few	the *spoken* word
a well-*done* hamburger	a well-*written* letter
the *stolen* camera	a *worn* garment

If you are not sure whether an adjective form is regular or irregular, look up the present form of the verb it comes from in the dictionary. The past participle (adjective) form comes after the past form of an irregular verb, as in the following example:

> shake (shāk), *vb.*, shook, shaken (shakən), shaking

In this example, the past participle (adjective) form, *shaken*, follows the past form, *shook*.

4c
Use adjectives and adverbs correctly after verbs like look, feel, seem, appear, taste, *and* sound.

Often these verbs mean the same as *is, are, was, were*, or some other form of *to be*. When they do, they are called *linking verbs* because they link adjectives with the words they describe.

> Strawberry shortcake *tastes* delicious.
> [Strawberry shortcake *is* delicious.]
> I feel restless.
> [I *am* restless.]

Whenever you use a verb like *look, feel, seem, smell*, or *taste* as a linking verb, use an adjective with it. When you are just telling how something is done, use an adverb.

LINKING VERB USE AN ADJECTIVE	NOT A LINKING VERB USE AN ADVERB
The teacher looked angry. [*looked = was*]	The teacher looked angrily at me. [*looked* does not = *was*]
She felt cautious about making a decision. [*felt = was*]	She felt cautiously under the bed, not knowing what she would find. [*felt* does not = *was*]
Your decision appears sudden. [*appears = is*]	She appears suddenly—out of nowhere! [*appears* does not = *is*]

Remember that you almost always want to say that someone feels *bad*, not *badly*. A person who feels badly is probably looking for something in the dark.

EXERCISE 6

Write the adjective to the left of each of the following sentences in the blank provided, or change the adjective to an adverb if necessary.

(hasty)   1. Your decision seems _____ to me.
(hasty)   2. We ate _____, not certain when the doorbell would ring.
(bad)   3. I felt very _____ after making a difficult decision.
(real)   4. Dave is a _____ good friend of mine.
(slow)   5. People who drive too _____ don't belong on the road.
(sad)   6. My sister looked _____ at the broken vase.
(sad)   7. She felt _____.
(fresh)   8. The hamburger I bought doesn't smell _____ to me.

4d
Use adjectives and adverbs correctly when comparing two or more persons or things.

Use a comparative form of adjectives and adverbs when comparing two persons or things; use a superlative form when comparing more than two.

4d-1

Short adjectives and some adverbs use an *-er* ending when they compare two persons or things (comparative form).

> Today is *hotter* than yesterday.
> Herb is *lazier* than Jim.
> Luis snores *louder* than Joe.

4d-2

The word *more* comes before longer adjectives and most adverbs that compare two persons or things (comparative form).

> Ted is *more* interesting than Shawn.
> I talk *more* freely when Sue is not around.

4d-3

Short adjectives and some adverbs use an *-est* ending when they compare more than two persons or things (superlative form).

> This is the *hottest* room in the house.
> The *largest* of the three backs is the powerback.
> Luis snores *loudest* of all.

4d-4

The word *most* comes before longer adjectives and most adverbs that compare more than two persons or things (superlative form).

> Ted is the *most* interesting person I know.
> I talk *most* freely when no one else is listening.

Do not use *more* or *most* before a descriptive word that ends in *-er* or *-est*.

WRONG	more prettier
RIGHT	*prettier*
WRONG	most funniest
RIGHT	*funniest*

If *more* or *most* comes before a descriptive word, do not put *-er* or *-est* at the end of that word.

WRONG	more likelier
RIGHT	*more likely*

WRONG	most wonderfulest
RIGHT	most *wonderful*

4d-5
Learn the special comparative and superlative forms of *good* and *well* and *bad* and *badly*.

Words That Describe or Compare Persons and Things

Janice is a *good* daughter.
Janice is a *better* daughter than Sarah. [comparative]
Janice is the *best* daughter anyone could have. [superlative]

I have a *bad* cold.
I have a *worse* cold than Earl. [comparative]
I have the *worst* cold I have ever had. [superlative]

Words That Describe or Compare Verbs

Leon obeys *well*.
Janice obeys *better* than Sarah. [comparative]
Janice obeys *best* of all [superlative]

I drive *badly* when I am tired.
I drive *worse* when I am tired than when I am rested. [comparative]
I drive *worst* of all when I am ill. [superlative]

4d-6
Summary of comparisons: adjectives and adverbs

BASIC FORM	COMPARATIVE FORM FOR TWO ITEMS	SUPERLATIVE FORM FOR MORE THAN TWO ITEMS
small	smaller	smallest
fast	faster	fastest
beautiful	more beautiful	most beautiful
rapidly	more rapidly	most rapidly
good, well	better	best
bad, badly	worse	worst
much, many	more	most

EXERCISE 7

Correct the incorrect adjectives and adverbs in the following sentences by using the right form to compare the persons or things. Write *C* next to any sentences that are correct.

1. The ten-speed is one of the most fastest bikes.

2. I like both neighbors, but one is more friendlier.

3. Mosquitoes are becoming a bigger problem than ever.

4. One of the loveliest places to visit in the fall is the mountains.

5. Saturday is the club's most busiest night.

6. The drydock is the most coldest place in the shipyard.

7. It often appears to someone in church that the harder the pew is, the more deeper the sleep.

8. Bill is the most funniest person I know.

9. Don't make matters worst than they are.

10. If a person pays back what he owes immediately, it will be much more simpler.

EXERCISE 8

Put the correct comparative or superlative forms of the adjectives and adverbs to the left of the following sentences in the blanks provided.

(good)   1. My father cooks _____ than my mother does.

(bad)   2. The lectures we get at orientation are _____ than you can imagine.

(good)   3. My friend Amy is the _____ listener I know.

(bad)   4. At boot camp we were treated _____ than animals.

(good)   5. Irene drives _____ than Frank does.

4e
Learn the special uses of good *and* well.

Good is always used as an adjective.

Bleak House is a *good* book.
Joe is *good* to me.
Al looks *good* in brown.

Well can be used as an adjective or an adverb. It is an adjective when it describes someone's health or appearance; it is an adverb when it describes how something is done.

A completely *well* person would not have spent the day in bed.
[adjective—describes someone's health]
The children usually play *well* together.
[adverb—describes the way the children played]

EXERCISE 9

Underline the correct descriptive word in parentheses.

1. That stew smells (good, well).
2. Homemade ice cream always tastes (good, well).
3. That red hat looks (good, well) with your purple skirt.
4. My father was sick, but today he feels as (good, well) as he ever has.
5. I get discouraged when I don't do (good, well) at something.
6. Look (good, well) under the bed, and maybe you'll find your other shoe.
7. At first Cynthia and I didn't get along very (good, well).

EXERCISE 10

Correct any incorrect adjectives or adverbs in the following sentences. Write *C* next to each sentence that is correct.

1. All my brothers have jobs that pay good.
2. I am feeling badly about losing your camera.
3. Music helps me release all of my build-up tension.
4. When you get married, it is for better or worst.
5. My aunt is a middle-age woman who loves hard rock music.
6. The expressway traffic situation is looking well today.

7. The children didn't want to sit in their assign seats.
8. Was your aunt really wearing a stripe shirt and well-wore jeans?
9. Drafting paper will not tear easily.
10. My mother said to me one day, "Stop watching those soap operas, and cook your husband some good, old-fashion soul food."

EXERCISE 11

Correct any errors in the use of adjectives or adverbs in the following paragraph.

It was a great day to play baseball. The sky was dark blue with plenty of fluffy white clouds. The well-mark play field looked cleanly for the big game. We were so excited about the game we couldn't wait to start practicing. Everybody seemed anxious to play ball. Finally, the umpire called out real loud, "Play ball," and threw a ball to the tobacco-chew pitcher. The pitcher struck out batters as quick as they came to bat, and batters that did hit balls were tagged out easy at first base. That was the most happiest day I can remember for our team, but the other team felt that it was the worse.

EXERCISE 12

Describe a room in your home or apartment, using adjectives for specific details, or describe someone you know well, using colorful adjectives so the reader can really picture the person you are writing about. Then exchange descriptions with someone in your class, and mark any errors you notice in the use of adjectives.

Chapter 5

NOUNS AND PRONOUNS

Use nouns and pronouns correctly.

You already know that nouns are the names of persons, places, things, or ideas.

> My sister (person) went to the mall (place) to buy a watch (thing) so she could tell time (idea).

You also know that a pronoun takes the place of a noun.

> She (my sister) bought it (the watch) for herself (my sister).

This chapter will help with some of the problems you may have using nouns and pronouns in your papers. It begins by showing the difference between singular and plural nouns and explaining how to use noun possessive forms correctly. Then it offers help with the use of pronouns as subjects and objects, with possessive pronouns, and with reflexive pronouns (*myself, himself,* and so on). The problem of agreement between noun and pronoun subjects and their verbs or antecedents is discussed in Chapter **6**.

5a
Use singular and plural nouns correctly.

5a-1
A singular noun does not add an ending.

A singular noun names only one person or thing. It is often used with a singular word like *a, one, much, each,* or *every.* Do not add an *-s* or another plural ending to any singular noun that appears by itself or with a singular adjective.

WRONG	each members of the group
RIGHT	each *member* of the group
WRONG	a new records
RIGHT	a new *record*

5a-2
Most plural nouns end in *-s.*

A plural noun names more than one person or thing. It is often used with a plural word like *six, many, all, some,* or *several* or with an expression like *a number, a few,* or *a group of* to describe more than one person or thing. Do not forget to mark the plural of a noun.

WRONG	forty hour per week
RIGHT	forty *hours* per week
WRONG	many student
RIGHT	many *students*
WRONG	all of the required adjustment
RIGHT	all of the required *adjustments*
WRONG	at least three time
RIGHT	at least three *times*
WRONG	a number of test
RIGHT	a number of *tests*
WRONG	I have a few ticket.
RIGHT	I have a few *tickets.*
WRONG	these kind of things
RIGHT	these *kinds* of things

Even when the number of persons or things is not mentioned in the sentence, use the *-s* or another plural ending when you mean to name more than one person or thing.

WRONG	Many people freeze up when they take test.
RIGHT	Many people freeze up when they take *tests*.

5a-3
A few nouns use special plural forms.

Instead of ending in -*s*, some nouns have special plural forms. Here are some common examples:

man	men	foot	feet
woman	women	tooth	teeth
gentleman	gentlemen	person	people
child	children	goose	geese

Do not use a plural noun when you mean to use a singular one.

WRONG	a women
RIGHT	a *woman*
WRONG	He is five foot tall.
RIGHT	He is five *feet* tall. OR He is a five-foot-tall man.

5a-4
Some nouns have no plural forms.

There are a few words that do not have plural forms. Some examples are abstract words like *happiness*, *violence*, *sincerity*, and *laziness*, and the common words *deer* and *sheep*. Do not add endings to these words.

WRONG	Think of the violences in the world!
RIGHT	Think of the *violence* in the world!

EXERCISE 1

Correct any incorrect singular or plural nouns.

1. Anesthesia is used in many hospital.

2. There are plenty of activities to keep all the guest entertained.

3. If you see your child display one of these symptom, act quickly.

4. I respect firefighters, who put their life on the line.

5. One of my friend is always trying to borrow money.

6. He eats at least six time a day.

7. It takes patience to change five or six diaper every three hour.

8. At one time a phone call cost five cent.

9. Being shy can sometime be a blessing.

10. Handicapped student need a special area to take test.

EXERCISE 2

Edit the following paragraphs, correcting any errors in the singular and plural forms of nouns.

(a) Timothy was one of my high school friend. We were in the same art class each years. Timothy was known as a comic book freaks because he loved to read comic book and draw all of his own comic character. He was a good artist, too, but he never wanted to do any of the assignment the teacher gave. Instead of sketching a glass or a bowl of peach, Timothy would draw comic strip of all his favorite comic hero, and his imagination was amazing. He drew strange character with weird names from planet 60 million light year away. Every chances Timothy got, he would think up a bunch of new comic strip to draw. I don't know what has become of Timothy since high school, but I hope he is living happily ever after in his fantasy world with all the super hero he created.

(b) "The inmate enjoy our fine city jail cuisine," said the sheriff of the Newport News City Jail in an address to about two dozen ministers and their guest at a special luncheon last week. As the sheriff continued speaking, four inmate dressed in white uniforms and head covering came into the room carrying tray of food, including bowl filled with tossed salad garnished with radishes and green onion, which they served professionally.

5a-5

Make it clear that a noun shows possession by adding an apostrophe (') and -s.

> the book belonging to John → John's book
> the playground for the children → the children's playground
> the health of a person → a person's health

Do not carelessly omit the ending that shows ownership.

WRONG   John book
RIGHT   John's book
WRONG   Children playground
RIGHT   Children's playground

For more information on the use of the apostrophe in showing possession, see **15a**, **b**, and **c**.

5a-6
Do not confuse a noun that shows possession with a word that merely ends in *-s*.

Be sure that you have a reason for putting an apostrophe before an *s*. Do not put an apostrophe before an *s* used to indicate the plural of a word or to mark the present form of a verb.

WRONG   She is alway's in the way.
RIGHT   She is *always* in the way.

WRONG   Joe work's on Saturday's.
[*Works* is the present form of *work*; *Saturdays* is the plural form of *Saturday*. Apostrophes are not needed.]
RIGHT   Joe works on Saturdays.

EXERCISE 3

Correct the following sentences for errors in the use of possessive nouns. Remove any apostrophes that are not needed to show possession.

1. I hope I can use Captain Kirk reason and initiative to solve problem's in my own life.

2. Some people homes are large enough to have sunroom's.

3. The walls in Larry room were filled with hubcaps.

4. Getting into a neighbor business can cause a lot of trouble.

5. I lock the bathroom door so my daughter won't wash her doll hair in the toilet.

5b
Use pronoun subjects and objects correctly.

Nouns (*children, woman*) look the same whether they are subjects or objects. The pronouns *I, he, she, we, they*, and *who* change when they become objects.

I	→	me
he	→	him
she	→	her
we	→	us
they	→	them
who	→	whom

We avoided the spiders,
> BUT

the spiders also avoided *us*.

Subjects

I, you, he, she, it, we, they, and *who* are used as subjects of sentences or dependent clauses. They tell who the subject is.

> *I* waited for hours.
> *They* listened carefully.
> This is the man *who* called you.

Objects

Me, you, him, her, it, us, them, and *whom* are used as objects. Pronouns (like nouns) can be objects of verbs or objects of prepositions. They are objects of verbs when they receive the action of these verbs.

> Three children live on our street. Harry saw *them* yesterday.

Pronouns are objects of prepositions when they appear in prepositional phrases like *to him, to her*, and *for me*. These pronouns are called *indirect objects*.

> I lent some money to *her* (the woman).

Sometimes the preposition *to* or *for* is omitted with indirect objects.

> I lent *her* some money. [I lent some money to her.]
> He did *me* a favor. [He did a favor for me.]

Caution: When a pronoun such as *I, me, he, him, she, he, they* or *them* follows *than* or *as* in a comparison, decide on the correct form of the pronoun by putting in mentally any missing words.

> She works harder than I.
> [harder than I *do*; *I* is a subject.]
> I like Darlene as much as her.
> [as much as *I like* her; *her* is an object.]

5b-1
Use *me* instead of *I* as an object. *I* can be used only as a subject.

In sentences like

> Sally gave the tickets to Jim and *me*.
> OR
> Mrs. Consalvo invited Joan and *me* to the party.

remember that *me* is used as an object even though it does not directly follow the verb.

> WRONG   She called to Ed and I to come in.
> RIGHT   She called to Ed and *me* to come in.

5b-2
Do not use *us* instead of *we* as the subject of a sentence.

> WRONG   Us girls go bowling every Friday.
> RIGHT   We girls go bowling every Friday.

Since *we* is the subject of the sentence, if you want to show that you are one of the girls, you have to say, "We [girls] go bowling."

5b-3
***Them* cannot be used to describe nouns.**

If you want to say that certain persons or things are in a particular place, use the words *these* or *those* to express that idea.

> WRONG   Them books are on the table.
> RIGHT   *Those* books are on the table.

5b-4

Remember to use subject pronouns (*I*, *he*, and so on) when a sentence or clause has a double subject.

Do not confuse
$\left.\begin{array}{l}\textit{I} \text{ with } \textit{me} \\ \textit{he} \text{ with } \textit{him} \\ \textit{she} \text{ with } \textit{her} \\ \textit{we} \text{ with } \textit{us} \\ \textit{they} \text{ with } \textit{them}\end{array}\right\}$ when your sentence has two subjects.

WRONG   Me and Althea always come home late.
RIGHT   Althea and *I* always come home late.

WRONG   Him and me lost a bet.
RIGHT   *He* and *I* lost a bet.

WRONG   Her and Joe are really close.
RIGHT   *She* and Joe are really close.

For a sentence that has a double subject, there is a simple test you can use to see whether you have used the right word. Try using each subject by itself as the subject of the sentence. In the sentence

Me and Althea always come home late.

you would not say

Me always come home late.

because *I*, not *me*, is the subject of the sentence. Therefore, if it is correct to say

I always come home late.

it is also correct to say

Althea and *I* always come home late.

5b-5

Use *whom*, not *who*, as an object.

WRONG   This is the man to who I gave the tickets.
RIGHT   This is the man to *whom* I gave the tickets.

EXERCISE 4

Underline all pronouns in the following expressions. Write *S* above all subject pronouns; write *O* above all object pronouns. Then use each expression in a sentence.

1. he and I

2. we brothers

3. who among you

4. Nancy and me

5. many of us

6. she or Sarah

7. the man whom I saw

8. a picture of Helen and me

EXERCISE 5

In the following sentences, underline the correct word in parentheses.

1. One morning my parents took my brother and (I, me) to Waffle House.
2. I told him that (we, us) ex-Marines would have to stick together.
3. When we were in Alaska, (my friends and I, me and my friends) camped near Prince William Sound. Will we ever camp there again?
4. Everyone left except (my brother and me, my brother and I).
5. To (who, whom) were you referring in your letter?
6. (He and I, Him and me) went downstairs to see what was going on.
7. All was going well until my friend Joey knocked over a bucket of crabs, sending my father and (I, me) overboard.
8. I just told you that (those, them) glasses have already been washed.
9. When (she and her husband, her and her husband) decided to go into politics, they gave up all rights to privacy.
10. I sent my boss, (who, whom) was unaware of the problem, a frantic e-mail.

5c
Show possession clearly by using the correct pronoun forms.

Possessives

My, mine, your, yours, his, her, hers, its, our, ours, their, theirs, whose, and so on are pronouns that show possession. These words cannot be used as subjects. Instead they tell who or what owns a particular thing. If you wanted to say, "I own a house, and it is large," you would probably say:

> My house is large.

If you wanted to say that the roof belonging to the house was large, you would say:

> Its roof is large.

5c-1
Be sure that you change *you* to *your*, *it* to *its*, and *who* to *whose* to show possession.

> WRONG   In an emergency you know who you friends are.
> RIGHT   In an emergency you know who *your* friends are.
>
> WRONG   Every nation has it secrets.
> RIGHT   Every nation has *its* secrets.

5c-2
Remember the two common ways that a pronoun can show possession.

THESE PRONOUNS COME BEFORE THE NOUN	THESE PRONOUNS SUBSTITUTE FOR A PRONOUN AND A NOUN
This is *my* cover.	This cover is *mine*. [my cover]
This is *your* cover.	This cover is *yours*. [your cover]
This is *his* cover.	This cover is *his*. [his cover]
This is *her* cover.	This cover is *hers*. [her cover]
This is *our* cover.	This cover is *ours*. [our cover]
This is *their* cover.	This cover is *theirs*. [their cover]

5c-3
Do not use an apostrophe with a pronoun to show possession.

The pronouns *yours, his, hers, its, ours,* and *theirs* do not have an apostrophe (') before the *s. Mine* does not have an apostrophe (') or an *s.*

WRONG   mine's, mines, your's, hi's, her's, it's, our's, their's
RIGHT   mine, yours, his, hers, its, ours, theirs

WRONG   That's mine's.
RIGHT   That's *mine.*

WRONG   I'm not using that pan because it's lid is missing.
RIGHT   I'm not using that pan because *its* lid is missing.

REMINDER: **Pronouns + Apostrophes = Contractions**

Remember that a pronoun with an apostrophe always means a contraction, not possession.

CONTRACTION	POSSESSION
You're here.	Use your head.
They're wrong.	Those are their raincoats.
It's raining.	Its tail is curly.

For more information on contractions, see 15d.

EXERCISE 6

Underline the word groups that are correctly written.

1. you raincoat; your raincoat
2. This is mines. This is mine. This is mine's.
3. its story; it story; it's story
4. What's mine is yours. What's mine's is your's. What's mine is your's.
5. That bar is theirs. That bar is their's.
6. Is it ours or his? Is it our's or hi's? Is it ours or hi's?

EXERCISE 7

Decide whether the following words or expressions show possession. Then use each in a sentence of your own: *your, there, you're,
its, whose, it's, who's.*

EXERCISE 8

In the following sentences change any italicized word that does not
show possession correctly.

1. The *Brady Bunch* taught *it's* audience that sometimes being
    unpopular is not so bad.

2. When shooting free throws, make sure *you* shoulders are in line
    with the goal.

3. They should put new shock absorbers on *they're* van because *it*
    ride is so rough it will knock *you* teeth out.

4. *Your* sure that no one knows *who's* books these are?

5. Does *your* sister always borrow *your* clothes without first asking
    if *your* planning to wear them?

6. *Their* children are grown up; *mine's* are still in their teens.

7. All people have *they* own meaning of Christmas.

5c-4
**When a word ending in *-ing* is used as a noun,
use a possessive pronoun to describe it.**

> WRONG   I don't like you sleeping until noon.
> RIGHT   I don't like *your* sleeping until noon.

Sleeping is a thing (an activity); therefore, it is a noun. The possessive pronoun *your* rather than the object pronoun *you* should then
be used to describe *sleeping*. The writer does not object to *you*; he
just objects to *your sleeping*.

EXERCISE 9

Correct all errors in words showing possession. Some items may be
correct.

1. Tom is a good friend of mine's.

2. Some baggers don't care how they handle you groceries.

3. It is almost impossible to go anywhere with Bob without him making a fool of himself.

4. On the soap operas both the husband and wife have something to hide; it's often a matter of who's secret comes out first.

5. My VCR has definitely reached the end of its useful life.

6. Park you vehicle under a street light.

7. Every marriage has its ups and downs.

EXERCISE 10

Edit the following paragraph, changing any incorrect possessive pronouns.

When I was nine years old my family lived in a community called Academy Park, which had it's own recreation center—a place where all the children and even a lot of adults liked to come in they're spare time. There was never any question about who's place the center was; it was our's. The center had games for the grown-ups, and many of them looked forward to enjoying it's facilities day after day. In addition to cards, checkers, and horseshoes, the center offered art and sewing classes and upholstery workshops. While I enjoyed these things, I have to admit that something else at the center was a favorite of mines—its lunchtime activities. After we ate, the director usually asked, "Whose interested in hearing a story today?" Then we had an hour of our favorite stories. The center gave grown-ups and children something that was fun to do in their free hours.

EXERCISE 11

Correct the following paragraph, eliminating any errors in noun and pronoun forms or the incorrect use of the apostrophe.

My mother's favorite brother, Uncle Francis, is undoubtedly my favorite relative. In fact, him and my aunt Jessie are the only people in my mother family who are even worth mentioning. Uncle Francis is a trucker, but he moonlight's as a bouncer in one of Chestertowns shadiest nightspot, the Midnight Cafe. I could not have survived to manhood without Uncle Francis's help. When I was small, I fell into a sewer and would probably have drowned had it not been for my uncle efforts. Although he has been married three time's to women who have divorced him, he doesn't let his marital problem's get him down. His helpfulness and good humor should explain me calling Uncle Francis my favorite relative.

5d
Myself, yourself, himself, herself, itself, ourselves, yourselves, *and* themselves *are never used alone.*

Use these words with subjects and objects to give them emphasis.

> I walked by *myself* when I was eleven months old.
> *Charles* thinks for *himself.*
> We *ourselves* want to get the job finished.
> The *lesson itself* is not difficult.

Do not use objects (*me*, *him*, *them*) for this purpose.

WRONG	I bought me a milkshake.
RIGHT	I bought *myself* a milkshake.
WRONG	My brother found him a good wife.
RIGHT	My brother found *himself* a good wife.

5d-1
Reflexive pronouns must come after the words they refer to.

WRONG	Myself and some friends moved all the furniture.
RIGHT	Some friends and *I* moved all the furniture.
RIGHT	Some friends and I moved all the furniture *ourselves.*

5d-2

Be sure to spell *himself, itself, ourselves,* and *themselves* correctly.

himself	NOT	hisself
itself	NOT	its self
ourselves	NOT	ourself
themselves	NOT	theirself
		theirselves
		themself

EXERCISE 12
NOUN AND PRONOUN REVIEW

Change any incorrect nouns or pronouns.

1. During the past five year there have been many changes in myself.

2. Did he mean to keep that letter a secret from you and I?

3. In cold weather most people bundle themself up in warm clothing.

4. Are these children their's or her's?

5. Her and I were planning to go to the dance until you called.

6. I went to the mall to buy me some socks.

7. That red motorcycle is mine's; the other one is his.

8. Remember that a sales tax takes money out of you pocket.

9. I call what he has on his face a rat nest, but he thinks it's a beard.

10. We always get us something good to eat.

11. This is a time when my relatives get together to spread the latest gossip and to enjoy themselves.

Chapter 6

AGREEMENT

Make a subject agree with its verb; make singular and plural words agree with the words they refer to.

6a
Make each subject agree with its verb.

Many of your papers will be written in the present tense. A verb in the present tense has an *-s* ending or no ending. It is important to be sure that every present tense verb you use agrees with its subject.

In the following lists you can see that most subjects agree with present-tense verbs that have no ending; only *he, she,* and *it*—or nouns that can be replaced by *he, she,* and *it*—agree with verbs that end in *-s*.

I ___sit___	we ___sit___	I _____	we _____
you ___sit___	you ___sit___	you _____	you _____
he ___sits___	they ___sit___	he ___s___	they _____
she ___sits___		she ___s___	
it ___sits___		it ___s___	

6a
—
agr

6a-1
In the present tense, singular (*he, she, it*) subjects agree with verbs that end in -*s*. Plural (*they*) subjects agree with verbs that do not end in -*s*.

The present tense tells what is happening now or what happens on a regular basis or as a matter of course. When you use the present tense, make sure to add -*s* to the verb with a singular (*he, she, it*) subject.

SOME SUBJECTS AND VERBS THAT AGREE

(*he* subject)	Michael *sends* e-mail to his friends every day. [*Michael* could be replaced by *He.*]
(*she* subject)	Lisa *smiles* and *looks* happy when she sees you. [*Lisa* could be replaced by *She.*]
(*it* subject)	A party sometimes *lasts* all night. [*A party* could be replaced by *It.*]
(*they* subject)	The neighbors always *finish* dinner before we do. [*The neighbors* could be replaced by *They.*]
(*they* subject)	The weird noises outside *keep* us awake. [*The weird noises outside* could be replaced by *They.*]

▽ **Caution:** Words sometimes come between a singular subject and the verb that goes with it. When this happens, be very careful to make the verb end in -*s* to agree with its subject.

WRONG   One of my best friends sing off key.
RIGHT   One of my best friends *sings* off key.
[*One,* not *friends,* is the subject of the sentence. Since *one* is singular, *sings* should end in -*s* to agree with it.]

1. The following singular (*he, she, it*) subjects agree with verbs that end in -*s*.

one	*One* of the children *plays* quietly by himself.
everyone	*Everyone tries* to get her attention.
someone	*Someone waits* for Jane after class every day.
something	*Something* always *makes* me late.
everything	*Everything happens* to me.

each	Each of the police officers *guards* one section of the mall.
kind	This *kind* of jewelry costs a lot.
sort	The best *sort* of candy *is* expensive.
type	One *type* of businessman *is* the workaholic.

2. The following plural (*they*) subjects agree with verbs that do not end in -*s*.

lots	*Lots* of my friends *attend* this school.
kinds	Many *kinds* of clothes *are* found in a thrift shop.
both	*Both* of their children *study* several hours a day.
many	*Many* of us *worry* about the future.
Mary and Joe	*Mary and Joe* often *visit* us on Sunday.

3. *All, some, most,* and *none* can be singular or plural, depending on meaning.

SINGULAR SUBJECT VERB ENDS IN -*s*	PLURAL SUBJECT VERB DOES NOT END IN -*s*
All candy *tastes* delicious.	All jellybeans *taste* delicious.
Some of the mail *seems* to be lost.	Some of the husbands *seem* to be male chauvinists.
Most of my morning *was* wasted.	Most of the books *are* mine.
None of the money *is* gone.	None (not any) of the children *are* here.

4. *Who, which,* and *that* are singular when they refer to singular subjects. They are plural when they refer to plural subjects.

SINGULAR SUBJECT VERB ENDS IN -*s*	PLURAL SUBJECT VERB DOES NOT END IN -*s*
He who *hesitates* is lost.	People who *work* hard need rest.

5. Units of money, time, and measure are considered singular subjects; they agree with verbs that end in -*s*.

Five dollars *seems* to be all the money I have.
Two hours *is* a long time to wait for a bus.

6. Two singular words joined by *or* or *nor* = a singular subject. They agree with a verb ending in -*s*.

Either the movie or the concert *seems* like a good idea.
Neither Jeff nor Mike *wants* to work very hard.

6a

agr

If one word is singular and the other one plural, the verb agrees with the subject that is nearer to it.

Neither Jeff nor the children *want* to work very hard.
Neither the children nor Jeff *wants* to work very hard.

EXERCISE 1

Write *S* for singular in the blank to the right of each singular subject. Write *P* for plural next to each plural subject.

woman _____   geese _____

anyone _____   somebody _____

one of you _____   all of the children _____

many of the reasons _____   none of the food _____

a book of stamps _____   ten dollars _____

a driver who _____   thoughts that _____

fashion _____   men _____

nothing _____   no one _____

a few _____   anything _____

several of my relatives _____   each of us _____

some of the apples _____   she and her cousin _____

everyone _____   all of the candy _____

EXERCISE 2

In the following sentences, underline the verb in parentheses that agrees with its subject.

1. Vernon (talks, talk) from the time he (start, starts) cutting your hair until the time he is finished.
2. Usually Susan (dresses, dress) very informally.
3. Every time Joe has some extra money, he always (spend, spends) it.
4. Those children (makes, make) you smile when you really don't feel like it.
5. The slow driver never (consider, considers) that other drivers have some place to go.

EXERCISE 3

In the following sentences, underline the verb in parentheses that agrees with its subject.

1. Someone who (find, finds) out your password can cause you no end of trouble.
2. The mall has several kinds of stores that (stays, stay) open late.
3. Some of my friends (spends, spend) their evenings in that bar.
4. Everything (bother, bothers) me today.
5. All of my new friends (seem, seems) to look up to me.

EXERCISE 4

Correct the incorrect italicized verbs in the following sentences so that they agree with their subjects. Write *C* next to each sentence that is correct.

1. The hallway *look* like a racetrack.

2. My aunt always *want* me to invest my money in her company.

3. Julius's neighbors *makes* annoying noises.

4. Ten cents *buys* very little these days.

5. The bimetal strip *expands* when the air surrounding it is warm.

6. Before a wedding even *start*, there always *seems* to be somebody crying.

7. Sammy told me about the parts of the movie that *scares* everyone.

8. Brushing out the curls in your hair *relaxes* it and *give* it body and bounce.

9. Writing often *help* me explore the world of imagination.

10. Not one of the students *realize* that the bell has rung.

6a-2

In the present tense, *I*, *we*, and *you* subjects agree with verbs that do not end in -s.

SOME SUBJECTS AND VERBS THAT AGREE
I like to visit him.
You always *finish* first.
I work every day from 8:00 to 4:30.
We understand your problem.
You treat John unfairly.

EXERCISE 5

Circle the verbs that can be used with the following subjects. There may be more than one for each subject.

EXAMPLE   I passes, thinks, (listen), (work)

1. People races, drinks, shout, dance

2. I sings, play, twirls, strut, take

3. Each of us swim, row, fishes, float, pretend

4. Not one of the snakes bite, hiss, strikes, rattles

5. Several newcomers in the area talk, smile, greets, waves

6. You cry, fights, scratch, sleep

7. I scream, laugh, hears, works

8. You collapse, jog, blinks, touch

9. Rusty, a member of the club for years, swims, wonder, sits, hide

10. We snores, delivers, act, thinks, ask, test

6a-3

Remember the forms of the verb *to be* that agree with their subjects.

The present tense of *to be* has three verb forms: *am*, *is*, and *are*. *Am* agrees with *I*; *is* ends in *-s* to agree with *he, she,* and *it* subjects; and *are* agrees with all other subjects.

SINGULAR	PLURAL
I *am*	we *are*
you *are*	you *are*
he, she, it *is*	they *are*

To be is the only verb that has two past forms that need to agree with their subjects: *was* and *were*. *Was* agrees with *I, he, she,* and *it*; *were* agrees with all other subjects.

SINGULAR	PLURAL
I *was*	we *were*
you *were*	you *were*
he, she, it *was*	they *were*

Caution: In *here is* (*are*), *there is* (*are*), and *where is* (*are*) sentences, the subject comes after the verb. Be sure to look after the verb for its subject in such sentences, and make the verb agree with its subject.

> Here is the key you have been looking for.
> [*Is* agrees with the singular subject *key*.]

> There are definitely mice in this attic.
> [*Are* agrees with the plural subject *mice*.]

> Where were those shoes when you found them?
> [*Were* agrees with the plural subject *shoes*.]

EXERCISE 6

In the following sentences, underline the correct verb form in parentheses.

1. Since we don't encourage good mechanics, the only ones we see (is, are) on reruns of the Andy Griffith show.
2. Eating vegetables (is, are) good for a person's health.
3. There (is, are) only a few days of vacation left.
4. Why do parents spank children when there (is, are) other forms of discipline?
5. In the bus a large group of students (was, were) pointing and laughing.
6. There (is, are) the shopaholic, the frequent shopper, and the in-a-hurry shopper.
7. On that shelf there (is, are) several of my favorite knickknacks.
8. The only things my brother has gained from his addiction (is, are) a $60-a-day habit, a stay at the Portsmouth City Jail, and a soulless existence.
9. Here (is, are) the books and tapes the language lab supplies.
10. A comfortable home, a family, and a good career (is, are) what I see when I gaze into my crystal ball.

6a-4
Singular subjects (*he, she,* and *it*) agree with the verb form *has*; all other subjects agree with the verb form *have*.

SUBJECT	VERB	SUBJECT	VERB
I	have	we	have
you	have	you	have
he, she, it	has	they	have

EXERCISE 7

Correct the incorrect italicized verbs in the following sentences so that subjects and verbs agree. Write *C* next to each correct sentence.

1. My father's appearance and attitude *has* changed.

2. Rave dancing *has* been around for more than ten years.

3. The roles of women these days *has* changed considerably.

4. He *has* to jog every morning to keep his weight under control.

5. One of the children *have* to be in bed by 9 p.m.

EXERCISE 8

Edit the following paragraph for incorrect use of *is, are, has,* and *have.*

The world of video games has three basic categories. The most popular is probably action games. One example of this type is *Mortal Kombat,* which has two or more people beating each other's brains out. Another action game is the sports simulators. These games are based on actual sports and is a means of allowing someone to play with the teams. The last type of action games are the "kill or be killed" games. These games often have one person who shoots hundreds of others. There is many examples of this type, but the most popular is *Goldeneye.* Adventure and puzzle games is also available to people who enjoy video games, but the game played most often, in my opinion, has to be the action game.

6a-5
Singular subjects (*he, she,* and *it*) agree with the verb forms *does* and *goes;* all other subjects agree with the verb forms *do* and *go.*

SUBJECT	VERB	SUBJECT	VERB
I	do	I	go
you	do	you	go
he, she, it	does	he, she, it	goes

SUBJECT	VERB	SUBJECT	VERB
we	do	we	go
you	do	you	go
they	do	they	go

EXERCISE 9

In the following sentences, underline the correct verb form in parentheses.

1. Rain and snow (do, does) not keep loyal fans away.
2. It looks as though they (go, goes) to all of the school activities.
3. Many young parents today (does, do) seem too busy to take care of their babies.
4. Tonya will see that everything (go, goes) well.
5. It just (go, goes) to show you that people (do, does) not always do what you would have done in their place.

6a-6

Remember the subjects that agree with the contracted forms of the verb + *not*.

Since -*n't* only adds *not* to verbs like *do, have, was,* and so on, the same subject that agrees with one of these verbs agrees with its contracted form.

I subjects agree with the verbs *don't, wasn't,* and *haven't. He, she,* and *it* subjects agree with the verbs *isn't, doesn't, wasn't,* and *hasn't. We, you,* and *they* subjects agree with the verbs *aren't, don't, weren't,* and *haven't.*

SOME SUBJECTS AND VERBS THAT AGREE

(*I* subject)	I *don't* understand you.
(*he* subject)	Dennis *doesn't* like Janis.
(*she* subject)	Rhonda *hasn't* heard the news.
(*it* subject)	My car *doesn't* start on cold days.
(*we* subject)	We *weren't* going to tell him.
(*they* subject)	Joe and Richard *weren't* always friends.
(*they* subject)	His teeth *aren't* straight.

EXERCISE 10

Correct the incorrect italicized verbs in the following sentences so that they agree with their subjects. Write *C* next to each sentence that is correct.

1. Buying everything on credit *don't* seem to be a problem for many people.

2. Your soap and shampoo *isn't* used for washing a baby's body and hair.

3. When my daughter takes a bath, she *doesn't* always clean the tub.

4. Some people *don't* look very good in hats.

5. *Aren't* the union supporters going to strike?

 CHECKLIST: When to Add an -*s* to the Verb

ADD AN -*s* ENDING	DO NOT ADD AN -*s* ENDING
in the present when the subject is singular (*he*, *she*, or *it* subject)	in the present when the subject is plural (*they* subject)
when *was* is used with a *he*, *she*, or *it* subject	when *were* is used with *we*, *you*, or a *they* subject

In contractions the -*n't* ending does not affect the verbs *is, are, has, have, was, were, does,* and *do. Is* becomes *isn't; are* becomes *aren't,* etc. when the verbs become negative.

EXERCISE 11

Write a sentence using each of the following subjects: *busybodies, Eddie, my sister, someone, a crate of oranges, several of my friends, one of you.* The verb of each sentence should be in the present tense.

EXERCISE 12

The student who wrote this paragraph at times forgot to use an -*s* ending where it was needed and sometimes used an -*s* where it was not really needed. Circle any errors in agreement, and write your corrections above them.

Some of my friends says that I treat my dog Nancy like a person instead of a dog. I enjoys my dog for the way she act and for the things she do. When Nancy want water, something makes her stands in front of the refrigerator and bark for ice to be put in it.

She don't like lukewarm water from the sink. Nothing can make her eat her food from a dog's bowl. She insist on using one of our china dishes. She also want to sleep in a regular bed just as we does. She have a special pillow that she drag around the house all the time. Nancy love to chew ice and eat candy. She adore ice cream. I treat Nancy like a person because she do act more like a person than a dog.

EXERCISE 13

Change all of the italicized verbs in the following paragraph to the present tense. Make sure that they agree with their subjects.
EXAMPLE I often *noticed* children playing on my way to work.

On the way to school I *observed* some men working on the road. One of them *started* by placing pylons on the road to direct traffic around the work area. Then they *started* digging up the asphalt. Next they *moved* the asphalt to the side of the road. In the trenches they *carved* in the street some of them *placed* pipes, which other men *covered* with asphalt. Finally, someone *removed* the pylon, and the traffic *resumed* its normal pattern.

6b
Make pronouns agree with the words they refer to.

You wouldn't expect to read a sentence like

> Joe reads Joe's book.
>   OR
> The children took the children's places in the classroom.

To keep from using the same word over and over, sometimes you might want to use another word to refer to that word. When you do this, it is important that the two words agree.

6b-1

Use singular pronouns *he, she, it, its, his, him, her,* or *hers* to agree with a singular noun or pronoun.

> Sam is careless. He often locks his keys in his car.
> The cider is too aged. Its taste is sour.

6b-2

Use plural pronouns *they, them, their,* or *theirs* to agree with a plural noun or pronoun.

> Students shouldn't write on *their* desks or leave *their* gum stuck to *them*.
> If I cleaned my room, perhaps my children would clean *theirs*.

SOME NOUNS AND PRONOUNS THAT AGREE

> A boy who prepares carefully for class will probably pass *his* exams.
> Since a school desk is used by so many students, *it* always loses *its* shine.

NOTE: When a subject could be either male or female, many writers like to make the subject plural and to use a plural pronoun to refer to it.

INSTEAD OF	A visitor should check his or her packages at the door.
IT IS LESS AWKWARD TO SAY	*Visitors* should check *their* packages at the door.

6b-3

Use a singular pronoun to agree with two or more singular subjects joined by *or* or *nor*. Use a plural pronoun to agree with two or more plural subjects joined by *or* or *nor*.

SOME NOUNS AND PRONOUNS THAT AGREE

> Either Mr. Lee or his son left *his* own work unfinished.
> Neither the daughters nor the sons ever clean *their* own rooms.

When one of the subjects is singular and the other is plural, the pronoun agrees with the nearer subject.

> Neither the teacher nor the *students* remembered *their* books.

EXERCISE 14

In the following sentences, underline the word in parentheses that agrees with the italicized words.

1. *Neither Barbara nor Pam* finished (her, their) paper in class.
2. Did *your truck or your trailer* fail (their, its) inspection?
3. *Neither my father nor the children* lost (their, his) temper.
4. *Either the rain or the wind* had (its, their) effect on the garden.
5. *Will Bill or Ed* take (their, his) vacation in August?

 CHECKLIST: Agreement

When you proofread a paper,

1. make sure all verbs agree with their subjects.
2. make sure all pronouns agree with the words they refer to.

EXERCISE 15

In the following sentences change any verb that does not agree with its subject and any pronoun that does not agree with the word it refers to.

1. Enablers are people who needs to redirect their lives in a more positive manner.

2. There is restrictions these days on the way parents discipline their children.

3. I babysit so often that when Charlene or her mother come to visit me, they get the impression that I am running a nursery.

4. The dachshund has one drawback as a pet. They are like potato chips; no one can stop at just one.

5. Duckpin bowling is one of those games that requires skill and patience.

Chapter 7
VERBS

Use verbs correctly.

In a sentence a verb is a word that tells what the subject is doing or what is happening to the subject. You can usually use verbs correctly if you know how verb forms are spelled and if you understand their purpose in a sentence.

A verb can stand by itself (*love, loves, loved*), or it can appear with another verb—often called a *helping verb*.

COMMON HELPING VERBS

has	is	do	can	will	must	shall
have	are	does	could	would	might	should
had	was	were				

VERB BY ITSELF	VERB WITH HELPING VERB
I *love* ice cream.	Ice cream *is loved* by many.
He *loves* ice cream.	I *have loved* ice cream.
We *loved* ice cream.	I *could love* ice cream.
	They *do love* ice cream.
	We *will love* ice cream.

A verb can be helped by one helping verb or by more than one helping verb.

I *have* loved ice cream.
I *could have* loved ice cream.

A verb that is sometimes used as a helping verb can also appear by itself as the main verb of a sentence.

I *have* ice cream every Sunday.

Most verbs have no more than four basic forms or principal parts. If you know the principal parts of a verb, you can express any number of ideas. Here are the four principal parts of the regular verb *learn* and the irregular verb *give*.

	PRESENT	PAST	PAST PARTICIPLE	PRESENT PARTICIPLE
Regular:	learn(s)	learned	learned	learning
Irregular:	give(s)	gave	given	giving

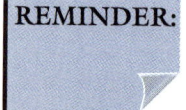

REMINDER: **Principal Parts of Verbs**

Here are the main ways these principal parts are used.

PRESENT: *ALLOWS(S), GIVE(S)*

1. Used to form the present tense; *-s* is added to present tense verbs that agree with *he*, *she*, and *it* subjects

    I allow; he *allows*; we give; it *gives*

NOTE: The tense of a verb shows when the action takes place. More information on verb tenses appears in Sections **7h** and **7i**.

2. Used after *will* to form the future

    I *will* allow; he *will* give

3. Used after helping verbs *can, could, will, would, should, must, might*, and *ought*, and with *do* and *did*

    I *can* allow; we *did* give

PAST: *ALLOWED, GAVE*
Used by itself to show past action

    She *allowed*; you *gave*

PAST PARTICIPLE: *LEARNED, GIVEN*

1. Used after a form of the helping verb *have*

    he *has allowed*; we *have allowed*; we *had given*

2. Used after a form of the helping verb *be*

    it *is allowed*; they *will be allowed*; I *was given*

PRESENT PARTICIPLE: *ALLOWING, GIVING*

Used after a form of *be* to show continuing action

    I *am allowing*; they *were giving*

The use of the present tense is covered in Chapter **6**. The uses of other verb tenses are dealt with in this chapter. The present, past, and past participle forms of irregular verbs are listed in **7c**.

7a
Learn the past tense of verbs.

Each verb except *be* has only one simple past form.

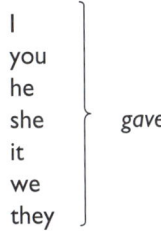

    I
    you
    he
    she   *gave*
    it
    we
    they

Be has two simple past forms: *was* and *were*; for more information, see **6a-3**.

The simple past says that something happened, and it says it by using one verb. No helping verbs are used. The italicized verbs in the following sentences all tell about something that happened in the past.

    I *sang* in the choir.
    You *lost* your way in the woods.
    We *laughed* on the way home.
    She *danced* all night long.
    My shoe *was* under the sofa.
    Your shampoo and conditioner *were* in the bathtub.

7a-1
Simple past forms (ending in -ed)

Each verb has a one-word form that expresses the past. It is called the simple past, and it usually ends in -ed. Only a -d is added when the verb already ends in -e (add + -ed → added; change + -d → changed). Sometimes the ending is not clearly heard in speech, but it always appears in writing.

WRONG	I notice that there were some buses full of people.
RIGHT	I noticed that there were some buses full of people.
WRONG	I watch the news last night.
RIGHT	I watched the news last night.

Be sure to add -d or -ed to express the past of use and happen. If you do not do this, it will sound as if you are talking about something happening in the present.

PRESENT	I use my commuter tickets. [I use them every day.]
PAST	I used my commuter tickets. [I used them earlier.]
PRESENT	I happen to be against the plan. [I am against it now.]
PAST	I happened to be against that plan. [I was against it.]

EXERCISE 1

If any of the following sentences show that something happened in the past, make the italicized verb simple past by adding -d or -ed. If you cannot tell whether the past or present is intended, do not change the verb.

1. Everybody *finish* eating an hour ago.

2. The last time Sid *play* cards was a year ago.

3. I *use* to let my nails grow, but I don't anymore.

4. I *realize* that you were right.

5. Pat Buchanan *work* on former President Reagan's campaign.

6. We sometimes *sneak* into my sister's closet to try on her clothes.

7. Something embarassing *happen* last week at the mall.

8. I *open* the box and found a pink and red tie.

9. People with allergies often *use* a special soap.

10. We *happen* to be wrong in this case.

7a-2
Irregular past forms (listed in 7c)

Some simple past forms are irregular. You need to learn these forms separately. Remember that simple past forms appear by them-selves—without helping verbs.

WRONG   He ~~has~~ ran home.
RIGHT   He *ran* home.

The chart in **7c** lists the most common irregular past forms. Con-sult this chart or your dictionary if you are not sure about the spelling of a simple past form.

7b
Learn to use regular and irregular past participles with helping verbs.

Four of the verbs used with helping verbs (such as *has, have, had, is, was, will be,* and *has been*) are the past participles *loved, given, done,* and *run.* The past participle *loved* is regular. It looks just like the past and is constructed by adding *-d* to the present form (*love* + *-d* → *loved*). The others (*given, done,* and *run*) are not regular, and you must learn them separately. The following are some of the different ideas you can express by using past participles with helping verbs.

I have loved (given, gone, run)
he has loved (given, gone, run)
I will have loved (given, gone, run)
I would have loved (given, gone, run)
I can have loved (given, gone, run)
I could have loved (given, gone, run)
it is loved (given, gone, run)
it was loved (given, gone, run)
they will be loved (given, gone, run)
they have been loved (given, gone, run)

 Caution: 1. Remember that the past participle does not always mean that the verb expresses past time.

Everyone *is loved* by someone.
Romeo *will be loved* by Juliet by the end of Act I.

2. Remember that a verb may be separated from its helping verb by other words in the sentence. Do not let this situation make you forget to use the correct verb form.

WRONG   I have never love you.
RIGHT   I *have* never *loved* you.

WRONG   Was her favorite doll gave to her sister?
RIGHT   *Was* her favorite doll *given* to her sister?

7b-1
Regular past participles (ending in -*ed*)

Regular past participles end in -*ed*. They are often used with helping verbs like *has, have, had, is, are, was, were,* and *has been.* Some regular past participles are *loved, danced, watched, waited,* and *listened.* Remember that you do not always hear the -*d* ending clearly in speech, but it always appears in writing.

WRONG   We were pack and ready to go.
RIGHT   We *were packed* and ready to go.

WRONG   The air is then push out of the carburetor.
RIGHT   The air *is* then *pushed* out of the carburetor.

Be especially careful to add -*d* or -*ed* to *use, happen,* and *suppose* when these words are used with helping verbs.

WRONG   My father is use to hard times.
RIGHT   My father *is used* to hard times.

WRONG   We are suppose to be there.
RIGHT   We *are supposed* to be there.

WRONG   Oil spills have happen many times.
RIGHT   Oil spills *have happened* many times.

EXERCISE 2

In the following sentences, underline the correct form of the verb in parentheses.

1. Was your brother (suppose, supposed) to work at the Mt. Olive pickle factory?
2. At an R-rated movie a child is (require, required) to be accompanied by an adult.
3. Please (call, called) Mr. Johnson about the job opening.

4. Moving to a dorm was a strange experience because I wasn't (use, used) to having roommates.
5. How strange that Crystal is working as a cleaner since she has never (pick, picked) up a broom in her life!
6. The Baltimore-Washington area is (consider, considered) the rave dancing capital of the United States.
7. Have you ever, even by accident, (finish, finished) your homework before midnight?

EXERCISE 3

Edit the following paragraph for errors in the use of *-ed* endings. Circle each error, and write your correction in the space above it.

My favorite hours have been pass working in my flower beds. Each plant has always seem special to me. When I have problems of one sort or another, my flowers become imaginary friends, and I have often talk to my flowers, confiding in them all the secrets of my life. In the past, when I have been upset, my flowers have always seemed understanding and have always nodded to show their agreement with all my decisions. My flowers are much cheaper than a psychiatrist.

EXERCISE 4

Complete the following paragraph, using the verbs below. When necessary, change the present form to a past participle.

> intend   pick   donate   seem
> cloud   dress   rescue   fasten

My aunt Esther is _____ in a very strange way today. Her shoes _____ to be bright pink, and her hat looks as though it had been _____ from the attic or _____ out of the Salvation Army donation box. Her dress was certainly _____ to her by her worst enemy. It has a yellow belt that is _____ together with a safety pin since it is much too big for her. To top it all off she is carrying a green umbrella that must be _____ to protect her from rain, even though the sky is certainly not _____ over.

7b-2
Irregular past participles (listed in 7c)

Some past participles are irregular and must be learned individually. The chart in **7c** lists the most common irregular forms. Consult it or a dictionary when you are unsure about the spelling of a form. Remember that past participles are used with helping verbs.

WRONG   I just begun working.
RIGHT   I *have* just *begun* working.

7c
Use a verb chart to find the correct forms of irregular verbs.

Sometimes you will need to consult a dictionary or a verb chart to find the correct form of an irregular verb. (See 20c for information on using a dictionary to spell verb forms.) You might find the following verb chart useful as a source of the most common forms of irregular verbs. Note that the verb *be* is not listed by its present form. Its forms are given in 7e.

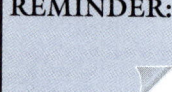

REMINDER: Common Irregular Verbs

PRESENT	SIMPLE PAST	PAST PARTICIPLE
arise	arose	arisen
beat	beat	beaten
become	became	become
begin	began	begun
blow	blew	blown
break	broke	broken
bring	brought	brought
build	built	built
burst	burst	burst
buy	bought	bought
can	could	been able
catch	caught	caught

IRREGULAR VERBS (*continued*)

PRESENT	SIMPLE PAST	PAST PARTICIPLE
choose	chose	chosen
come	came	come
cost	cost	cost
cut	cut	cut
deal	dealt	dealt
dig	dug	dug
dive	dove (dived)	dived
do	did	done
drag	dragged	dragged
draw	drew	drawn
drink	drank	drunk
drive	drove	driven
eat	ate	eaten
fall	fell	fallen
feed	fed	fed
feel	felt	felt
fight	fought	fought
find	found	found
fly	flew	flown
forget	forgot	forgotten
forgive	forgave	forgiven
freeze	froze	frozen
get	got	got (gotten)
give	gave	given
go	went	gone
grow	grew	grown
have	had	had
hear	heard	heard
hide	hid	hidden
hit	hit	hit
hold	held	held
hurt	hurt	hurt
keep	kept	kept
know	knew	known
lay	laid	laid
lead	led	led
leave	left	left
let	let	let
lie	lay	lain

IRREGULAR VERBS (*continued*)

PRESENT	SIMPLE PAST	PAST PARTICIPLE
lose	lost	lost
make	made	made
meet	met	met
pay	paid	paid
put	put	put
quit	quit	quit
read	read	read
ride	rode	ridden
ring	rang	rung
rise	rose	risen
run	ran	run
say	said	said
see	saw	seen
seek	sought	sought
sell	sold	sold
send	sent	sent
set	set	set
shake	shook	shaken
shine	shone	shone
show	showed	shown (showed)
shrink	shrank (shrunk)	shrunk
shut	shut	shut
sing	sang	sung
sink	sank	sunk
sit	sat	sat
sleep	slept	slept
speak	spoke	spoken
spend	spent	spent
spring	sprang	sprung
stand	stood	stood
steal	stole	stolen
swim	swam	swum
swing	swung	swung
take	took	taken
teach	taught	taught
tear	tore	torn
tell	told	told
think	thought	thought

IRREGULAR VERBS (*continued*)

PRESENT	SIMPLE PAST	PAST PARTICIPLE
throw	threw	thrown
understand	understood	understood
wake	woke (waked)	woken (waked)
wear	wore	worn
win	won	won
write	wrote	written

For the following exercises, consult the verb chart when necessary.

EXERCISE 5

Change any of the italicized verbs that do not express the past correctly.

1. George and Steve *run* all the way home.

2. Leo *has swore* to tell the truth, the whole truth, and nothing but the truth.

3. I *knowed* that verb should have been a subjunctive.

4. Jo *wore* my dress three times before I ever *had* it on.

5. The Riveras *growed* gardenias in their yard.

6. I *have wrote* about three types of parents.

EXERCISE 6

Complete the following sentences or questions. Use an irregular past or past participle form from the chart in 7c in each of them.

1. Have you ever _____?
2. This morning the alarm clock _____.
3. I could have _____.
4. Yesterday, my friends and I _____.
5. By next year I will have _____.

EXERCISE 7

In the following sentences, change any italicized verb that is incorrect.

1. It would have *took* even longer if I hadn't called for some help.

2. Larry has often *spoke* to me about Jess.

3. If you haven't *forgotten*, you haven't *forgiven*.

4. My money problems had just *began*.

5. My father has to be *driven* to work every morning because our car is still in the shop.

6. I've finally *did* it!

7. How many times have you *sang* that song?

8. Who *drank* all the sodas while we were watching the game?

9. Sonny waited all night, but the phone never *rung*.

10. The disaster has *took* away all their hopes for the future.

EXERCISE 8

Write the correct form of the verb given in parentheses in each of the blanks provided.

1. Joe Riddick has _____ from the shipyard. (retire)

2. A student from my school was _____ to represent Dayton in the debating finals. (choose)

3. That would not have _____ if you had been on time. (happen)

4. Bob should have _____ the car more gas. (give)

5. None of us was really _____ to be there. (suppose)

6. After an hour had _____, I went to look for Brian. (pass)

7. Fried chicken is often _____ with the fingers. (eat)

8. Only fresh whole eggs are _____ in making an orange dream cake. (use)

9. I sometimes think the government is _____ by idiots. (run)

10. The Merrimac was _____ in the Atlantic after a famous sea battle. (sink)

7c
—
vb

EXERCISE 9

Write at least ten sentences using the past participles *run*, *begun*, *sung*, *sprung*, and *shrunk* with the helping verbs *is*, *was*, *has*, and *had*.

EXERCISE 10

Respond to the following commands by writing a sentence using *have* and the past participle of the underlined verb in each command.
EXAMPLE Please beat the eggs.

I have already beaten the eggs.

1. Write me a letter.
    I have _____.

2. Eat all of your lunch.
    I have _____.

3. Take as much time as you need.
    I have _____.

4. Forget what you just saw.
    I have _____.

5. Give me your promise.
    I have _____.

6. Begin preparing for your exam.
    I have _____.

EXERCISE 11

In the following paragraph, blanks appear where verbs have been omitted. Supply your own verbs to complete the paragraph.

My car has a unique appearance. When it was just (1) _____
_____, it must have (2) _____ one of the
finest cars on the road. Now, twelve years later, it has (3) _____
_____ an eyesore. It has (4) _____ rust
spots from one end to the other. The vinyl roof is badly (5) _____
_____, and many dents can be (6) _____
on the fenders. When people see the paint job, they think the

painter must have (7) _____ asleep when he did it. When it rains, you get the benefit of a shower while you ride down the road. The only good thing that can be (8) _____ _____ about my car is that it is reliable. In fact, I have (9) _____ _____ myself that, ugly or not, my car will have a home with me for many years to come.

EXERCISE 12

Write two sentences using each of the following verbs: *happen*, *write*, *begin*, *use*, and *take*. One sentence should use the simple past of the verb, and the other should use the past participle.

7d
Use the present participle (ending in -ing) to tell the reader that something is continuing.

In addition to saying that something is happening now,

> He *bothers* me.
> He *is bothered* by a fly.

or that something happened in the past,

> He *bothered* me.
> He *has bothered* me.
> He *was bothered* by a fly.

or that something will happen,

> That fly *will bother* him.
> He *will* not *want* to be bothered.

verbs also distinguish between something that happens all at once and something that happens over time. Verbs that end in *-ing* (for example, *bothering*, *saying*, *doing*, *wanting*, *loving*) tell the reader that something is, was, or will be going on or continuing. They appear with helping verbs like *am*, *is*, *are*, *was*, *were*, and *will be*. These verb combinations are called *progressive forms* and are listed and described in **7h**.

> ALL AT ONCE   I *worked* at the credit union. [I worked there at one time.]

CONTINUING	I *am working* at the credit union. [I am still working there.]
CONTINUING	I *was working* when you saw me. [I was working over a period of time.]
ALL AT ONCE	I *will work* late tonight. [I will work at one particular time.]
CONTINUING	I *will be working* tomorrow. [I will be working for some time.]

 Caution: Remember that the present participle does not necessarily mean present action.

When you came in, I *was saying* something to a friend.

EXERCISE 13

Write five sentences that include a helping verb and the present participle. At least one verb should express past action.
EXAMPLES It *is* already *raining.*
          I *was playing* cards when you arrived.

7e
Use the verb **be** *correctly.*

Be is the most useful verb in English. A form of *be* can appear either by itself or with other verbs.
    These are the basic forms of *be*:

INFINITIVE	PRESENT	PAST	PAST PARTICIPLE	PRESENT PARTICIPLE
be	am, is, are	was, were	been	being

The present tense of *be* tells what is happening.

I *am*
You *are*
He *is*
She *is*   very silly.
It *is*
We *are*
They *are*

The past tense of *be* tells what has happened.

I *was*
You *were*
He *was*
She *was* } very silly.
It *was*
We *were*
They *were*

A form of *be* can be used as a helping verb to help the verb say something about the subject. It can express present time.

The library *is* located in this building.

It can express past time.

My father *was* waiting for me.

Sometimes a form of *be* appears with other helping verbs to tell what the subject is doing.

I *have been* studying for an hour.
Edith *is being* left behind.
You *will be* waiting.

7e-1
Use *is* and *are* correctly.

Be sure not to leave out the verbs *is* and *are* when they are needed to complete the meaning of a sentence.

WRONG   My roommate snores sometimes, but otherwise he great.
RIGHT   My roommate snores sometimes, but otherwise he *is* great.

WRONG   What happening?
RIGHT   What's happening? or What *is* happening?

WRONG   They gone!
RIGHT   They're gone! or They *are* gone.

Do not use *be* in place of *is* or *are* to complete the meaning of a sentence.

WRONG   Joe be waiting here.
RIGHT   Joe *is* waiting here.

7e-2
Use *being* and *been* correctly.

Remember that a helping verb is needed with *being* and *been* to complete the meaning of the sentence.

WRONG	He being stubborn.
RIGHT	He *is* being stubborn.
WRONG	We been here a long time.
RIGHT	We *have* been here a long time.

EXERCISE 14

Write two sentences using *being* and two sentences using *been* with helping verbs.

EXERCISE 15

Correct the following paragraph by inserting *is* or *are* when necessary.

EXAMPLE The value of the dollar ^*is*^ rising against the Japanese yen.

Don't you find family reunions frustrating? First, you expected to prepare a lot of food for large numbers of people. Sometimes you find that you entertaining your relatives as well as feeding them. You have to make sure that everything done before everyone ready to eat. Then after everyone finished eating, you left with the job of removing the dishes from the table and washing them. As the family members leaving, they telling you how nice everything, but you really wishing they would hurry up and go. After the reunion concluded, you relieved and happy that everyone gone.

7e-3
Use the forms of *be* such as *is, are, was, were,* and *will be* with the past participle when you want to express the passive.

In most sentences, you should use the active form, not the passive form, of the verb because you want to tell what the subject is doing. Your emphasis is on the doer of the action.

We set the table.

Sometimes, however, you want to emphasize what is being done, or you may not know who is performing the action. You may then use a passive verb form. This passive form is a form of *be* and the past participle.

The table *was set.*

It is not a good idea to use the passive except when you do not know who is performing the action or when you want to emphasize the action itself. If you overuse the passive, you will probably produce wordy or awkward sentences.

PASSIVE   A mistake *has been made* by Harry. (wordy)
ACTIVE   Harry *has made* a mistake. (better)

▼ **Caution:** Do not shift from the active to the passive within a sentence. Such a shift may confuse the reader.

CONFUSING   The building inspector *examined* the work carefully, but no violations *were found.*
BETTER   The building inspector *examined* the work carefully, but he *found* no violations.

EXERCISE 16

In each of the following sentences, the passive form of the verb is underlined. Rewrite each sentence, making the emphasis active.
EXAMPLES   A good time <u>was had</u> by everyone.

Everyone had a good time.

1. The Christmas presents <u>are opened</u> by the children.
2. The books <u>were checked out</u> by the students.
3. Current issues of magazines <u>were displayed</u> by the librarian.
4. A thorough knowledge of the subject <u>is required</u> by that teacher.
5. Joey <u>is liked</u> by many people.

7e-4
Were can signal the subjunctive.

Were is usually the past form of the verb *be* that is used with a plural subject (they *were*). Sometimes, however, you will want to use it to express a wish or suggest a situation that might be true (but is not). This way of using *were* is called the *subjunctive.*

I wish I *were* president. [I am not.]
He acts as though he *were* president. [He is not.]

When *were* is used as a subjunctive, it does *not* agree with *he*, *she*, or *it* subjects (for example, I wish he *were*). A subjunctive expression uses *were* no matter what the subject is when the writer wants to suggest a wish or a possibility.

EXERCISE 17

In the following sentences, underline the correct verb forms in parentheses.

1. I told the doctor that if I (was, were) well, I wouldn't be in her office.
2. I wouldn't do that if I (was, were) you.
3. If there (was, were) no such thing as love, where would we be now?
4. I wish I (was, were) a millionaire.
5. I knew that his decision (was, were) the right one.
6. Even if he (was, were) rich, he would never spend money on himself.

7f
Learn the verb forms used with the helpers will, would, do, can, could, *and so on.*

You may find that you are occasionally confused about how to spell a verb form. You cannot always depend on what you hear because the verb ending does not always have a distinct sound. You remember that a verb has a special ending when used with a helping verb like *has, have, had, is, are, was,* or *were*:

NO HELPING VERB	They *dance.*
HELPING VERB	They *have danced.* [past participle ending]
NO HELPING VERB	We *sing.*
HELPING VERB	We *are singing.* [present participle ending]

But *has, have, is, was,* and other forms of *have* and *be* are not the only helping verbs. Verbs like *do, can,* and *would* are also helping verbs, but they are used with present forms, not with participles. These present forms have no endings. The following are some of the most common helpers.

will	do	should
would	does	may
can	did	might
could		

After these helpers and their negative forms (*won't, wouldn't,* and so on), use the present form of the verb.

WRONG   You did needed to study.
RIGHT   You *did need* to study.

WRONG   They would reacted badly.
RIGHT   They *would react* badly.

WRONG   He will tries to jump over the fence.
RIGHT   He *will try* to jump over the fence.

WRONG   A roofer can used both sides at once.
RIGHT   A roofer *can use* both sides at once.

WRONG   Alice won't wanted to be too early.
RIGHT   Alice *won't want* to be too early.

7f-1

When there are two helpers (*will be, could have, can be,* and so on), the one directly before the verb controls the spelling of the verb.

will be visited. [*Be* controls the spelling of *visited.*]
could have gone. [*Have* controls the spelling of *gone.*]

The helping verbs *be* and *have* change the spelling of the verbs that follow them.

WRONG   In time, I would have react better.
RIGHT   In time, I *would have reacted* better.
         [*Have* comes before the verb, so you must add *-ed* to *react.*]

WRONG   Meanwhile, I can be use the book.
RIGHT   Meanwhile, I *can be using* the book.
         [*Be* comes before the verb, so you must add *-ing* to *use.*]

7f-2

Use *have* (not *had*) after helping verbs such as *will, would, should, could, can, may,* and *might.*

Since *will, would,* and so on do not influence the spelling of the verbs they help, use the present form *have* after them, not the past participle *had.*

| WRONG | They might had encountered some problems while looking for a job. |
| RIGHT | They might *have* encountered some problems while looking for a job. |

| WRONG | I should had given up my old habits. |
| RIGHT | I should *have* given up my old habits. |

EXERCISE 18

Correct any errors in the italicized verbs in the following sentences. If a sentence is already correct, write *C* to the left of it.

1. When she did *arrived*, everyone was ready to go.

2. If children are forced to do what does not *interests* them, they will put forth little effort.

3. If I had known Lisa was going to be at the dance, I might *had* gone somewhere else.

4. I can't *decided* what I want.

5. Perry Mason never did *found* the evidence.

6. Jimmy does *wants* some rock candy.

7. My mother-in-law did *come* early, as usual.

8. Mrs. Fernandez realized the children needed help, but she didn't *realized* that they would refuse it.

9. If you get overtired, you can *began* to lose your patience with others.

7g
Use the correct forms of lay *and* lie *and* set *and* sit.

The verbs *lay* and *lie* and *set* and *sit* have been bothering students for a long time. Here are the guidelines you need to remember to use these verbs correctly.

7g-1
Be sure to use the correct forms of *lay* and *lie*.

Lay means "place" or "put something down."

WHEN WRITING ABOUT	USE	EXAMPLES
the present:	lay	They *lay* canvas over the equipment each night.
with a helping verb:	laying	She is *laying* it on the counter.
the past:	laid	He *laid* the book on the table.
with a helping verb:	laying	They *were laying* the bricks too far apart.
	laid	We *have laid* boards over the muddy spots.

Lie means "rest" or "be in a horizontal position."

WHEN WRITING ABOUT	USE	EXAMPLES
the present:	lie	They *lie* on the grass every afternoon.
with a helping verb:	lying	The pen *is lying* on the desk.
the past:	lay	He *lay* there for an hour.
with a helping verb:	lying	The muddy dog was *lying* on our new chair.
	lain	It *has lain* there for an hour

Present

Lay (or *laying*) in the present means "place" or "put." It needs an object (the person or thing receiving the action). When you lay something or someone down, you are doing something to that person or thing. In the following sentences, *lay*, *laying*, and *lays* take objects.

> We *lay* the packages down on the table.
> [packages = the object]
> They *are laying* aside their prejudices.
> [prejudices = the object]
> She *lays* the sleeping baby on his bed.
> [baby = the object]

Lie (or *lying*) in the present means "stretch out and rest." When you lie down, you are not doing anything to another person or thing.

The verbs *lie*, *lying*, and *lies* have no object in the following sentences; in other words, there is nothing receiving the action.

We often *lie* on the beach for hours.
The alligators *are lying* in the sun.
My aunt *lies* in bed too long every morning.

Past

Laid (or *laying*) in the past means "placed" or "put." When you laid something or someone down, you did something to that thing or person (the object).

We *laid* down our brushes.
[brushes = the object]
They *laid* their sleeping children on the mattress.
[children = the object]
The workers *were laying* brick.
[brick = the object]

Lay (or *lying*) in the past means "stretched out." When you lay down last night, you were not doing anything to anyone else; you were just resting.

The verbs *lay* and *lying* have no object in the following sentences:

Yesterday we *lay* on our backs in the calm water.
A jellyfish *was lying* near the shore.

REMINDER: **Using *Laid* and *Lain* with Helping Verbs**

Laid with a helping verb means "put down." It takes an object.

I *have laid* aside my work.
[work = the object]

Lain with a helping verb means "stretched out." It does not take an object.

The dog *has lain* under the rosebush for a long time.
[This form is not often used. Most writers prefer to write: "The dog *has been lying* under the rosebush."]

EXERCISE 19

In the following sentences, underline the correct form of *lay* and *lie* in parentheses.

1. A bank employee who was (laying, lying) in the corner got a look at both the robbers.
2. He ordered me to (lay, lie) face down on the floor.
3. Engine parts are (laying, lying) in huge piles in the garage.
4. Putin was (laying, lying) the groundwork for the talk.
5. The junk food addict will (lay, lie) around the house and eat sweets all day.

7g-2
Be sure to use the correct forms of *set* and *sit*.

Set means "arrange" or "put in place."

WHEN WRITING ABOUT	USE	EXAMPLES
the present:	set	Please *set* the flowers here.
with a helping verb:	setting	The committee *is setting* guidelines.
the past:	set	Professor Jensen *set* the time for the meeting.
with a helping verb:	setting	They *were setting* the chairs in a row.
	set	Jean *has set* the books down.

Sit means "rest in a sitting position" or "occupy a place."

WHEN WRITING ABOUT	USE	EXAMPLES
the present:	sit	They *sit* here every day for lunch.
with a helping verb:	sitting	My uncle *is sitting* in the car.
the past:	sat	The cat *sat* in the warm sunshine.
with a helping verb:	sitting	The boys *were sitting* on the fence.
	sat	They *have sat* there each evening.

Present

Set (or *setting*) in the present means "arrange in place." It needs an object (the thing receiving the action). When you set something down, you are doing something to that thing.

> We *set* down certain rules each year. [rules = the object]
> The girls *are setting* their hair. [hair = the object]
> Joe *sets* the timer for the roast. [timer = the object]
> *Set* your priorities. [priorities = the object]

Sit (or *sitting*) in the present means "rest in a sitting position" or "occupy a place." When you sit, you do not do something to anything.

> Are you going to *sit* around and do nothing?
> She *is* always *sitting* in the same spot.

Past

Set (or *setting*) in the past means "arranged" or "put into place." When you set something down, you were doing something to that thing or object.

> Last week we *set* up a summer schedule.
> [schedule = the object]
> My mother and sister *were setting* out tomato plants.
> [plants = the object]

Sat (or *sitting*) in the past means "rested" or "occupied a seat."

> My grandmother often *sat* for hours, rocking back and forth.
> My boyfriend and I *were sitting* on the sofa when my father entered the room.

REMINDER: **Using *Set* and *Sat* with Helping Verbs**

Set with a helping verb means "arranged."

> I *have set* the alarm for 6:00 A.M.
> The time *is set* for the match.

Sat with a helping verb means "occupied a seat."

> How long *have* you *sat* in that position?

EXERCISE 20

Change any incorrect form of *sit* or *set* in the following sentences. Write *C* next to any correct sentence.

1. While I was setting on the porch, I was also thinking.

2. There is a house sitting on that land across the river.

3. You should have sat down and set up some concrete plans.

4. Sometimes water sets in my backyard.

5. Set that package down over there on the table.

7b
Use verbs to help you tell time.

Whenever you use a verb, you are telling time. This is true because verbs give you an idea of when something is happening. They can tell you that something is happening now.

> I *surrender.*
> He *surrenders.*
> We *are surrendering.*
> They *do surrender.*
> The fort *is being surrendered.*

They can tell you that something happened in the past.

> I *surrendered.*
> We *did surrender.*
> We *have surrendered.*
> The fort *was surrendered.*
> They *had* all *surrendered.* [before the fighting stopped]
> The fort *had been surrendered.* [before we realized it]

They can tell you that something will happen in the future.

> I *will surrender.*
> He *is going to surrender.*
> We *are surrendering.* [tomorrow]
> They *will* all *have surrendered.*

There is another way that verbs tell time. They tell you whether something happened all at once or continues to happen.

ALL AT ONCE   I *hid* from the pirates.
CONTINUING   We *are hiding* from the pirates.
CONTINUING   We *would hide* whenever the pirates approached.

To tell time accurately, English uses six tenses. (The word *tense* refers to the time expressed by the verb.) The tenses are formed from the four principal parts of the verbs. The following is a chart showing the six tenses for a regular and an irregular verb. For each of these four tenses, there is an -*ing* (progressive) form listed. This form, like the others, not only tells the reader whether the time is present, past, or future, but it also suggests that the action is continuing rather than being completed all at once.

REGULAR VERB (*finish*)		IRREGULAR VERB (*begin*)	
SINGULAR	PLURAL	SINGULAR	PLURAL

Present tense (one-word verb)

I finish	we finish	I begin	we begin
you finish	you finish	you begin	you begin
he, she, it finishes	they finish	he, she, it begins	they begin

Present progressive (*am, is,* or *are* + present participle)

I am finishing	we are finishing	I am beginning	we are beginning
you are finishing	you are finishing	you are beginning	you are beginning
he, she, it is finishing	they are finishing	he, she, it is beginning	they are beginning

Past tense (one-word verb)

I finished	we finished	I began	we began
you finished	you finished	you began	you began
he, she, it finished	they finished	he, she, it began	they began

Past progressive (*was* or *were* + present participle)

I was finishing	we were finishing	I was beginning	we were beginning
you were finishing	you were finishing	you were beginning	you were beginning
he, she, it was finishing	they were finishing	he, she, it was beginning	they were beginning

Future tense (*will* + present)

I will finish	we will finish	I will begin	we will begin
you will finish	you will finish	you will begin	you will begin
he, she, it will finish	they will finish	he, she, it will begin	they will begin

REGULAR VERB (*finish*)		IRREGULAR VERB (*begin*)	
SINGULAR	PLURAL	SINGULAR	PLURAL

Future progressive (*will* + *be* + present participle)

I will be finishing	we will be finishing	I will be beginning	we will be beginning
you will be finishing	you will be finishing	you will be beginning	you will be beginning
he, she, it will be finishing	they will be finishing	he, she, it will be beginning	they will be beginning

Present perfect tense (*has* or *have* + past participle)

I have finished	we have finished	I have begun	we have begun
you have finished	you have finished	you have begun	you have begun
he, she, it has finished	they have finished	he, she, it has begun	they have begun

Present perfect progressive (*has* or *have* + *been* + present participle)

I have been finishing	we have been finishing	I have been beginning	we have been beginning
you have been finishing	you have been finishing	you have been beginning	you have been beginning
he, she, it has been finishing	they have been finishing	he, she, it has been beginning	they have been beginning

Past perfect tense (*had* + past participle)

I had finished	we had finished	I had begun	we had begun
you had finished	you had finished	you had begun	you had begun
he, she, it had finished	they had finished	he, she, it had begun	they had begun

Past perfect progressive (*had* + *been* + present participle)

I had been finishing	we had been finishing	I had been beginning	we had been beginning
you had been finishing	you had been finishing	you had been beginning	you had been beginning
he, she, it had been finishing	they had been finishing	he, she, it had been beginning	they had been beginning

REGULAR VERB (*finish*)		IRREGULAR VERB (*begin*)	
SINGULAR	PLURAL	SINGULAR	PLURAL

Future perfect tense (will + have + past participle)

I will have finished	we will have finished	I will have begun	we will have begun
you will have finished	you will have finished	you will have begun	you will have begun
he, she, it will have finished	they will have finished	he, she, it will have begun	they will have begun

Future perfect progressive (will + have + been + present participle)

I will have been finishing	we will have been finishing	I will have been beginning	we will have been beginning
you will have been finishing	you will have been finishing	you will have been beginning	you will have been beginning
he, she, it will have been finishing	they will have been finishing	he, she, it will have been beginning	he, she, it will have been beginning

These are the most common uses of the six tenses:

Present

1. The present tense tells the reader that something is happening now.

    Al *begins* his work cheerfully.
    Al *is finishing* his work now.

2. It tells that something happens on a regular basis.

    Al usually *begins* his work early.
    Al always *finishes* on time.

3. It emphasizes the present action by using *does* or *do*.

    Al *does finish* on time.

Past

1. The past tense tells that something happened; it does not suggest that the action is still going on.

   I *finished* at 7:30.
   I *was finishing* that book when you arrived.

2. The past form *did* emphasizes something the subject did.

   I *did finish* the book.

3. The past form *used to* tells that the subject did something on a regular basis.

   I *used to finish* on time.

Future

The future tense tells that something will happen.

   Sue *will finish* at 7:30.
              OR
   Sue *will be finishing* at 7:30.
              OR
   Sue *is going to finish* at 7:30.

Present Perfect

The present perfect tense tells about something that happened in the past and is or may be still continuing.

   You *have begun* to improve. [You may still be improving.]
   You *have been finishing* your chores for hours now. [You still are.]

Past Perfect

The past perfect tense tells about a past action that took place before another action that happened in the past.

   We *had finished* the inventory before the manager arrived.
   We *had been finishing* our chores when our mother made an untimely appearance.

Future Perfect

The future perfect tense describes something that will happen in the future before something else that will happen.

   By the time you get here, I *will have finished* the project.
   When 4:00 arrives, I *will have begun* my homework.

7i
Use a logical sequence of verb tenses to show when something happened.

A sentence can be very simple or it can be complex.

SIMPLE   There were buses full of people.
COMPLEX   I saw that there were buses full of people.

In the first sentence, time or tense is no problem. (There were buses full of people at some time in the past.) In the second sentence there are two verbs (*saw* and *were*). When you write a sentence with more than one verb, it is important to be accurate in telling time—that is, in telling the reader whether something has happened, is happening now, will happen in the future, or happened before something else that has already happened. Otherwise, you will confuse the reader.

CONFUSING   I saw that there are some buses full of people.
             [Did you see yesterday that there were buses, or
                 do you see now that there are buses?]
CLEAR   I *saw* that there *were* buses full of people. OR I *see*
             that there *are* buses full of people.

When you are telling a story, do not get so caught up in the experience of telling a story that you think something is really happening while you tell it. If you do, you may find that you are using the present tense, even though you are telling about a past event. Use a logical sequence (order) of verb tenses. In other words, when you use more than one verb, be sure that the reader can tell when something happened.

WRONG   I saw him cross the street. I knew he wanted to talk to
         me, so I stop right in front of him.
RIGHT   I *saw* him cross the street. I *knew* he *wanted* to talk to
         me, so I *stopped* right in front of him.

For more help on sequence of tenses, see **11a**.

EXERCISE 21

Change one of the verbs in each of the following sentences to make clear whether you are talking about past, present, or future time.

1. When giving artificial respiration, blow into the victim's mouth until you see his chest began to rise.

2. Denise doesn't like to take orders because she wants to feel free, able to do what she wanted.

3. I saw a red light flashing behind me, so I pull my car to the side of the road.

4. The reason I enjoy the job so much was that I could make fifty dollars a day.

5. When Carl was away from home for a week, he starts to get homesick.

6. While my date waits for me to come downstairs, my baby sister annoyed him with a million questions.

7i-1

Show clearly when events occur at the same time by using verb tenses logically.

If both events take place now, both verbs should be present:

> I *know* that I *am* wrong.
> Because we *have* a pool, Rita *can swim* all day.

If both events took place earlier, both verbs should be past:

> I *knew* that I *was* wrong.
> Because we *had* a pool, Rita *could swim* all day.

7i-2

Show that one past event happened before another past event by using the past perfect (*had* + past participle).

> I *knew* that I *had been* wrong.
> [Being wrong happened before knowing about it.]
> She *had known* for years that a disaster *was going to happen.*
> [Knowing about the disaster happened before the disaster.]

 Caution: Be sure that the verb using *had* and the past partici-ple really describes an event that took place before the other past event.

WRONG   While I was in the dentist's office, he had told me my tooth was bad. [Both events took place at the same time.]

RIGHT   While I was in the dentist's office, he told me that my tooth was bad.

7i-3
Show that a past event is or may still be continuing by using the present perfect (*have* + past participle).

> Aunt Lianne *has* always *liked* roses.
> [She has liked them in the past and still likes them.]

Do not use *have* and the past participle when you are referring to a particular time period.

> CONFUSING   My mother *has left* the house early this morning.
>   [The time, *this morning*, is stated.]
> CLEARER   My mother *left* the house early this morning.

EXERCISE 22

In the following sentences, correct each italicized verb, if necessary, so that the sentence shows clearly when events happened. Write *C* next to any correct sentence.

EXAMPLE   After the earthquake *occurred*, Californians saw a need for tougher building standards.

> *After the earthquake had occurred, Californians saw a need for tougher building standards.*

1. I realized too late that you *requested* the same vacation time.
2. I try not to worry about things that never *change*.
3. Carrie said that Sylvia *had called* an hour earlier.
4. *Had* the doctor *diagnosed* the illness before the patient was hospitalized?
5. Before Tracey *had recognized* my voice, she had asked who I was.
6. I want my children to feel as though they *could* tell me anything.
7. My father, the man who tells everyone what to do and how to do it, *has retired* from the U.S. Navy this February.
8. Shortly after that, we *had heard* the news that my sister had been married.
9. I *haven't done* any work before you got here.

7i-4

Use verbs in *if* clauses and main clauses logically to show what might happen.

a. Use the simple past in the dependent (*if*) clause and *would, could,* or *might* in the main clause when you want to say that if something happened, something else would, could, or might happen.

If I saw him, I *would* tell him the truth.
If we had a pool, Rita *could* swim all summer.

Notice that the above examples have two parts:

1. *If* something happened (dependent clause),
2. something else *would* or *could* happen (main clause).

Be sure not to use *would* in the dependent clause after *if;* use the past instead.

WRONG   If they would be able, they would visit him.
         [You want to say that if they *really were* able, they would visit him.]
RIGHT   If they *were* able, they would visit him.

b. Use the past perfect (*had* + past participle) in the dependent clause and *would have, could have,* or *might have* in the main clause when you want to say that if something had happened, something else would, could, or might have happened.

WRONG   If they would have known that he was sick, they would have visited him.
         [You want to say that if they *had really known* that he was sick, they would have visited him.]
RIGHT   If they *had* known that he was sick, they would have visited him.

Sometimes the main clause comes before the dependent (*if*) clause.

They *would* visit him *if* they were able.
They *would* have visited him *if* they had known that he was sick.

EXERCISE 23

You are given the main clause of each of the following sentences. Complete each sentence by adding a dependent clause, using the beginning you are given.

EXAMPLES If *she learned the truth*, she would be furious.

We would have called you last week if *there had been time.*

1. If _____, he would certainly do it.
2. If you _____, you would not have gotten into trouble.
3. If I _____, I could find it somewhere.
4. I would have made a million dollars if _____.
5. My friends might not have listened if _____.

7i-5
Use *would have* + an infinitive to suggest something you wanted to do or thought about doing.

I *would have* liked to see her. [but I didn't see her]

Be sure to express this idea clearly.

WRONG   I would have liked to have seen her.
RIGHT   I would have liked *to see* her.

This first sentence suggests that you would have liked yesterday to have seen her a month earlier. What you mean is that you would have liked yesterday to see her yesterday.

WRONG   I would have wanted to have gone.
RIGHT   I *would have* wanted *to go*.

 Caution: Remember that *would have*, not *would of*, is the correct form.

WRONG   I would of told you.
RIGHT   I *would have* told you.

7i-6

Use *would* logically both by itself and in time sequences.

Would has special meanings when used by itself and in time sequences. *Would* tells about something someone wishes to do or is considering doing. It can suggest possibility.

> The boss *would* like to see you.
> If I were you, I *would* study harder.

Would also tells about something that was done often or regularly in the past.

> After church we *would* visit my grandmother.
> On Saturday mornings, my father and I *would* pick up our fishing rods and head for the lake.

Do not use *would* instead of *will* to describe something that is going to happen in the future.

> WRONG   Next Sunday Joe would definitely be at her house.
> RIGHT   Next Sunday Joe *will* definitely be at her house.

In time sequences you want to show what might happen *if* something else happened. Use *will* in the main clause when the verb in the *if* clause suggests a possible action in the future.

> If I have plenty of money (in the future), I *will* have no worries.

Use *would* in the main clause when the verb in the *if* clause is past.

> If I had plenty of money, I *would* have no worries.

For more information on *if* clauses and main clauses, see **7i-4**.

EXERCISE 24

Edit the following paragraph to ensure the correct use of *will* and *would*.

Inconsiderate moviegoers can really ruin your evening. First they will arrive after the movie has already started, so they would have to find seats in the dark. If there are no seats left at the end of the row, they would have to walk in front of you, blocking your view of the screen. They will yell at the actors, telling them what they should do next. If they've seen the movie, they would talk about what is going to happen at the end. Sometimes they will have a baby with them, but they would not take the baby to the lobby because they don't want to miss any of the movie. Next time you are at the movies, if you are unlucky enough to be sitting next to one of these moviegoers, change your seat right away. Maybe you will be able to avoid some of these problems.

EXERCISE 25

In the following sentences, change the italicized verbs if they are incorrectly used. Write *C* next to any sentence in which the verb is used correctly.

1. If I *wouldn't have known* what to do, the results would have been worse.

2. We knew you would have wanted *to have visited* Elaine then.

3. Whenever I *called* Ann, she always found an excuse not to go out with me.

4. If you *had studied* the map, you would have known what trails to take.

5. Use great caution in working underneath your car, so you *would* not let it fall on you.

6. If I had known you were going to be there, I would have wanted *to have gone* too.

7. If there were lights in the park, we *will* play basketball until curfew.

8. I would have helped my brother if he *would have* let me.

9. After I collect all the ingredients, I *would* beat the egg with a fork.

EXERCISE 26

In the following sentences, underline the correct form of the verb in parentheses.

1. If there were no trust in marriage, just think of all the suspicions that (will, would) arise over the most insignificant things.
2. The criminals threatened that if they heard one word from a single individual, he (will, would) be sorry.
3. If the original inhabitants of the house (returned, had returned), they would have found many changes.
4. He had the reputation of being unscrupulous because in the past he (forged, had forged) some documents.
5. If you (had, would have) owned a VCR, you would have been able to record the space launch.
6. You should have called your mother. She would have wanted to (see, have seen) you.
7. If the phone rings while you are gone, I (will, would) definitely answer it.

EXERCISE 27

Edit the following paragraph for errors in verb tenses.

My little brother Joey is clumsy, messy, and babyish. After dinner last night, he had walked to the trash can to scrape in his leftovers, tripped over the rug, and hit his head on the oven. What amazes me is that he was still able to hold on to his plate. He always manages to make a mess while he is eating. If he would eat an ice cream sandwich, he would have it all over his mouth. He is also a big baby. Last Sunday he asked me if he can go to the movies with me. When I explained that I was taking a friend, he started to cry. If you meet Joey one day, you would have to agree that he has all the faults of a typical little brother.

7j
Recognize words that look like verbs but are not verbs.

Some words look like verbs but are not verbs. They have other important uses.

7j-1
Recognize -ing words that are not verbs.

Words like *buying*, *being*, *singing*, and *running* can be verbs when they appear with helping verbs. They say something about a subject.

> Liz *is buying* a new car.
> Dave *is being* stubborn.

Sometimes, however, they are not really verbs. Besides appearing with helping verbs to say something about the subject, words ending in *-ing* have other uses.

A word ending in *-ing* can be a noun (gerund); it can name a person or thing.

> *Eating* is my uncle's favorite pastime.
> [*Eating* names a thing; it names my uncle's favorite pastime.]
> Unhappiness can cause *overeating*.
> [*Overeating* names a thing; that thing is caused by unhappiness.]

A word ending in *-ing* can also be an adjective or a participle.

> My brother Billy reminds me of a *laughing* hyena.
> [*Laughing* tells what kind of hyena my brother reminds me of.]
> *Being stubborn*, my father wouldn't listen to my explanations.
> [*Being stubborn* describes my father.]

REMINDER: Using -ing Words Correctly

There are some things to remember about *-ing* words when they are not used as verbs.

1. Do not write an *-ing* fragment.

> WRONG   Licensing my car in the state of Kentucky.
> RIGHT   *Licensing my car* in the state of Kentucky caused me
>   problems I hadn't expected.

2. The *-ing* ending suggests that something is going on or continuing. Be sure to add this ending to a word expressing continuing action.

> WRONG   She often eats a snack while watch the news on TV.
> RIGHT   She often eats a snack while *watching* the news on TV.

| WRONG | Charlie finally went home, have no other place to go. |
| RIGHT | Charlie finally went home, *having* no other place to go. |

7j-2
Use infinitives like *to swim, to walk,* and *to find* correctly.

An infinitive is a verb form with no ending. It is usually used after *to* in an expression like *to swim* or *to walk*. It looks like a main verb, but it usually serves as the subject or object of a verb.

> *To swim* well demands much practice.
> [*To swim* is the subject of the sentence.]
> A baby tries *to walk* at the age of six months.
> [*To walk* is the object; it tells what the baby tries to do.]

With the exception of the infinitive form *be*, the infinitive form of a verb is the same as the present.

> I try *to enjoy* what I do.
> I try *to listen* to others.
> I try *to be* as cheerful as possible.

Be sure not to add an *-s* or an *-ed* ending to an expression like *to swim, to walk,* or *to find*.

| WRONG | In basketball you need four people to assists you in a fast-break execution. |
| RIGHT | In basketball you need four people *to assist* you in a fast-break execution. |

Caution: In some infinitive expression the *to* is omitted because the verbs that come before these infinitives do not require *to*.

> Sam allows Linda *to help* him.
> Sam lets Linda *help* him.

In both cases, *help* is an infinitive, but *to* is omitted in the second example because *let* does not require the use of *to*. Some other verbs do not require *to* when followed by an infinitive.

| help | He *helps* me work. OR He *helps* me to work. |
| make | Lenore *makes* me laugh. |

EXERCISE 28

The following sentences contain -*ing* words and infinitives. Underline the correct form in parentheses.

1. I have to (use, used) a good shampoo.
2. A walk will help a person (get, gets) some exercise.
3. I felt that all those parades and street lights only helped to (commercialize, commercialized) Christmas.
4. A cup of coffee makes a dinner (seem, seems) better.
5. If you use a little arch, you will have a good chance of (make, making) the shot.

EXERCISE 29
VERB REVIEW

In the following sentences, change any of the italicized words that are incorrect.

1. After I collect all the ingredients, I *would* use a fork to *beat* the eggs.

2. I *use* to think that having a million dollars *will* solve all my problems.

3. In the summer, all I want to do is *lay* around and *rest.*

4. Last week I *have let* the building superintendent *moved* my bike.

5. One of these days I am going to *sit* down and *have* a talk with my brother.

6. Were you *suppose* to call this week before *going* on vacation?

7. If our neighbors *would have* received our message, they would have *water* our garden while we were gone.

8. We could *listened* to good music instead of what you *have* on the stereo.

9. After my father *arrive* at the supermarket, he remembered that he *forgot* his grocery list.

10. As the days *past*, my father *begun* to get worried.

Chapter 8

MAKING SENSE
OF SENTENCES

Make your sentences logical;
give them direction.

8a
Avoid the mixed-up sentence.

Sometimes you know that something is wrong with a sentence, but you cannot figure out what it is. In this chapter we are going to look at some sentences that are mixed up and try to see how they can be corrected. You will see several kinds of sentence mistakes that you will not find explained anywhere else in this handbook.

8a-1
Avoid falling into the *in which, for which,* or *of which* trap.

Suppose you write:

> We had been told to follow the instructions, in which we had received that morning.

If you were trying to say that we followed instructions that we received, the *in* has no place in the sentence. You really meant to say:

> We had been told to follow the instructions, which we had received that morning.

In this sentence, *of* is not needed; it only confuses the reader:

WRONG   A man sold a list of bogus names to an insurance com-
         pany for a million dollars, of which he pocketed himself.

RIGHT   A man sold a list of bogus names to an insurance com-
         pany for a million dollars, which he pocketed himself.

EXERCISE 1

Correct the following sentences, crossing out *in, on,* and *of* when they are not needed. Write *C* next to any sentence that is correct.

1. My first surfboard was a six-foot "fish," in which I purchased with my employee discount.
2. My living room has three desks, for which I use for different purposes.
3. Jealousy is a powerful emotion, of which most people feel at some time.
4. The handle is the wooden part, on which the blade is attached to.
5. Eddie likes the school in which he is enrolled.

8a-2
Avoid using *who, which,* or *that* unless they have specific references.

The words *who, which,* and *that* are commonly used to refer to words that you have just used. It is correct to say:

Rudolph Valentino is the actor *who* broke a million hearts in the movies of the 1920s. [*who* refers to the actor]

It is also correct to say:

Here are the keys that I have been looking for all day. [*that* refers to the keys]

a. *Who, which,* or *that* cannot be used as a joining word in place of *and.*

When you write:

He is very bright which he is always telling me about his accomplishments.

you probably meant to use *and* instead of *which* because you have joined two complete thoughts or finished sentences. You should have written:

He is very bright, *and* he is always telling me about his accomplishments. [*and* used as a joining word]

OR

He is very bright, a fact *that* I never realized. [*that* used as a referring word]

b. Do not use *which* or *that* when you really need a clause introduced by *in which, to which, on which,* or *of which.*

WRONG   He is content to get a job that he has no room for advancement.

RIGHT   He is content to get a job *in which* he has no room for advancement.

EXERCISE 2

If the word *which* or *that* is incorrectly used in any of the following sentences, change it to a comma plus *and* or use it in a clause introduced by *in which, to which, on which,* or *of which.* Write *C* next to any correct sentence.

EXAMPLES   I found his notebook, which I carefully put it away for him.

I found his notebook, and I carefully put it away for him.

Scientific American is a magazine that you find "computer re-creations."

Scientific American is a magazine in which you find "computer re-creations."

1. My cousin is always buying expensive clothing which she can't really afford it.

2. I looked through the rack until I found a dress that I really liked.

3. *Rolling Stone* is the magazine that the information you are looking for can be found.

4. In the Greek play *Antigone,* the heroine says that King Creon does not believe in the gods, which she is right.

5. In the Black History contest held on my campus, there were five questions each week that you have to find the answers.

8a-3
Avoid mixing up a statement and a question in the same sentence.

When you say:

> He asked me did I want to go.

you are mixing two things. You meant to say:

> He asked me if I wanted to go.
>
> OR
>
> He asked me, "Do you want to go?"

WRONG	The first thing my sister asked me was where was my ring.
RIGHT	The first thing my sister asked me was *where my ring was.*
WRONG	The mechanic asked me did I keep my car tuned up nicely.
RIGHT	The mechanic asked me *whether I kept my car tuned up nicely.*

EXERCISE 3

Change the following direct questions to statements by following these five steps:

1. Put the asker or wonderer first.
2. Write *if* or *whether*.
3. Write the thing being asked.
4. Make sure you put the subject before the verb in Step 3.
5. You may need to change the second verb and its subject. For example, *you will* may become *I would.*

EXAMPLE My brother asked me, "Will you be home at 4:00?"

My brother asked me if I would be home at 4:00.

1. John asked my sisters, "Are you going home?"

2. Lisa asked, "Will he be at the party?"

3. Sarah wondered, "Will there be a meeting at the recreation center?"

4. My wife wondered, "Should we have been stricter in raising our son?"

5. I asked her, "Did you have to go to court on Tuesday?"

6. Doctors all ask you, "How long has it been since your last visit?"

8a-4

Avoid writing a mixed-up sentence when you are trying to give someone a definition of a word you are using.

It is hard to define something, so instead of telling the reader what a word means, you may find yourself giving an example of when or where it happens. When you say:

> Moshing is when teenagers smash into each other at a rock concert for no apparent reason.

you are forgetting that *moshing* is not *when* teenagers do something; it is the practice itself. You should instead say:

> Moshing is the practice engaged in by teenagers who smash into each other at a rock concert for no apparent reason.

Often the best way to define a word is to decide to what class or general category the word belongs and to make that class the first part of the definition.

WORD	CLASS	DEFINITION
clutch	device	A *clutch* is a device used for holding an object firmly.
home run	hit in baseball	A *home run* is a hit in baseball that allows the batter to touch all the bases and score.

EXERCISE 4

Look over the following definitions. The write two of your own, remembering to make the class the first part of the definition.

1. *Cool* is a word that describes people who run their affairs in a very capable way.
2. A *pop rivet tool* is a device used to fasten parts made of thin metal.
3. *Envy* is a feeling that makes you dislike someone who has something you would like to have yourself.

EXERCISE 5

Correct the following definitions by saying *what* something is, not when or where it is.

1. *Greed* is when you want something that you don't need.

2. A *chokehold* is when a fighter blocks the airway of his opponent.

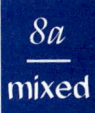

8a

mixed

3. A *carburetor* is where you mix air and gasoline.

4. *Laziness* is where a person misses the trash and never bothers to pick up what has fallen.

8a-5
Avoid writing a mixed-up sentence that has no subject.

If you are trying to say two different things in the same sentence, you sometimes write a sentence without a subject (the person or thing you are talking about in the sentence). For example, suppose you say:

> After finishing your education will assure you of a job in the future.

What will assure you of a job in the future? You have not answered that question. You meant to say:

> After finishing your education, *you* will be assured of a job in the future.

OR

> *Finishing your education* will assure you of a job in the future.

Here is another example:

> WRONG   In the writing lab has enough word processors for all the students.
>
> RIGHT   The writing lab has enough word processors for all the students.

EXERCISE 6

Correct the following items, making sure each sentence has a subject.

1. With only having lunch for 25 minutes creates a problem.

2. For students living away from home have to decide what kind of housing is best suited to them.

3. Even though I am hurting on the inside is no reason to give up on myself.

4. Underneath the hood consists of many parts.

5. The band Minor Threat made a song called "Straight Edge." With its catchy line "I'm a person just like you, but I've got better things to do" made teens think more about the meaning behind being "straight."

6. By singing in a church choir helped Bessie Smith become a great blues singer.

8a-6
Avoid mixing two thoughts so completely that the reader cannot tell which of the two ideas you are trying to get across.

Sometimes your problem is not the absence of a subject. Suppose you write:

> The shelf life of the supermarket's goods are constantly rotated.

You have two ideas here. One idea is

> The shelf life of goods in the supermarket is short.

The other idea is

> The goods in the supermarket are constantly rotated.

Here is another example of this problem.

> WRONG   Vicki is too nice a person until people like to take advantage of her.
>
> RIGHT   Vicki is such a nice person that people like to take advantage of her.
>
> OR
>
> Vicki is a nice person until people take advantage of her.

EXERCISE 7

Correct the following sentences by rewriting them, after deciding which idea you want to emphasize.

1. If going on a trip, you will enjoy it more if it has been planned in advance about where you are going, what you are taking, and how long you are going to stay.
2. After about an hour had passed before my father and mother decided to let us go to the dance.
3. In the other corner there is a closet where you can put your clothes in it.
4. When I am waiting in the express line at the supermarket, and the person in front of me has a shopping cart full of items makes the situation more difficult than it needs to be.

EXERCISE 8

This exercise contains all of the types of mixed-up sentences described in **8a**. Rewrite each of the sentences.

1. Turn off the engine, turn on the emergency flasher, and apply the emergency brake are the next three things to do.

2. A lazy person is when you always wait for other people to do your work for you.
3. After Crystal finished eating, I asked her how did it taste.
4. Mrs. Howard is one woman that you would not forget her after you had met her.
5. CBS has good coverage of the topics in which it reports on.
6. To be a student, that girl seems to think she should be teaching the class.
7. Ann's letter was very well written, which I feel it showed much planning.
8. There are equally good women attorneys as there are men attorneys.

8b
Cure your seriously mixed-up sentences.

Be your own doctor. Diagnose the illness in your mixed-up sentences, and cure them by saying what you meant to say. In the last section, you looked at some mixed-up sentences and saw how easy it is to mix two thoughts in the same sentence so that neither thought comes across clearly. Sometimes a mixed-up sentence can get so out of hand that it is hard to make just one single correction. When that happens, about all you can do is resort to drastic surgery. Look at the sentence again, decide what you wanted to say, and say it. Then delete everything that does not relate to your main point.

> MIXED-UP   Not like soul music, which is slow and meaningful, rock is a fast-moving age in the years before me, the present years and the years to come.

It is difficult to be sure, but the writer might have been saying one of three things:

> Unlike soul, rock is fast moving.
>
> Rock is part of a fast-moving age.
>
> Rock has its own place in history.

Let us say that the writer is talking about the place of rock music in this age.

> BETTER   Unlike soul—which is a slow, meaningful form of music—rock is part of a fast-moving age.

You can see that it is impossible to give a prescription to cure all mixed-up sentences. You must be your own doctor. Diagnose why the sentence is mixed up, and cure it. It will be easier to make this diagnosis if you ask yourself what one thing you meant to say in the sentence and eliminate anything that gets in the way of saying it.

EXERCISE 9

Cure the following sentences. Decide what the writer meant to say. Then rewrite the sentence, eliminating anything that does not help the writer make the point.

1. My friend's wife considers him to be heavy handed in the discipline department of his children and even calls the children names.
2. Now there is Chrysler, who just a few years ago was one step from being bankrupt now are the industry leaders in getting a car from concept car to full production models.
3. The students of today will have to run this country one day, and it's going to be in bad shape when the student who breaks his back to pass the exam and others break theirs to see the other's paper.
4. Unlike a house you have large heating bills and yearly taxes which increase annually, high mortgages, a lot to worry about for couples and single people just getting out on their own.

8c
Give your sentences direction.

Avoid rambling sentences. Decide what you are going to write before you write it. A rambling sentence seems to go nowhere. It suggests that you have forgotten what you wanted to say, yet you feel the need to fill space on the paper. When you find a rambling sentence in your writing, rewrite it so that it takes you somewhere. Decide what you meant to tell the reader in the first place.

> RAMBLING   Carelessness is shown when children leave their toys on a stairway or sidewalk where others can trip over them and be seriously injured, which may result in a tremendous loss of income.

The direction of this sentence is not clear because it is difficult to decide whether the writer is listing the results of carelessness, worrying about a possible lawsuit, or warning a potential victim. The

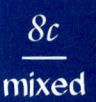

writer has to decide where the sentence is going and then eliminate what is not needed or put it into another sentence.

BETTER   Carelessness is shown when children leave their toys on a stairway or sidewalk where others can trip over them. (An injury resulting from such carelessness can lead to disability and possible loss of income.)

The following sentence has too much unnecessary information at the beginning.

RAMBLING   Since I was a technical consultant on diesel electric power plants to the Turkish Air Force, which had fifteen radar sites and thirty air force bases with this type of equipment, I traveled most of the time.

The writer does not need all the information about radar sites and bases to make the point.

BETTER   Since I was a technical consultant to the Turkish Air Force on their many diesel electric power plants, I had to travel most of the time.

EXERCISE 10

Give the following sentences direction. Decide what the writer is telling you, and eliminate all unnecessary information or put it into another sentence.

1. It may have been a busy day or my uncle may have gotten on his nerves, but sometimes my father can be an understanding man as long as nothing goes wrong.

2. For a woman who is already neglected because she is the wife of a successful lawyer and the member of a prominent family and has many family problems, the time spent playing golf when he could be at home would make the situation even worse.

3. Kevin doesn't allow anybody to enter his garage because after he finishes cleaning it up and putting his tools in place, he doesn't want people coming in here because they may knock things out of place.

Chapter 9

SENTENCES WITH MISPLACED AND DANGLING PARTS

Improve your sentences by eliminating misplaced and dangling parts.

9a
Relocate the misplaced parts in your sentences.

Sometimes a sentence will sound awkward because one or more words are out of place. These words need to be relocated or placed next to the person or thing they are describing.

OUT OF PLACE   I see a boat beside this man that is green and looks as if it is tied to a tree.

[The man is not green or tied to a tree; to make this sentence clear, put the words describing the boat next to the word boat.]

IN PLACE   Beside this man I see a boat *that is green and looks as if it is tied to a tree.*

OUT OF PLACE   Television coverage puts the president on the air anytime he suggests which includes all available channels.

[It is the television coverage that includes available channels.]

139

IN PLACE   Television coverage, *which includes all available channels*, puts the president on the air anytime he suggests.

EXERCISE 1

Relocate the misplaced parts so that the following sentences are clear.
EXAMPLE My aunt bought an antique clock at the auction last week and an old steamer trunk.

> *My aunt bought an antique clock and an old steamer trunk at the auction last week.*

1. Most of the time when a team is playing on TV that we like, we watch the game together.
2. I saw your advertisement in the *Los Angeles Times* of November 28, 2000, for a clerk-typist.
3. Two types of waitresses at a restaurant that I despise are those that never check up on customers and those that won't leave customers alone.
4. One thing you can do in your home is to keep all lights turned off that are not necessary.
5. A friend pushed my car with the help of a mechanic to the garage.
6. In the 1930s she became chief clerk and knew all the farmers in our county by name and most of the businesspeople.
7. Hand tools are used for doing the required work such as pliers, wire cutters, screwdrivers, and wrenches.
8. Don't ask my brother to help you do anything because you will end up doing the job yourself and his work too.

9b
Give any dangling part in your sentences something to describe.

Sometimes, without really wanting to, you can make your reader laugh. Suppose you had written the sentence:

> After leaving the highway at the Witchduck Road off-ramp, the street is brightly lit.

A reader would probably have found this sentence funny because it certainly does not mean what it seems to mean. You do not want to suggest that the street is leaving the highway. The words *after leaving the highway* are dangling in the sentence like a loose part. Make it clear that they refer to a person instead of the street by giving them a subject to describe. The sentence should read:

> After leaving the highway at the Witchduck Road off-ramp, *a driver* will find that the street is brightly lit.

Here are some other sentences with dangling parts. Notice in each case that the corrected sentence supplies a clear subject for the dangling part to describe.

DANGLING   Being a beautiful woman, a man is naturally attracted to you.
[Is the man a beautiful woman?]

CLEAR SUBJECT   *Because you are a beautiful woman*, a man is naturally attracted to you.

DANGLING   Passing through the door on my right, bizarre posters showing a lion, the Taj Mahal, a dog with suitcases, and a sign saying "I Won't Stay in a World Without Love" can be seen.
[Who is passing through the door?]

CLEAR SUBJECT   *A person passing through the door on my right* can see bizarre posters showing a lion, the Taj Mahal, a dog with suitcases, and a sign saying "I Won't Stay in a World Without Love."

Be careful not to allow a group of words to dangle without a subject for it to describe.

Caution: A dangling part is not always at the beginning of a sentence.

DANGLING   By watching for ads of special sales, grocery shopping can be more efficient.

DANGLING   Grocery shopping can be more efficient by watching for ads of special sales.

In the first example shown above, the dangling part comes at the beginning. In the second example, the dangling part is at the end. Both examples are incorrect. The problem can be corrected only by giving the dangling part a clear subject to describe, not by moving it from one part of the sentence to another.

CORRECT   **By watching for ads of special sales,** *we can make grocery shopping more efficient.*

EXERCISE 2

Identify the dangling part in each sentence. Then rewrite the sentence and supply a clear subject for that part to describe.

EXAMPLE   Hoping to keep awake in class, a lot of coffee was consumed.

Hoping to keep awake in class, we consumed a lot of coffee.

1. When taking cuttings from a plant, the correct utensils are needed.
2. Her feet are small and nicely shaped with hands that are soft and smooth.
3. When buying gasoline, 93 octane fuel is required for many cars.
4. Upon entering the house, the sight of beautiful marble and slate floors is very impressive.
5. After searching over an hour for a new battery, the snow began to pile up on the ground.
6. Upon receiving my wetsuit, the neoprene hood was not with it.
7. By being more alert, the collision rate in the United States would be drastically reduced.
8. Homeless people are seen on the street every day while growing up, and nothing is done about it.
9. By careful proofreading, your papers can be free of serious errors in punctuation and grammar.
10. Amazed at the brightly colored animals on his mobile, my nephew's baby blue eyes tried desperately to follow them.

EXERCISE 3

Edit the following paragraph, eliminating all misplaced or dangling parts of sentences.

The rock-a-thon is becoming a popular fund-raising event on campuses which has students taking to their rocking chairs to raise money for charity. When well-organized, profits from this kind of event can be surprising. The first step in planning a rock-a-thon is recruiting people to sponsor and chaperone the event who will be reliable and hard working. Recruiting participants who will do the actual rocking is the next task. After locating participants, sponsors will be asked to pledge a certain amount of money for every hour the participant rocks. By providing good entertainment, rockers will not become bored or fall asleep. Finally, supplying the rockers with food that can be eaten with the fingers, they will be able to rock for twelve to fourteen hours without taking a break. If good participants and sponsors have been recruited and if refreshments have been provided such as cookies and other finger foods, the rock-a-thon should be a success.

9b

dang

Chapter 10

NONPARALLEL SENTENCES

Write parallel sentences.

10

Make the parts of your sentences parallel.

A sentence with nonparallel parts does not say what you want it to say. For example, a student wrote the following description.

> He was wearing a bandana, dark sunglasses, combat boots, and he had a hat pulled down over his eyes.

You can easily see that this sentence contains parts that are not parallel in form. The writer made the fourth item different from the other three. The writer should have corrected the sentence by adding a fourth noun (a hat) to the other three.

NOT PARALLEL

He was wearing
- a bandana
- dark sunglasses
- combat boots
- he had a hat pulled down over his eyes

PARALLEL

He was wearing
{ a bandana
dark sunglasses
combat boots
a hat pulled down over his eyes

He was wearing a *bandana*, dark *sunglasses*, combat *boots*, and a *hat* pulled down over his eyes.

In the following sentences, two or more things are not parallel. In each case, making the things like one another helps the writer say what he or she wants to say.

The park is a place where everyone can have a good time or just to be sitting around doing nothing.

NOT PARALLEL

The park is a place where everyone can
{ have a good time
just to be sitting around doing nothing

PARALLEL

The park is a place where everyone can
{ have a good time
sit around doing nothing

The park is a place where everyone can *have* a good time or just *sit* around doing nothing.

Web users at the college scan the Internet for their own purposes, do research for classes, or just because they are bored.

NOT PARALLEL

Web users at the college
{ scan the Internet for their own purposes
do research for classes
just because they are bored

PARALLEL

Web users at the college
{ scan the Internet for their own purposes
do research for classes
go online just because they are bored

Web users at the college *scan* the Internet for their own purposes, *do* research for classes, or *go* online just because they are bored.

10
//

The more options a car has and the larger it is, it will cost more and its maintenance will be greater.

NOT PARALLEL

The more options a car has $\left\{\begin{array}{l}\text{the larger it is}\\\text{it will cost more}\\\text{its maintenance will be greater}\end{array}\right.$

PARALLEL

The more options a car has $\left\{\begin{array}{l}\text{the larger it is}\\\text{the more it will cost}\\\text{the more maintenance it will require}\end{array}\right.$

The *more* options a car has and the *larger* it is, the *more* it will cost and the *more* maintenance it will require.

Sometimes you will have to eliminate one or two items from a sentence because they cannot be made like the others. If you want to mention these items, you will have to put them into a new sentence.

Barbara is medium-sized, 5′5″ tall, always neatly dressed and wears glasses.

NOT PARALLEL

Barbara is $\left\{\begin{array}{l}\text{medium-sized}\\\text{5′5″ tall}\\\text{always neatly dressed}\\\text{wears glasses}\end{array}\right.$

PARALLEL

Barbara is $\left\{\begin{array}{l}\text{medium-sized}\\\text{5′5″ tall}\\\text{always neatly dressed}\\\text{[eliminate item]}\end{array}\right.$

Barbara is *medium-sized, 5′5″ tall*, and *always neatly dressed*.

Sometimes, just correcting an item on a list is not enough to make the sentence make sense. In the example

Karen's eyes are dark brown, thin eyebrows, a smooth complexion, and a thin mouth.

not all the things listed describe Karen's eyes. The writer is really describing Karen's features.

Confusing

Karen's eyes are
- dark brown
- thin eyebrows
- a smooth complexion
- a thin mouth

Clear and Parallel

Karen has
- dark-brown eyes
- thin eyebrows
- a smooth complexion
- a thin mouth

10
———
//

Karen *has dark-brown eyes, thin eyebrows, a smooth complexion*, and *a thin mouth*.

EXERCISE 1

Make the items parallel in each of the following sentences. Decide what you are listing, and make a chart like the one in the example. Change wording if necessary.

EXAMPLE   He has thick eyebrows, long eyelashes, sideburns, and has a few strands of hair under his chin.

He has (1) thick eyebrows
(2) long eyelashes
(3) sideburns
(4) a few strands of hair under his chin.

1. My brother's positions are forward and sometimes he plays guard.
2. The super-jock is always worried about his hair, clothes, and the pimple on his forehead.
3. My mother always tells me how angry she is and that she is going to punish me.
4. The acetylene torch is used to heat metals, free bolts, bend steel pipes, and numerous other things in workshops.
5. Sometimes I can't find any shoes, my car keys, or the phone rings as I am about to slam the door.

EXERCISE 2

Rewrite each of the following sentences, being sure that the items in them are parallel.

EXAMPLE I'm glad I am young, handsome, and never been married.

I'm glad I am young, handsome, and unmarried.

1. If deadbeat parents have no jobs, no form of income, and make no child support payments, they will have their driver's licenses revoked.
2. I was taught how to take a phone order, log on to my computer, and other important information.
3. When you vote, consider the candidate's political background, his point of view on different issues, and if you think he will get the job done.
4. I think the reasons teenage girls are depressed are financial problems, lack of support from their parents, and many girls have low self-esteem.
5. My car has a five-speed transmission, a blue interior, chrome rims, a four-speaker sound system with a CD player, and is good on gas.
6. My father never gets upset about our grades or when we make mistakes.
7. Hakeem Olajuwon uses his size well in rebounding, jump shots, blocking shots, and keeping up with the other players.
8. The following are advantages of having a VCR: being able to record programs when you are not at home, to rent tapes of recent movies, and a chance to buy some of the old film classics at an affordable price.

Chapter 11

AVOIDING SHIFTS AND CONFUSING REFERENCES

Guide your readers so that they
will not feel puzzled.

Your readers should not have any doubts about when things are taking place or whether what you have written is intended to be serious, funny, sad, or exciting. You, the writer, should be clear in your own thinking and should make it clear to the reader: *when* things are happening, *who* is telling about events, and *who* is referred to.

11a
Tell your readers clearly **when** *events are happening. Do not shift tenses.*

If you are writing about things that are happening now, the verbs you use should tell about the present. If you are writing about things that happened at some time in the past, let the reader know. Do not confuse the reader by mixing the time of the verbs.

149

CONFUSING   Although learning to play the trombone takes time and practice, in the end it proved to be worthwhile.

CLEAR   Although learning to play the trombone *took* time and practice, in the end it proved to be worthwhile.

▼ **Caution:** When you write about a story, a play, or another work of literature, you usually use the present tense. Avoid shifting from the present to the past tense unless you want to show that one event takes place before another.

CONFUSING   In *Hamlet*, Shakespeare gives us a memorable hero who cannot decide to avenge the death of his father even though he realized that he had a responsibility to do so.

CLEAR   In *Hamlet*, Shakespeare *gives* us a memorable hero who cannot decide to avenge the death of his father, even though he *realizes* that he *has* a responsibility to do so.

More information on using the correct tense of a verb can be found in **7i**.

EXERCISE 1

In each of the following sentences, one verb should be changed so that the time of the action is clear. Decide on the changes to be made and correct the sentences.

1. The wind was blowing, and the sun was shining; the children are digging in the sand while I played volleyball with my friends.

2. As Eileen entered the shop, she sees the different colors of wax and the various sizes and shapes of candles.

3. When Sherlock Holmes has a particularly difficult case, he often played his violin while thinking of a solution.

4. My Army written examination went smoothly, but the physical seems to take all day.

5. In *The Glass Menagerie*, Amanda wanted her daughter to marry a suitable gentleman. She doesn't care what Laura herself wants.

11b
Tell your readers clearly who *is telling about events and* who *is being referred to. Avoid shifting person.*

Many of your papers will be about personal experiences, and you will make frequent use of the words *I* and *we*. Some papers may give directions for doing something or may ask for some action and will be directed to *you*. Other papers may be stories, or narratives, that are about someone else, and you will use the words *he, she, it,* or *they*.

The pronouns you use suggest a focus for your paper. If you are telling things from your point of view, you are using first person (*I, we,* and so on). If you are writing to someone, you are using second person (*you, your, yours*). If you are writing about someone, you are writing about a third person other than *I* or *you*. In that case you use the pronouns *he, she, it,* and so on. Here is a chart suggesting the appropriate pronouns to use, depending on whether you are writing about yourself, to others, or about others.

POINT OF VIEW	SUBJECT PRONOUNS	POSSESSIVE PRONOUNS	OBJECT PRONOUNS
First person (writing about yourself)	I, we	my, our, mine, ours	me, us
Second person (writing to others, as in instructions)	you	your, yours	you
Third person (writing about other persons or things)	he, she, it, they	his, her, hers its, their, theirs	him, her, it, them

Before beginning your paper, decide whether you are writing about yourself, to others, or about other persons and things, and use the correct pronouns throughout your paper. Do not shift person.

CONFUSING   The cafeteria should offer salads and fruit. Even if students don't want to limit themselves to health food, you should give them a choice of some tasty items, not just prepackaged sandwiches.

[Avoid shifting from third person (*students*) to second person (*you*).]

BETTER   The cafeteria should offer salads and fruits. Even if students don't want to limit themselves to health food, *they* should have a choice of some tasty items, not just prepackaged sandwiches.

CONFUSING   There are always trash cans available. That means throw your garbage in them, not on the street.
[The second sentence shifts the focus to *you* (understood).]

BETTER   There are always trash cans available. People should throw their garbage in them, not on the street.

 Caution: Most formal papers that do not give instructions or directions should avoid the use of *you* as a point of view.

EXERCISE 2

Rewrite the following paragraph, eliminating all shifts in person.

I keep physically fit by working on all my muscles. First I lift weights and do push-ups and sit-ups. These exercises help you tone your upper body. I start out with two hundred sit-ups. Then I do a hundred push-ups with my feet elevated on a chair or table. Finally I curl a twenty-five-pound hand weight two hundred times to tone my arms and shoulders. Try to do these exercises every day. I also work on my lower body and stamina. I run at a medium pace for about two miles every other day. In addition, I try to swim an hour a day during the summer. Swimming uses almost every muscle in your body. Not everyone can swim every day, but you should be able to lift weights and run. Physical exercise is vital for your health.

11c
Use *a* singular noun *to refer to a person or thing you have already written about; use a* plural noun *to refer to more than one person or thing. Avoid shifts in number.*

WRONG   Some husbands are not the sole provider in a household.

RIGHT   Sometimes *a husband* is not *the sole provider* in a household.

Caution: When writing a paper in which you classify persons or things, be especially careful not to shift from singular to plural.

WRONG   Two-stroke dirt bikes require much more maintenance than a four-stroke bike.

RIGHT   Two stroke dirt bikes require much more maintenance than *four-stroke bikes.*

11d
Guide your readers by using clear pronoun references.

Most of the time, when writers want to refer to a person or thing they have just named, they use a pronoun to avoid using the same word or group of words again. For example, writers would not say:

My friends laughed because my friends thought I was joking.

Writers would almost certainly use the word *they* in place of the second *my friends.* When pronouns like *they, he, she, it,* and *this* are used in place of other words, however, it is important that they refer clearly to definite persons or things that come before them.

UNCLEAR   Several teachers complained about those noisy students. We thought they were being unreasonable.
[Did we think the teachers or the students were being unreasonable?]

CLEAR   Several teachers complained about those noisy students. We thought *those teachers* were being unreasonable.

UNCLEAR   Snow on a highway gives drivers steering problems. This can be a major cause of accidents.

[What can be a cause of accidents—snow, bad steering, or the dangerous situation itself?]

CLEAR   Snow on a highway gives drivers steering problems. *These problems* can be a major cause of accidents.

11d-1

Be sure that when you use a pronoun like *it*, *they*, or *them*, you have already given your readers a clear reference for this word.

Do not expect your readers to guess something that you have not told them.

UNCLEAR   My paper looks okay, but my teacher with her 20/20 vision will spot them every time.

[You know that *them* refers to the mistakes in your paper, but you should not expect your readers to guess this fact.]

CLEAR   My paper looks okay, but my teacher with her 20/20 vision will spot *my mistakes* every time.

UNCLEAR   If they put yield signs at the major intersections, my neighborhood would be safer.

CLEAR   If *the traffic department* put yield signs at the major intersections, my neighborhood would be safer.

11d-2

Use *this* and *that* to refer to specific persons or things.

Do not use the words *this* and *that* when you mean *a*, *an*, or *the*. When you are describing or referring to a person or thing that you have not previously mentioned to the reader, write *a* boy or *the* boy instead of *this* boy. Never use the incorrect expressions *this here* or *that there*.

WRONG   I met this here girl I liked in Knoxville.
RIGHT   I met *a* girl I liked in Knoxville.

WRONG   I walked into this store, and I saw this really great bargain.
RIGHT   I walked into *a* store, and I saw *a* really great bargain.

EXERCISE 3

In each of the following sentences, if there is no clear reference for a pronoun or if the pronoun could refer to more than one person or thing, correct the sentence to clear up the confusion.

EXAMPLE This is a badly written article. Instead of giving the readers more specifics, they avoid the issue.

This is a badly written article. Instead of giving the readers more specifics, the authors avoid the issue.

11a
ref

1. Nowadays people buy computers and sound systems as if it were no more than writing a check.

2. Security in high school is so important that they have metal detectors at the entrance.

3. The first thing you notice about the roads is the gravel. This can be a hazardous situation.

4. On TV they are always advertising a new soap or a new deodorant.

5. My friend James makes a lot of money doing almost nothing. He wants me to do something like that too.

6. There are many ruts and holes in the road. This makes it impossible to stay on your side of the road.

7. They should give more benefits to the elderly and the unemployed.

8. When a police officer stopped us, this was the third time they had stopped us that night.

11d-3

Use a singular pronoun like *he, she, his, it, its, him, this,* or *that* to refer to one person or thing. Use a plural pronoun like *we, they, their, them, these,* or *those* to refer to more than one person or thing. (See 6b.)

WRONG   The wise shopper looks inside the garment to see that they have adequate seams.

RIGHT   The wise shopper looks inside the garment to see that *it* has adequate seams.

11d-4
Use *you* and *your* only to refer directly to the reader; do not use these words to make general statements.

Some writers use *you* and *your* in general observations when *a, an,* or *the* is appropriate or when no pronoun at all is needed.

WEAK   Take your jack from your trunk. This is your first step in changing your tire.

[*Your* here suggests you are referring to a particular reader and his particular car.]

BETTER   Take *the* jack from the trunk. This is *the* first step in changing *a* tire.

[Here it is clear that you are just giving general instructions.]

WEAK   In any jail you have your hardened criminal and your first-time offender.

[*You* suggests you are referring directly to the reader.]

BETTER   In any jail there are hardened *criminals* and first-time *offenders.*

[Here it is clear that you are just making an observation.]

 CHECKLIST: Providing Clear References

In order to guide your readers accurately, here are some questions to ask yourself:

1. Do I give a clear reference for pronouns such as *it, they, them, you,* and *your*?
2. Do I always use a singular word to refer to one person or thing?
3. Do I use a plural word to refer to more than one person or thing?

EXERCISE 4

Correct any of the following sentences that contain shifts or unclear references.

1. Every viewer of pay TV receives a TV guide so they don't need previews to keep the viewers informed of upcoming programs.

2. Some people think that women cannot be the equal of a man.

3. One of the reasons I love to cook is that you can alter recipes to suit your taste.

4. A person performing venipuncture should first check the patient's I.D. bracelet. Then apply your tourniquet.

5. I hope whoever starts smoking stops, and for those who do not smoke never start.

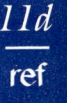

11d

ref

6. A shopper sometimes can't get through the checkout lane because they are talking with their friend.

7. Someone who likes to be considered sophisticated often acts as though they are not enjoying themselves, even when they are.

8. When it comes to eating, gourmands are very different from the gourmet.

9. Three types of hockey players are your puck hog, your lazy players, and your 110% contributor.

10. Now the race was on to the connecting flight, and do it all over again.

Chapter 12

WRITING
EFFECTIVE
SENTENCES

Improve your sentences by giving them
variety, emphasis, and interest.

You are on your way to writing well if your sentences are free from errors in spelling, punctuation, and word choice. However, good writing has another important quality: It seems to "flow." That is, the writer has written each sentence in such a way that it clearly emphasizes its point and moves smoothly to the next sentence. The result is a piece of writing which is interesting, pleasurable, and easy to read. You can help your writing flow by varying the lengths and beginnings of your sentences and by arranging your words so that your sentences clearly emphasize your points.

12a
Vary the lengths of your sentences. Avoid a series of short, choppy sentences.

As you read the following paragraph, notice that although there are many excellent details to help you imagine the place described, the writing seems choppy and monotonous. The paragraph does not flow for two reasons. First, most of the sentences are short, and second, all of the sentences except the first one begin with the sentence's subject.

> There is a chapel in North Carolina. I love to visit it. It is situated among tall pine trees. The trees are covered with Spanish moss. It looks like a storybook cottage. It is a red brick building trimmed in white. The patterns of the stained-glass windows seem to glow with a life of their own, even on the cloudiest days. The most impressive of these windows depicts Christ kneeling in prayer. The chapel always makes me feel that I have been transported to a serene, almost holy place. This is a place where even the most troubled person would find peace.

12a
var

Now read the revised paragraph. Notice that many of the sentences have been combined to create variety in both the lengths and beginnings of the sentences.

> There is a chapel in North Carolina that I love to visit. Situated among tall pine trees which are covered with Spanish moss, it looks like a storybook cottage. It is a red brick building trimmed in white. The patterns of the stained-glass windows seem to glow with a life of their own, even on the cloudiest days. The most impressive of these windows depicts Christ kneeling in prayer. Whenever I see that chapel, I always feel that I have been transported to a serene, almost holy place, somewhere that even the most troubled person would find peace.

EXERCISE 1

The following paragraph contains choppy, monotonous writing. Rewrite the paragraph by combining several sentences and starting some sentences with something other than their subjects.

Gossip tabloids all appear to have "amazing facts" inside. One fact I read recently was about a newborn. The newborn supposedly gave birth seconds after she was born. Another fact concerned a mother who saved her son's life. That mother removed a ten-ton boulder from the front of a cave to free him. Some tabloids have miracle cures. One cure I saw was a garlic-and-orange-juice recipe guaranteed to cure baldness. Another was washing the face with vegetable oil to treat acne. Gossip tabloids really depend on miracles.

12b
Emphasize the right points in your sentences.
Use coordination and subordination effectively.

12b-1
Use coordination to emphasize points equally.

Coordination is the joining of two ideas of equal importance by using a comma and *and, but, so, for, or, nor,* or *yet* instead of using two short sentences. Joining them in this way shows emphasis or contrast.

> I moved here when I was twelve years old, and I mean to stay here until I die.
> I thought you would be here, but I was wrong.

However, it is important to avoid stringing together sentences with *and, but, so, for, or, nor,* or *yet* when the ideas in the sentences are not equal. Ideas generally are not equal if one causes another, one comes before or after another in time, or one makes a point which the other only contributes to.

NOT EQUAL	He didn't study for the exam, and he failed it.
BETTER	Because he didn't study for the exam, he failed it.
NOT EQUAL	John went to work, but he got sick.
BETTER	After John went to work, he got sick.
NOT EQUAL	Mary applied for the job, so she wasn't hired and had to look for another job.
BETTER	Although Mary applied for the job, she wasn't hired and had to look for another job.

Caution: Never join more than two complete sentences with *and, but, so, or, nor, for,* or *yet.* If you do, your writing will seem to ramble without a point.

RAMBLING	Harold broke up with her last week, and he called her yesterday, but she didn't call him back.
BETTER	Although Harold broke up with her last week, he called her yesterday, but she didn't call him back.

12b-2

Use subordination to show cause and effect. When something in one sentence causes or is caused by something in the next sentence, join the sentences with *because* or *since*.

Subordination is the showing of a relationship between two ideas by putting one of them into a dependent clause. Subordination helps the reader see the point that you are making.

When one thing happens because another thing has happened, you can make the relationship between those two ideas clearer by using *because* or *since* to join the sentences in which those ideas are expressed. Remember that if your new sentence begins with *because* or *since*, you need to put a comma where the sentences are joined. (See **13b** for more information.) As you compare the ways the following two ideas can be written, note the combination which best expresses a cause/effect relationship.

TWO IDEAS	His bus was not on time. He was late for work.
JOINED WITH *AND*	His bus was not on time, and he was late.
BEST COMBINATION	Because his bus was not on time, he was late for work.
	OR
	He was late for work because his bus was not on time.

12b-3

Use subordination to show relationships in time. When something in one sentence happens before, after, or during the time something happens in the sentence next to it, join the sentences with words like *before, after, when*, or *while*.

Often when you are describing an event which has happened, you will write sentences explaining that one thing happened and then another thing happened after that. For instance, if you were describing the day you graduated from high school, you might write "The school band started to play. We began to march down the aisle." However, it would be better to write "After the school band started to play, we began to march down the aisle." As you can see, the relationship between various things that happen is expressed more clearly if you join sentences with words like *before, after, when*, or *while*. Remember that if your sentence begins with *before, after, when,* or *while,* you need to put a comma where the sentences are joined.

TIME RELATIONSHIP   We went to the mall. We ate dinner at a
NOT CLEAR   new restaurant close to my house.

BETTER   After we went to the mall, we ate dinner at a new restaurant close to my house.

OR

Before we went to the mall, we ate dinner at a new restaurant close to my house.

12b-4

Use subordination to create emphasis. When two sentences next to each other state parts of the same point, emphasize the main point by joining the sentences with words like *if, unless,* and *although.*

Often sentences which are next to each other express parts of one larger point. For instance, if you were explaining how you feel about fast food restaurants, you might write "I fear that most fast food restaurants serve food that is high in calories. Junk food is my favorite kind of food." Although both sentences make a point about fast food, your reader will be confused about your feelings toward your subject because the first statement seems negative and the second positive. However, if you join the sentences in such a way that one point is emphasized over the other, your reader will no longer be confused. You might write "Although I fear that most fast food restaurants serve food that is high in calories, junk food is my favorite kind of food." Now your reader will understand that you will probably eat at fast food restaurants because your love of junk food is stronger than your fear of calories. Using words like *if, unless,* and *although* helps your reader to make sense of sentences whose points are closely related. Remember that if your sentence begins with *if, unless,* or *although,* you need to put a comma where the related ideas are joined.

CONFUSING   See a doctor about your high temperature. You may have to postpone your business trip.

BETTER   Unless you see a doctor about your high temperature, you may have to postpone your business trip.

CONFUSING   I might see Susan at the party. I will tell her to call you.

BETTER   If I see Susan at the party, I will tell her to call you.

EXERCISE 2

In each pair of sentences, decide which sentence contains the point to be emphasized and which sentence merely contributes to that point. Then combine the sentences by using *when, after, before, while, although, because, since, if,* or *unless.*

EXAMPLE   I didn't go out that day. It was raining hard.

Because it was raining hard, I didn't go out that day.

OR

I didn't go out that day because it was raining hard.

1. My best Christmas vacation was spent working in a day-care center. It was fun to see the children looking forward to the holiday.
2. Robert introduced me to his sister. He told me we both had the same name.
3. Rabbits really do dig up a garden. They make nice pets for children.
4. My husband washes the dishes. I tune up the car.
5. Sally might go to Europe next summer. She will visit her aunt in Germany.
6. My alarm goes off at 7:00. I am enjoying the last of my dreams.
7. Spring is a welcome relief to winter's snow. I dread summer's heat and humidity.
8. We have never been very close. We have known each other for ten years.

12b-5

Use subordination to create interest. When you describe a person or thing, one well-developed sentence is often more interesting than two short sentences.

WEAK	My father's old felt hat looks as though it has been through the wars. It is sitting on the mantel.
MORE INTERESTING	My father's old felt hat, *which looks as though it has been through the wars*, is sitting on the mantel.

WEAK	Joe Louis was undoubtedly the greatest heavyweight fighter of all time. He died practically penniless.
MORE INTERESTING	Joe Louis, *who was undoubtedly the greatest heavyweight fighter of all time*, died practically penniless.
WEAK	Jack Nicholson is a versatile comic actor. He has played the devil, an astronaut, and the Joker in *Batman*.
MORE INTERESTING	Jack Nicholson, a versatile comic actor, has played the devil, an astronaut, and the Joker in *Batman*.

EXERCISE 3

Rewrite the following paragraph, varying the lengths of the sentences and using subordination to replace sentences that are joined with *and*, *but*, or *so*.

I try to study, but I am always distracted by several things. First, my mother starts asking me too many questions. She asks things like what time a TV program comes on or what I am doing. The telephone rings, and it's my friend. She just wants to talk about nothing and to make noise, so I make an excuse to get off the phone. And then somebody knocks at the door, wanting to know what I am doing, so I don't open the door and I go back upstairs, and I try to study. Now I start watching talk shows, and they are so interesting that I stop studying. Then I get hungry. You can see now why I have trouble studying. I try, but everything distracts me.

EXERCISE 4

Combine each of the following pairs of sentences, following one of the patterns given in the example.

EXAMPLE   Tom Cruise is my favorite actor.
            He sends goosebumps down my spine.

Tom Cruise, my favorite actor, sends goosebumps down my spine.

OR

Tom Cruise, who is my favorite actor, sends goosebumps down my spine.

1. Uncle Jack watches all the horror movies on TV. He sometimes can't sleep at night because he is thinking about them.
2. My dog Fred never bit a soul. He has a sign on his outdoor kennel which reads "Beware of Dog."
3. Marilyn's mother-in-law has never been sick a day in her life. She is always worried about her health.
4. My mother thinks she is an expert on politics. She was positive that George W. Bush would never be elected President of the United States.
5. Janet's mother goes fishing every Saturday morning. She believes that weekends should be reserved for fun and relaxation.
6. Carl's father is a Navy pilot. He is going to speak to our class on Tuesday about careers in aviation.
7. My sister is the biggest baby in the world. She cried when she stubbed her toe on the screen door.

12b
sub

EXERCISE 5

Combine each of the following pairs of sentences, using one of the patterns given in the example.

EXAMPLE The aspidistra is called the cast-iron plant. It is the only one that will grow in my daughter's New York apartment.

> *The aspidistra, called the cast-iron plant, is the only one that will grow in my daughter's New York apartment.*

OR

> *The aspidistra, which is called the cast-iron plant, is the only one that will grow in my daughter's New York apartment.*

1. My sister's hope chest is a standing joke in our family. It will probably never leave our house.
2. Our garbage can is about to overflow. It should have been emptied two days ago.
3. Betsy's car is a great car for a family with no children. It is a convertible with only two seats.
4. Brighton Beach is a recreation area. It is not very far from downtown Manhattan.

12c
Vary the beginnings of your sentences so that your writing will flow better and will be more interesting.

You may already have noticed that when you begin to combine sentences to vary their lengths, you also begin to vary their beginnings. For instance, notice what happens when you combine the following sentences.

TWO SENTENCES	Julia is a nurse. She is good at diagnosing childhood illnesses. [The first sentence begins with the subject.]
COMBINED SENTENCE	Because Julia is a nurse, she is good at diagnosing childhood illnesses. [Now the sentence begins with a dependent clause.]
TWO SENTENCES	I saw a deer on my way to the village. It was in Mr. Jones's yard.] [The first sentence begins with the subject.]
COMBINED SENTENCE	On my way to the village, I saw a deer in Mr. Jones's yard. [Now the sentence begins with a prepositional phrase.]

A sentence which begins with its subject can be very effective because it is a direct and powerful statement of an idea. However, if your writing contains too many subject-first sentences, your writing will quickly seem dull and predictable to your reader. Therefore, make sure you begin some sentences with prepositional phrases, some with dependent clauses, and some even with verbs, adjectives, and adverbs; use subject-first sentences between the other sentences, not in a row.

EXERCISE 6

Study the following paragraph, and then answer the questions that follow it.

¹Almost every store is visited at some point by the all-day bargain hunter. ²He is the person who arrives at the store before the em-

ployees. ³He stays until closing time. ⁴This shopper frantically collects coupons and ads. ⁵He has stuffed his pockets with clippings from every magazine and newspaper he can get his hands on. ⁶He begins his shopping by rummaging through a table of sale merchandise at the front of the store. ⁷He searches for the best buys. ⁸He touches every item on the table. ⁹He then moves to the back of the store, and the sales racks are usually there. ¹⁰He goes through every piece of clothing, and he selects all those which can possibly fit him. ¹¹Finally finished with his survey of sale merchandise, he gathers all the items he has selected. ¹²He takes them to a fitting room. ¹³He spends the rest of the day trying on things. ¹⁴The clerk starts to remind him that the store will close in five minutes. ¹⁵He keeps right on trying on clothes as if he had all night. ¹⁶The all-day bargain hunter can be annoying to sales clerks even if he does manage to buy a lot by the end of the day.

1. List the numbers of the sentences which begin with their subjects.
2. List the numbers of the sentences which use coordination (*and*, *but*, *so*, *for*, *nor*, *or*, or *yet*).

Now study the rewritten version of the same paragraph. Then answer the questions that follow it.

¹Almost every store is visited at some point by the all-day bargain hunter. ²He is the person who arrives at the store before the employees, and he stays until closing time. ³This shopper, who frantically collects coupons and ads, has stuffed his pockets with clippings from every magazine and newspaper he can get his hands on. ⁴Beginning his shopping by rummaging through a table of sale merchandise at the front of the store, he searches for the best buys, touching every item on the table. ⁵He then moves to the back of the store because the sales racks are usually there. ⁶After he goes through every piece of clothing, he selects all those which can possibly fit him. Finally finished with his survey of sale merchandise, he gathers all the items he has selected, takes them to a fitting room, and spends the rest of the day trying on things. ⁸Although the clerk starts to remind him that the store will close in five minutes, he keeps right on trying on clothes as if he had all night. ⁹The all-day bargain-hunter can be annoying to sales clerks even if he does manage to buy a lot by the end of the day.

3. List the numbers of the sentences which begin with their subjects.
4. List the numbers of the sentences which use coordination (*and*, *but*, *so*, *for*, *nor*, *or*, or *yet*) to emphasize points equally.

12c
—
sub

5. List the numbers of the sentences which use subordination (*because* or *since*) to show cause and effect.
6. List the numbers of the sentences which use subordination (*before*, *after*, *when*, or *while*) to show relationships in time.
7. List the numbers of the sentences which use subordination (*if*, *unless*, or *although*) to create emphasis.
8. List the numbers of the sentences which use subordination (*who* or *which*) to create interest.

EXERCISE 7

Write a sentence using each of the following beginnings.

1. Although I didn't expect it,
2. Unless you get a letter tomorrow,
3. I didn't like my daughter's last boyfriend, and
4. Although I didn't like my daughter's last boyfriend,
5. If I hadn't stopped smoking,
6. After Jessica registered for classes,
7. I didn't go on vacation last year, but
8. In the middle of the park
9. Sue Ellen, who worked for her father last year,
10. James, my nephew,

EXERCISE 8

The following paragraph contains short, choppy sentences. Rewrite it, varying the lengths and beginnings of the sentences so that the paragraph flows better. Use each of the following methods at least once.

1. Coordination to show ideas that are equally important (*and*, *but*, *so*, *for*, *nor*, *or*, or *yet*)
2. Subordination to show cause and effect (*because* or *since*)
3. Subordination to show relationships in time (*before*, *after*, *when*, or *while*)
4. Subordination to create emphasis (*if*, *unless*, or *although*)
5. Subordination to create interest (*who* or *which*)

The worst childhood accident I ever had occurred on the day of my ninth birthday. I shared a room with my eleven-year-old sister, and so neither of us had a place where we could enjoy any privacy.

On the day of my birthday, I decided to go to my (our) room to read *A Wrinkle in Time*. It was a book my parents had given me for my birthday. My sister was outside playing softball, and I didn't think she would come in and bother me. I got settled on the bed with both pillows behind my head and my favorite comforter over me and opened my book. My sister burst through the door and started begging me to join her softball game because her team needed another player. I told her I would rather read my book, so she jumped on the bed and started tickling me to annoy me. I begged her to stop. She wouldn't. Soon the tickling turned into fighting. Before long, we were both so mad that we were really trying to hurt each other. Suddenly, my shoulder slammed into the footboard. I heard a crack. A quick trip to the emergency room revealed that I had broken my collarbone. I consider my sister my best friend today. When we were children, she could be my worst enemy.

12c
sub

Chapter 13

COMMAS AND NO COMMAS

Use commas correctly.

A comma is a punctuation mark which helps the reader get meaning from the sentences you write. Just as pauses and changes in the tone of your voice help convey meaning when you speak, commas (and other punctuation marks) assist the reader in understanding what you have written. A comma usually signals a pause. Thus, using commas correctly helps you and your reader communicate.

13a
Use a comma and a coordinating conjunction to separate main clauses.

You cannot separate main clauses by using a comma alone (see **3e**). Instead, use a comma followed by a *coordinating conjunction (and, but, or, nor, for, so,* or *yet).*

WRONG	Once I lived on a farm, I had a horse named Chessie.
RIGHT	Once I lived on a farm, *and* I had a horse named Chessie.
WRONG	Two years ago Chessie died, I still cannot accept losing her.
RIGHT	Two years ago Chessie died, *but* I still cannot accept losing her.

EXERCISE 1

Use a comma followed by a coordinating conjunction to separate main clauses in the following sentences.

1. My daughter-in-law asked me to show her how to make biscuits, I quickly agreed.

2. I knew this would pass on a family tradition and I was pleased.

3. The baking session went well, the biscuits looked, smelled, and tasted good.

4. Thelma, my oldest granddaughter, wanted to learn, I showed her the baking routine.

5. Making biscuits is not difficult nor does it take much time.

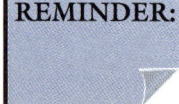 **REMINDER:** **Separating Clauses with Periods or Semicolons**

You can separate main clauses by using periods or semicolons instead of commas and coordinating conjunctions.

> WRONG   Yesterday the weather was hot and humid, it's cooler today.
>
> RIGHT   Yesterday the weather was hot and humid, but it's cooler today.
>
> RIGHT   Yesterday the weather was hot and humid. It's cooler today.
>
> RIGHT   Yesterday the weather was hot and humid; it's cooler today.

13b
Use a comma between a dependent clause and a main clause when the dependent clause comes first in the sentence.

The words *after, although, as, because, before, if, since, unless, until, when, whenever,* and *while* (subordinating conjunctions) often introduce dependent clauses. Add a comma only when the dependent clause comes before the main clause. If the main clause comes first, a comma is usually *not* used.

	(dependent clause)	(main clause)

WRONG   *Because* I am so busy at school I have no time for camping this summer.

	(dependent clause)	(main clause)

RIGHT   *Because* I am so busy at school, I have no time for camping this summer.

	(main clause)	(dependent clause)

RIGHT   I have no time for camping this summer *because* I am so busy at school.

For help in recognizing sentences and dependent clauses, see **1b-5** and **2b-1**.

EXERCISE 2

13a
,

Underline the dependent clauses in the following sentences. Then insert any needed commas and cross out commas that are not needed.

1. When you are not busy with other activities take time to clean your car.
2. Although their salaries are low, many young people enjoy working in summer camps.
3. NASCAR is my favorite spectator sport because it is exciting to watch.
4. Maria is usually more outgoing, when she is pleased with her appearance.
5. If I had my way all classes would meet for two hours three days a week.
6. While strolling through the old section of downtown Cincinnati, it is easy to imagine the living conditions there in an earlier time.
7. If it fails to move the football ten yards after three downs the team possessing the ball must either punt or attempt to kick a field goal.

EXERCISE 3

Add or remove commas between clauses in the sentences below. Write *C* if the sentence is correct.

1. The children ran across the street without looking for passing cars, although no one was hit.

2. The twins never dress alike nor do they look alike.

3. Most compact cars are easy to park, they get good gas mileage, too.

4. When I finish at TCC I hope to transfer either to Old Dominion University or to Christopher Newport University.

5. If you follow the directions I just gave you you will have no trouble finding my home.

6. My first plane ride was an ordeal, because I was so nervous.

7. Although you may purchase a dog with the idea that he is really yours, you will soon learn that you are really his.

13c
Use a comma between words or groups of words in a series or a list.

Study the use of commas in the following sentences.

COMMAS BETWEEN WORDS	The new student's name is either *Tom*, *Dick*, or *Harry*.
COMMAS BETWEEN PHRASES	We usually have Thanksgiving dinner at Grandma's house, which is *on a farm*, *over a river*, and *near dense woods*.
COMMAS BETWEEN CLAUSES	Fans *who purchase season tickets*, *who are serious about the game*, and *whose families attend* also are the ones most coaches like to see at high school games.

13d
Use commas between adjectives in place of the word *and*. If *and* cannot be used, do not use a comma.

Either the comma or *and* shows that both of the adjectives refer to the person or thing being described.

She came running into the large, empty room.
She came running into the large *and* empty room.

It was a noisy, exciting race.
It was a noisy *and* exciting race.
The only clue was a small, dark stain on the carpet.
The only clue was a small *and* dark stain on the carpet.
[The words *small* and *dark* both describe *stain*. The word *and* can substitute for the comma.]

In the following sentences, one of the adjectives does not refer to the thing or person described.

He wore a bright blue sweater.
He wore a bright and blue sweater.
[*Blue* describes *sweater*, and *bright* describes the color *blue*. Neither a comma nor *and* is needed.]
Both of the girls had dark brown hair.
Both of the girls had dark and brown hair.
[*Dark* describes *brown*, and *brown* describes *hair*. Neither a comma nor *and* is needed.]

13d
,

REMINDER: **Testing Whether a Comma Is Needed**

One test to see whether you need a comma is to reverse the order of the adjectives. If doing so creates an expression that no longer makes sense, you do not need a comma.

Both of the girls had brown dark hair.
[There is no such hair; therefore, do not use a comma between *dark* and *brown*.]

EXERCISE 4

Add or remove commas as necessary in the following paragraph.

When I worked in a restaurant at Nags Head last summer I lived with three friends. At the beginning of the summer everybody was happy. We all hung out surfed and partied. As the summer went on we started disagreeing about chores, and the dishes were rarely washed.

Piles of dirty greasy stained, dishes were stacked on the cupboards. However, because our supply of dishes was limited we finally had to wash them. Keeping the place neat, and tidy was not important until visitors came. Then we all helped by clearing off the tables, emptying the trash and shoving dirty clothes under our beds. Soon the long lazy summer days ended and we came home to start college, to find jobs or to join the Navy. Maybe my childhood ended then, but no matter what happens next I'll always remember that summer at Nags Head.

13e
Use commas in direct address to separate the name of the person (or persons) to whom someone is speaking from the rest of the sentence. Remember that commas signify pauses and changes in tone.

Notice the use of commas in the following sentences.

> *Rick*, do you agree with John's plan to raise money for Children's Hospital?
> No matter how busy you are, *Maria*, you always complete your assignments.
> *Animal lovers*, this is not the time to boycott the zoo.
> According to a survey, friends, 75% of those watching news programs push the mute button during commercials.

In the sentences above commas are needed because someone is speaking to each person or group.

13f
Use commas to separate the names of speakers from their exact (quoted) words.

> "The longer I live," *writes Charles Swindall*, "the more I realize the impact of attitude on life."
> When my aunt scolded Grandma for forgetting to take her medicine, *Grandma replied*, "Please forgive me, Carrie, but I've never needed pills before."

Notice that the quotation marks enclose the speaker's exact words. See also **16a**.

13g
Use commas to separate names of places, dates, and addresses.

Places, dates, and addresses usually contain more than one part. Use commas to separate these parts.

> Many farms near *Suffolk, Virginia,* produce large crops of peanuts each year.
> [Commas are needed to separate the city from the state and the state from the rest of the sentence.]

> Write to me at *710 York Court, San Diego, California* 92109
> [Commas are needed to separate the street address, city, and state; however, a comma is not needed between the state and zip code.]

> On *Sunday, July 9, 2000,* my grandparents celebrated their Golden Wedding Anniversary.
> [Commas are needed to separate the day of the week from the month, the day of the month from the year, and the year from the rest of the sentence.]

> During *July 1950,* shortly after Grandpa's discharge from the Navy, my grandparents were married.
>
> OR
>
> On *9 July 1950,* shortly after his discharge from the Navy, Grandpa married his high school sweetheart.
> [If the day of the month is not given or if the day appears before the month, the comma is omitted.]

EXERCISE 5

Add commas where they are needed in the following sentences, and be able to explain your additions.

1. Portsmouth Virginia and Portsmouth England are both seaport cities.

2. I can hardly believe that you've finished all your assignments Jason in such a short time.

3. Before you begin making the cake you should turn on the oven get the baking dishes ready and assemble the ingredients.

4. Mary's new car has a sunroof a CD player and a large monthly payment.

5. Baltimore Maryland is a large metropolitan area and it is located on the east coast.

6. Dave's new address is 279 Hallston Drive Columbus Ohio 43219.

7. My mom asked "Nicholas will you please take this note to school and give it to Miss Sparrow?"

13h
Use commas to separate nonrestrictive expressions (words that add nonessential information) from the rest of the sentence.

13h-1
Place commas around words that add nonrestrictive information about a person or thing.

> Marlo, *my brother's girlfriend*, is an honor student.
> [Marlo and *my brother's girlfriend* are one person. However, the meaning of the sentence does not depend on this information.]

> Mrs. Greene, *our next-door neighbor*, is very active in her children's school.
> [*Our next-door neighbor* adds information not needed to understand this sentence.]

13h-2
Use commas around a *who* or *what* expression (that is, a relative clause) when the expression is not essential to the meaning of the sentence.

When a clause beginning with *who, which, whoever,* or *whose* does not restrict or limit the person or thing it describes, separate the clause from the rest of the sentence with commas.

> Samantha, whose nickname is Sam, is my favorite niece.
> [The fact that Samantha's nickname is Sam is additional, nonessential information.]

Some teachers, *who are often very busy*, frequently have conferences with their students.

[*Who are often very busy* is not needed to complete the meaning of this sentence.]

13h-3
Use commas to separate parenthetical expressions such as *therefore, however,* and *for example* from the rest of the sentence.

Words such as *therefore, however, in fact*, and *for example* are parenthetical because they could be put into parentheses or omitted without changing the meaning of the sentence. Also called transitionals, these words may be used at the beginning, in the middle, or at the end of a sentence. They help take the reader from one idea to another.

> Rangers in U.S. National Parks have, *in fact*, warned visitors not to pollute land or lakes. *As a result*, campers are being careful to put trash into garbage containers. Yesterday, *however*, someone ignored the warning and threw bottles into the lake. *As a matter of fact*, that person could be fined as much as $100.

 Caution: When words such as *however, therefore, for example, as a result, in fact*, or *in that case* are used between main clauses, a semicolon is used before the word or words, and a comma is used after them.

> The day dawned cool and pleasant; *therefore*, the class trip was not cancelled.

13h-4
Use commas to separate introductory expressions (participles, infinitives, or long prepositional phrases) from the rest of the sentence.

> *Much embarrassed*, Lance Corporal Smith left the room.
> *Moving cautiously*, the troops approached the quiet barracks.
> *After finishing our essays in class*, we were excused.
> *To get full credit*, you must attend all sessions of that class.

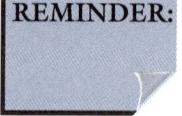

REMINDER: No Comma Needed With Short Prepositional Phrase

A short prepositional phrase may be used without a comma.

In high school my friends were always hanging out in the gym.

13h-5

Use commas after words such as *first, next, last, finally,* and *in conclusion* when they begin a sentence. These words show the order (sequence) of the events.

First, turn on the oven and set the temperature at 350 degrees.
Next, gather all of the ingredients needed to make lemon pie.

13h-6

Use commas to separate words such as *I hope, I believe,* and *he* or *she says* from the rest of the sentence when these expressions are used as interrupters.

This is, *I believe,* a very unusual situation.
No wars will be fought, *I hope,* in my lifetime.

Notice in the following sentences that when the expression is used at the beginning, the remainder of the sentence tells what is hoped or believed or said. In this case the expression is not an interrupter, and a comma should not be used.

I believe this is a very unusual situation.
I hope no wars will be fought in my lifetime.

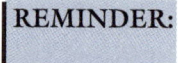

REMINDER: Using a Comma After *Yes* and *No*

Use a comma to separate *yes* and *no* from the rest of the sentence.

Yes, I am going to have my research paper in on time.
No, my family and I are not going to our beach house during August.

13h-7
Use commas to separate concluding parenthetical expressions from the rest of the sentence.

These concluding expressions usually begin with participles which end in *-ing* or *-ed*.

> Some teachers write creative lesson plans, *hoping* to motivate their students.
>
> Rene left the room, *embarrassed* by the quarrel.

REMINDER: **When To Use a Comma**

13i
,

You can usually tell when to use commas by the way you read a sentence aloud. If you pause before and after reading a group of words, usually these words are not needed to complete the meaning of the sentence and should be separated from the rest of it by commas.

13i
Use commas to make your meaning clear.

When you write your papers, think carefully about what you mean to say. The way you punctuate usually determines your meaning. For example, in the following sentences the same words appear in the same order. As you see, however, the meaning of this sentence changes when the punctuation changes.

> The ringmaster believes that clown is the funniest in the circus.
> [In this sentence the *ringmaster believes . . .*]
> The ringmaster, believes that clown, is the funniest in the circus.
> [In this sentence the *clown believes . . .*]

EXERCISE 6

Add commas where they are needed in the following sentences.

1. As we the students entered middle school our interests started to change.

2. Mike said "The team will never win without Darell in the lineup."

3. May 21 1914 is an important date in that little town.

4. She lives in Norton Iowa at 2115 Graham Street.

5. Cross the bridge taking a right at the first stoplight.

6. I know of course that I will never be the person that I dream about but it is pleasant to think of myself as a hero.

7. My oldest child a girl of fourteen is energetic stubborn single-minded and athletic.

8. Andy delighted his fellow shipmates by wolfing down his sandwich peanut butter jelly and mayonnaise on white bread before swallowing a cold cherry cola.

9. If you follow these simple directions you will arrive at 4512 Weatherly Lane my home.

10. Go to the fourth stoplight which is the big intersection after you leave TNC.

11. Next at that stoplight make a right turn onto Route 17.

12. Then go straight for about four miles being careful to avoid speeding.

13. To be sure you are going the right way look for a Texaco station on your left.

14. The next driveway is the one you are looking for.

15. My younger sister a child of three may be noisy rude and stubborn at that time of day.

16. I know of course that she's tired hungry and spoiled.

13j
Do not use a comma to separate a subject from its verb(s).

Be on your guard for this problem when your subject has more than one verb and when the second verb is not close to its subject.

	(subject)	(verb)
WRONG	*Utensils* needed for plant propagation, *are* hand pruners and rubber bands.	

	(subject)	(verb)
RIGHT	*Utensils* needed for plant propagation *are* hand pruners and rubber bands.	

	(subject) (verb)	(verb)
WRONG	*Biff* never *accepts* life as it is, but *wants* life to conform to his dream.	

	(subject) (verb)	(verb)
RIGHT	*Biff* never *accepts* life as it is but *wants* life to conform to his dreams.	

13k
Do not use a comma to separate the verb from its object(s).

Be on your guard when the verb has more than one object.

	(verb)	(object)
WRONG	My sister *completed* her history *assignment*, and her	
	(object)	
	term *paper.*	
RIGHT	My sister *completed* her history *assignment* and her term *paper.*	

	(verb)	(object)
WRONG	In first grade my classmates and I *practiced reading,*	
	(object)	
	and *social skills.*	
RIGHT	In first grade my classmates and I *practiced reading* and *social skills.*	

EXERCISE 7

In the following sentences, omit any commas that are not needed.

1. King Henry VIII broke away from the church, and made himself head of the Church of England.

2. I am a vegetarian, and I abstain from using all forms of animal products.

3. Hawaii's ocean stays warm year round, and is crystal clear.

4. In my room are my chest of drawers, and a few posters of my favorite bodyboarders.

5. I came and saw, but didn't conquer.

13l
Do not use commas around relative clauses (who or which expressions) or any words or phrases essential to the meaning of the sentence.

Do not put commas around a word, phrase, or clause which is needed to make the meaning of the sentence clear.

> Freshmen *who do not like to study* should not enroll in History 125.
> [The italicized clause identifies *specific* freshmen (who do not like to study); therefore, *the clause is needed* to complete the meaning of the sentence.]
>
> My sister, *trying to be helpful,* tells everyone *who asks* the secret of her success.
> [The first group of italicized words in this sentence is a *general phrase not needed* to complete the meaning of the sentence. The second italicized clause refers to a *specific group of people (people who ask)* and, therefore, *is needed.*]

13m
Do not use a comma between adjectives if and cannot substitute for the comma.

Notice the use of commas in these sentences.

> WRONG   In the past two years I have purchased several, plain, dark, blue, skirts.
> [If you substitute *and* for the commas, this sentence does not make sense.]
>
> RIGHT   In the past two years I have purchased several plain, dark blue skirts.
> [The skirts are *plain* and *dark blue.*]

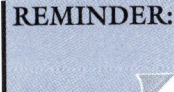

REMINDER: Deciding if a Comma is Needed

To decide whether a comma is needed, reverse the order of the adjectives.

WRONG   In the past two years I have purchased *plain several, blue dark* skirts.

EXERCISE 8

Cross out any unneeded commas in the following sentences and explain the reasons for your changes.

1. Jason is a pretty, neat little stepbrother.

2. Although the forecaster predicted a pleasant, clear day, rain fell in a constant, heavy, dismal, downpour last Sunday.

3. The huge, light, green, van has a dark, green stripe around each door.

4. The noisy, garbage truck, rumbled through the sleeping neighborhood.

5. I find it difficult to concentrate on my frequently boring, often dull, assignments.

13n
,

13n
Do not use a comma to separate a dependent clause from a main clause if that clause is last in the sentence.

                                            (dependent clause)
WRONG   Ask for an extension, *if you cannot complete your paper by May 15.*
                    (dependent clause)
RIGHT   *If you cannot complete your paper by May 15*, ask for an extension.

13o
Do not use a comma between the name of a state and the zip code.

WRONG   Michael and Sue Ramos live at 710 LaJolla Drive, San
         Diego, CA, 92109.

RIGHT   Michael and Sue Ramos live at 710 LaJolla Drive, San
         Diego, CA 92109.

13p
Do not use a comma without having a reason.

Leaving out commas is usually better than adding them where they are not needed. Always have a reason for adding a comma.

EXERCISE 9

Add or remove commas as needed in the following sentences. Be prepared to explain your reasons.

1. The music sounded, as though it were in this room.

2. The resolution was introduced, and was quickly passed.

3. My address has changed to 5534 Wilshire Blvd., Austin, TX, 88234.

4. In the meantime, after classes are over for the semester, I'll be going to my quiet cabin on the shore of the lovely large, fresh, water lake up north.

☑ **CHECKLIST: Deciding When to Use Commas**

Use a comma:
1. before coordinating conjunctions (*and, but, or, for, nor* or *so*) between main clauses;

Do *not* use a comma:
1. between a dependent clause and a main clause when the main clause comes first;

2. between a dependent clause and a main clause when the dependent clause beginning with a subordinating conjunction (*after, although, as, because, if, since, unless, until, when, whenever* or *while*) comes first;

3. between words or groups of words in a series or list;

4. between adjectives or adverbs when *and* can substitute for the comma;

5. around words that are nonessential to the meaning of the sentence;

6. to separate parts of names, places, dates, and addresses;

7. to separate speakers from their exact (quoted) words.

2. before a coordinating conjunction that separates a subject from its verb;

3. before a coordinating conjunction that separates a verb from its object;

4. between adjectives and adverbs when *and* could not substitute for the comma;

5. around words, phrases, or clauses that are essential to the meaning of the sentence;

6. between the state and zip code in an address;

7. unless you have a reason to use one.

13p
,

EXERCISE 10

In the following sentences, remove commas where they are not needed.

1. Since getting involved in racing, I have had difficulty, explaining my lifestyle to my young, curious friend, to my middle-aged brother, and to the IRS.

2. Charlie Brown's ability to take what life gives him and live with it, is one of his most endearing qualities.

3. I went back to sleep immediately, after I had turned off the alarm clock.

4. Since more women than ever before are working outside the home, men are taking over many domestic responsibilities.

5. The winter has been a cold, snowy one.

6. The reporter was not there, when the crowd came down the street.

7. Send the package to Mr. Harding in Jewett, Illinois, 62436.

8. Start washing from the top of the car, making sure you are loosening the dirt.

9. Clothes, such as fur coats and military uniforms, often suggest a person's social position or occupation.

10. Where is the 7-Eleven, that is closest to school?

EXERCISE 11

Add any necessary commas and remove any that are unnecessary in the following paragraph.

If you are a canine, the term, *dog's life*, is not very derogatory these days especially where diet is concerned. In fact the yuppy puppy can now enjoy a dinner of microwave meatloaf salmon and canine ice cream. For the pet, who is a bit plump, and health-conscious, there are low-salt dog delights, "all-natural" snacks and high-fiber goodies and for the sleek trim dog Porterhouse and Delmonico cuts of beef can be had at only slightly, exhorbitant prices. In spite of inflation any dog, who is intelligent enough to find the right master, or should I say "provider," can find himself living on the best street in town Easy Street.

Chapter 14

THE SEMICOLON

Use a semicolon between closely related main clauses and between groups of words that already contain commas. Use a semicolon only when the parts to be joined are equal in importance.

14a
Use a semicolon between two main clauses that are closely related.

The semicolon is sometimes called a "weak period"; when it is used between two main clauses, it takes the place of a period at the end of the first sentence. The second sentence does not begin with a capital letter because it has been joined to the first sentence by the semicolon.

> The use of actors and athletes in commercials is misleading; it implies that all of us can be handsome or athletic if we use the right product.

The above sentence is made up of two main clauses that have been joined by a semicolon. The sentences could be written separately:

> The use of actors and athletes in commercials is misleading. It implies that all of us can be handsome or athletic if we use the right product.

When the two main clauses are closely related, you can choose to use either a period or a semicolon between them. Because you have a choice, you can vary the length of sentences and make your papers more interesting than they would be with only short, choppy sentences. The following example shows how the semicolon can be used effectively.

> There is something for everyone, or should I say every canine? For the fashion-conscious pet there are evening gowns, jewelry, and pajamas; for the flabby pet there is the jog-a-dog machine.
>
> [Here the semicolon helps to characterize two types of pets.]

14b
After a semicolon, use transitional words like also, however, still, or then to introduce a main clause.

Some words or groups of words tell something about when or how the action of the sentence is taking place. These words are different from the coordinating conjunctions *and*, *but*, *or*, *so*, *yet*, *nor*, and *for*, which can be used with a comma to connect two finished sentences. (See also **13a**.) The transitional words have a semicolon in front of them and are usually followed by a comma. Some of these words are

also	however	nevertheless
as a result	in addition	on the other hand
besides	in fact	still
for example	instead	then
furthermore	meanwhile	therefore

> Children today see their heroes driving expensive cars and wearing gold chains; *therefore*, they want the same things.
> I am really hungry; *in fact*, I am starving.
> So far my flight had been uneventful; *then* something happened.

Words such as *also* and *however* can be used to introduce main clauses. When they are used as interrupters, however, they are usually set off from the rest of the sentence with commas.

USED AS CONNECTOR   It is my book; however, you are welcome to use it.

USED AS INTERRUPTER   Maria needs the book, *however*, by tomorrow.

14c
Use semicolons between groups of words that already contain commas.

This use of the semicolon helps the reader find the main divisions of the sentence and makes the ideas clear.

> Mr. Howard bought a pot, knives, and bowls; two folding tables; and three kinds of bread from Poffenbarger's Bakery.
> Some drivers seem to count every fence post; examine, discuss, and reject every side road; and enjoy delaying traffic.

14d
Do not use a semicolon in place of a comma.

14d
;

14d-1
Do not use a semicolon between a dependent clause and a main clause.

> WRONG   While everyone else is working hard; the lazy person is thinking of a way to avoid work.
>
> [The first part of the sentence is not complete. It should be separated from the complete portion by a comma.]
>
> RIGHT   While everyone else is working hard, the lazy person is thinking of a way to avoid work.

If you have trouble identifying dependent clauses or the conjunctions that introduce them, see **3d-1** and **3d-2**.

14d-2
Do not use a semicolon between two main clauses separated by a coordinating conjunction.

A comma is the correct mark to use in front of a coordinating conjunction that joins two main clauses. (See also **13a**.)

> WRONG   Everyone thinks her parenting style is best; but a person is a good parent if she cares about her child.
>
> RIGHT   Everyone thinks her parenting style is best, but a person is a good parent if she cares about her child.

14e
Do not confuse the semicolon and the colon.

The semicolon separates two main clauses, but the colon calls attention to what follows. (See also **17d**.)

SEMICOLON	Now I have many goals; some are short term and some are long term.
COLON	Now I have many goals: short term and long term.
SEMICOLON	Pick up your supplies tomorrow; be sure to have everything with you on Friday.
COLON	On Friday, bring the following supplies: a tack hammer, large tacks, a yard of burlap, and two yards of denim.

14f
Do not use a semicolon unless you have a reason for it.

Some writers seem to use the semicolon for no particular reason. The punctuation in these sentences may help you see how a semicolon can really make your meaning clear.

This class thinks its teacher is the best in the world.
[You are telling what the class thinks. Commas or semicolons would obscure meaning.]
This class, thinks its teacher, is the best in the world.
[You are telling what the teacher thinks. Commas make this meaning clear.]
This class thinks; its teacher is the best in the world.
[The second main clause is commenting on the first. The proof that the teacher is the best in the world is the fact that the class thinks. The semicolon makes that meaning clear.]

 CHECKLIST: Deciding When to Use Semicolons

When you use a semicolon, make sure you are using it for one of the following purposes:

1. to divide two closely related main clauses.
2. to separate items that already contain commas.

EXERCISE 1

Use semicolons and commas correctly in the following sentences.

1. A mechanic who works for a car dealership is paid by the hour it usually doesn't matter to him how long it takes to repair a car.

2. According to the Greek myth Pandora brought us all our troubles she opened the box containing the evils of the world.

3. Weightlifting develops certain muscles however it does not exercise all parts of the body.

4. When I told my father what had happened he laughed because he thought I was foolish.

5. Cassandra always told the truth however unpleasant it was but no one wanted to believe her.

EXERCISE 2

In some of the following sentences, the semicolon is incorrectly used. Correct any errors by omitting unnecessary semicolons and substituting commas when necessary. Write *C* next to any sentence in which the semicolon is correctly used.

EXAMPLE The price of gas, the number of traffic accidents, and mechanical, car-related problems lead me to think that we would be better off͵ by returning to the horse and buggy for transportation.

1. You can talk to and love a horse; people would think you were crazy if you did this with an automobile.

2. When you feed your horse at home; you eliminate the need for gas stations and the lines that often are associated with them.

3. The horse can graze in your yard; and keep the grass trimmed.

4. The output of a horse is excellent fertilizer; while the output of cars is only pollution.

5. I believe the rate of collisions will be greatly reduced; because your mind will be working with that of the horse.

6. Let's face it; two heads are better than one; even if one of the two belongs to a horse.

14f
;

7. Finally, horses will never have mechanical problems; and they respond to care in a personal way.

8. Cars come from assembly lines; horses come from other horses through a natural process that has enabled them to survive and be useful for many years.

Chapter 15

THE APOSTROPHE

Use the apostrophe (') to show possession or
omission and to form some plural words.

15a

Use the apostrophe to show that something belongs to or is related to something else.

The idea of possession or relationship can be expressed in other
ways, but the apostrophe and -*s* make it possible to write that idea
in fewer words.

WITH APOSTROPHE	WITHOUT APOSTROPHE
Jamie's book	the book that belongs to Jamie
everyone's hope	the hope of everyone
the cat's favorite food	the favorite food of the cat
the night's activities	the activities of the night
in harm's way	in the way of harm
the day's work	the work accomplished in a day
tomorrow's class	the class for tomorrow
a dollar's worth of jellybeans	the number of jellybeans that is worth a dollar

For things that are not alive, the -'*s* is frequently dropped or
replaced by the words *of* or *in*.

the table leg   the leg *of* the table
the kitchen stove   the stove *in* the kitchen

There are certain ways to add -*'s* to words to show possession, as in the following examples.

15a-1

If the noun (name of a person or thing) *does not* end in -*s*, add -*'s*.

I took Stacey**'s** shopping cart by mistake.
We get a month**'s** vacation this year.

15a-2

If the noun *does* end in -*s*, add either -*'s* or only -*'*.

If the extra *s* makes pronunciation difficult, the apostrophe by itself is acceptable.

Mr. Hopkins**'s** car was stolen.
Mr. Hopkins**'** car was stolen.

15a-3

If a plural noun does *not* end in -*s*, add -*'s*. If a plural noun *does* end in -*s*, add only -*'* to show possession.

The children**'s** feet made muddy tracks on the floor.
The men**'s** hats were on the table.
[*Children* and *men* are plural words that do not end in *s*, so you must add -*'s*.]

Some days Oprah has gifts under all the guests**'** seats.
The boys**'** jackets had disappeared.
[*Guests* and *boys* are plural words that do end in -*s*. Add -*'* only.]

EXERCISE 1

Rewrite each of the following expressions, using an -*'* or -*'s* where needed to show possession.

EXAMPLE the house of my sister *my sister's house*

1. the room of my friend _____
2. the hats of the ladies _____

3. the work of a scientist _____

4. the drills of dentists _____

5. the rights of women _____

6. the business of the family _____

7. the end of the day _____

8. the shoes of my aunt _____

9. the tie of my boss _____

10. the checks of travelers _____

EXERCISE 2

Write five sentences that each use an apostrophe to show possession. Add an -s after the apostrophe when necessary.

15b
───
apos

15b
Learn the special rules for the use of the apostrophe with nouns and pronouns.

15b-1
Use apostrophes with nouns to show possession. Do *not* use apostrophes with pronouns to show possession.

Pronouns use apostrophes only in contractions. Unlike nouns, pronouns show possession without the aid of apostrophes.

> *Mary's* book
> > BUT
> *her* book

Do *not* use the apostrophe to show possession in *mine, yours, his, hers, its, ours, theirs,* or *whose.* These special words already show ownership without the apostrophe.

WRONG		RIGHT	
hi's	her's	his	hers
it's	our's	its	ours
your's	their's	yours	theirs
who's		whose	

Every marriage has *its* ups and downs.
[the ups and down of every marriage]
The decision is *hers*.
[her decision]

For more information about the use of the apostrophe to show possession, see **5a-5** and **5c**.

15b-2
Treat pronouns that end in *-one* or *-body* like nouns. Add -'s to them.

anyone**'s** guess
nobody**'s** business

EXERCISE 3

Select the correct word to complete each of the following sentences.

1. (Everybody's, Everybodies) beliefs are different.

2. It could have been (anybody's, anybodys) mistake

3. The car lost (it's its) muffler when we hit a bump.

4. The central character is Aeneas, (who's, whose) task it is to find a home for the Trojans.

5. (Someone's, Someones) car is in my parking place.

EXERCISE 4

Add apostrophes where they are needed in the following sentences.

1. I never knew I had any writing problems until I was in Ms. Robeys class.

2. My brother doesn't have a drivers license so he is always asking for a ride.

3. Pollution of our harbors is not only a few peoples problem; it is everyones problem.

4. Mrs. James party was talked about for a week.

5. In boxing the only goal seems to be to beat the opponent senseless with ones bare hands.

6. Is Joan Jones name really Joan Jones?

7. I bet that Hillary and Bill Clinton wish that they still lived in the governors mansion in Arkansas.

8. The idea of a little house with a white picket fence sounds ludicrous to todays woman.

15c
If something belongs to two or more people (joint ownership), use -'s with only the last of the names.

I went to Jane and Luisa**'s** apartment.
[Two people live in one apartment.]
I went to Jane**'s** and Luisa**'s** apartments.
[Two people each have their own apartment.]
The new coffee shop is named Mike and Ed**'s**.
[Two people own the business.]

Words with hyphens have *-'s* added to the last word only.

Jack drove his brother-in-law**'s** car.
The governor-elect**'s** speech was very boring.

EXERCISE 5

Add -' or *-'s* where needed in the following sentences.

1. An enabler is a drug addicts best friend.

2. Whose house has a purple door?

3. George and Steve restaurant serves good Greek salads.

4. The man was wearing my father-in-law new hat.

5. He was quite impressed by the senator-elect article on tax reform.

6. I continue to walk daily, mentally preparing for next years event.

15d
Use an apostrophe in contractions to show omission.

15d-1
Use an apostrophe to show that one or more letters have been omitted in order to shorten a word or to combine two words into one.

This shortening is called a *contraction*.

CONTRACTED FORMS	LONG FORMS
o'clock	of the clock
we'll	we will
can't	cannot
don't	do not
class of '99	class of 1999
rock 'n' roll	rock and roll
they're	they are
let's	let us

Remember to spell contractions correctly by placing the apostrophe where the letter or letters have been omitted.

isn't	NOT	is'nt	doesn't	NOT	does'nt
aren't	NOT	are'nt	don't	NOT	do'nt

15d-2
Do not confuse *its* and *it's*.

Its is a possessive pronoun, which means that something belongs to *it*.

> Turn down that radio; *its* volume is too loud.
> [The volume of the radio is too loud.]

It's is a contraction meaning *it is* or *it has*.

> Turn down that radio; *it's* too loud.
> [The radio (it) is too loud.]

For more information on the use of the apostrophe with pronouns, see **5c-3**.

15d-3
Know the meaning of some common contractions so that you do not confuse them in writing.

Sometimes writers confuse certain contractions because they do not pronounce them distinctly. Here are the meanings of some frequently confused contractions.

I'm (I am)	I'll (I will)	I've (I have)	I'd (I had or I would)
you're (you are)	you'll (you will)	you've (you have)	you'd (you had or you would)
he's (he is or he has)	he'll (he will)		he'd (he had or he would)
she's (she is or she has)	she'll (she will)		she'd (she had or she would)
we're (we are)	we'll (we will)	we've (we have)	we'd (we had or we would)
they're (they are)	they'll (they will)	they've (they have)	they'd (they had or they would)

 Caution: In formal writing some people find it preferable to avoid contractions. It is always correct to write out the two words (for example, *is not* instead of *isn't*; *we will* instead of *we'll*).

EXERCISE 6

Change any incorrect contraction in each of the following sentences.

1. She's always on time.

2. In some schools there are'nt any desks for left-handed students.

3. I'd find my wallet sooner if you helped me.

4. He'll better wait for me.

5. He'd heard from me earlier.

6. You've heard all the excuses by now.

7. They'll come if they were able.

8. They'd know the answer when you call on them.

EXERCISE 7

Add apostrophes where needed to show contractions in the following sentences.

1. My brother graduated in the class of 78.

2. Its necessary to have at least an hour when you use my hairdryer; its nickname is the fevered mouse.

3. I dont know whats happening, but its something important.

4. Wed said that we wouldnt be late.

5. You cant imagine what a hurricane is like if youve never been through one.

6. A woman who lives with a workaholic doesn't stay up long enough to find out when he goes to sleep.

7. Dont buy a dress you wouldn't wear in public.

8. My brother does what most bachelors do, and thats hang around the local sports bar.

EXERCISE 8

Write five sentences that use apostrophes in contractions.

15e
Use an apostrophe to form the plural of numbers, letters, and words referred to as words.

> The printer put s's after all of the names, and half of the 5's are upside down.
> Put circles around the *and*'s.
> He spells his name with two *l*'s.
> Your paper would be better if you left out the *hopefully*'s.
> The 1920's were called the Jazz Years.

NOTE: Decades can also be written without the apostrophe.

> The 1920s were called the Jazz Years.

15f
Do not use an apostrophe unless you have a reason for it.

Do not get into the habit of using an apostrophe any time you write an -*s*. Here are some times that you *do not* need an apostrophe.

a. *Do not* use an apostrophe before a noun plural ending unless the noun shows possession.

> WRONG   Rush Limbaugh is never afraid to voice his opinion's.
> RIGHT   Rush Limbaugh is never afraid to voice his opinions.

b. *Do not* use an apostrophe before a present verb -*s* ending.

> WRONG   My poster let's you know that I am a Clemson Tigers fan.
> RIGHT   My poster lets you know that I am a Clemson Tigers fan.

c. *Do not* use an apostrophe before the -*s* of a possessive pronoun.

> WRONG   My washer has reached the end of it's useful life.
> RIGHT   My washer has reached the end of its useful life.

For more information on possessive pronouns, see **5c**.

15f
apos

EXERCISE 9

Remove any unnecessary apostrophes in the following sentences.

1. Everything has it's limitations.

2. In a basic armlock, make sure the opponent's arm is between your legs and that your bodie's form a 90-degree angle.

3. All the patients' needs have been met.

4. Surfing is an excellent cardiovascular exercise because of it's constant demand for endurance.

5. Partie's can be great fun, but sometime's they are disastrous.

6. I worked at Mike's Custom Woodwork's.

7. Everyone has a New Year's Eve anecdote.

CHECKLIST: When to Use Apostrophes

This summary should help you remember when you do and when you do not need an apostrophe:

1. Use an apostrophe with a noun to show possession.
   Mary's book

2. Use an apostrophe in a contraction to show omission.
   can't, isn't

1. Do not use an apostrophe with a pronoun to show possession.
   The book is *her̶s*.

2. Do not use an apostrophe before a noun plural or a verb *-s* ending.
   two reason̶s
   She look̶s happy.

EXERCISE 10

Edit the following paragraph, correcting all errors in the use of apostrophes.

My always-borrowing sister Edith came dashing up the stair's wearing a coat that was definitely not her's. She tossed Kevins' book on the table and gasped when she saw that it was seven o clock and that she was already late for a date with Francis brother. "Its late, and he alway's seem's to be early," she said to herself. "If he doesnt hurry, though, Ill make it. Ive no clothes to wear; however, maybe I can borrow Jill's shirt, my mothers sweater, and my aunts bracelet. I cant believe theyll miss those things tonight."

Chapter 16

QUOTATION MARKS

Use quotation marks around
the exact words of a speaker,
some titles, and words
used in a special sense.

16a

16a
Use double quotation marks to enclose the exact words of a speaker or writer.

Speakers or writers are directly quoted when their exact words are put within quotation marks and they are named somewhere in the sentence. The speaker may be named after, before, or in the middle of a quotation. The name of the speaker is not included in the quotation marks.

> "Everything is funny as long as it is happening to someone else," Will Rogers said.
>
> Will Rogers said, "Everything is funny as long as it is happening to someone else."
>
> "Everything is funny," said Will Rogers, "as long as it is happening to someone else."

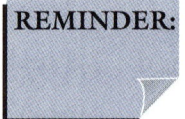

REMINDER: Using Double Quotation Marks

Use double quotation marks when quoting thoughts. "That is the correct answer," I thought to myself.

16a-1
If the quotation has more than one sentence, place the end quotation mark at the end of the last sentence.

> "The dictionary is like a miniature encyclopedia," our instructor said. "It helps us learn new words and their definitions, thus increasing our reading skills. Fortunately, it's easier to carry than an encyclopedia."

Notice that the quotation marks are placed after the comma or period which ends a quoted section.

16a-2
**If more than one speaker is quoted,
begin a new paragraph with each speaker.**

> "I love everything about my bedroom!" Kim said enthusiastically.
> "What's so great about it?" Joanie wondered aloud.
> "It's my sanctuary," Kim replied, "a special place of peace and quiet."

Notice that a comma is not used between the quotation and the name of the speaker if an exclamation point or question mark is required.

EXERCISE 1

Place quotation marks where they are needed in the following sentences.

Occasionally my friend Juanita and I stop at a local grocery store on the way home from classes. One day recently we were detained in the store longer than usual. Of course, the delay became the subject of our conversation.

What was the problem today? I asked.

I think, she replied, that today's delay was caused by two kinds of shoppers: those in a hurry and those taking their time.

What do you mean? I questioned.

I've noticed, Juanita explained, that the hurried shoppers rush past others and cut in front of carts, sometimes causing a pileup. On the other hand, the slow shoppers often get in the way by standing in the aisle reading labels and comparing prices.

Which people are more troublesome? I asked.

My friend replied, Both can cause problems, but we can't complain because we probably have done the same things at one time or another.

16a-3
Enclose a quotation within a quotation in single quotation marks.

> My brother and I occasionally sought our Dad's advice before buying anything expensive. The last time we did he replied, "I would like to help you, fellows, but I think it would be better if you helped each other because, as your grandma often said, 'I won't be around forever.'"

16a-4
Do not enclose an indirect quotation within quotation marks.

A quotation is *indirect* if the exact words of the speaker are not used but the speaker's words are repeated in sentences that usually begin with *for*, *that*, *whether*, or *if*. It is *direct* if the speaker's exact words are used.

DIRECT QUOTATION   Asked what she thinks soul food is Gloria replied, "Soul food is a combination of Grandma's spicy collard greens, Aunt Martha's baked chicken and yams, and Mom's black-eyed peas, baked beans, and fried chicken."

INDIRECT QUOTATION   Gloria thinks *that* soul food is a combination of her grandma's spicy collard greens, her aunt's baked chicken and yams, and her mother's black-eyed peas, baked beans, and fried chicken.

16a-5
Use quotation marks correctly when you are quoting from a book, a newspaper, or another source.

If a prose quotation is short (four lines or fewer), use quotation marks.

> One definition of *rap* in the *American Heritage Dictionary* is "talk, conversation, or discussion."
> A U.S. political maxim from around 1888 is "As Maine goes, so goes the nation."

If a quotation has more than four lines, do not use quotation marks. Instead, indent ten spaces and double-space the quotation. If you are omitting any part of the quotation, use ellipsis marks (…) where the omission occurs. For more help with ellipsis marks, see **17i**.

> Henry Thoreau defends being by one's self in *Walden*:
>
> I find it wholesome to be alone the greater part of the time. To be in company . . . is soon wearisome and dissipating. I love to be alone. I never found the companion that was so companionable as solitude. We are for the most part more lonely when we go abroad among men than when we stay in our chambers. A man thinking or working is always alone. . . . Solitude is not measured by miles of space that intervene between a man and his fellows. The really diligent student . . . is as solitary as a dervish in the desert. (p. 113)

The number in parentheses is the page of the book from which this quotation was taken. For additional assistance with quoting from books, magazines, and newspapers, see **27b**.

16a-6
When other punctuation marks are used with quoted material, put them in correct order.

Place periods and commas inside quotation marks, unless the period or comma follows identification of the speaker.

> "If you wait," I said, "you'll miss the bus."

Place colons and semicolons outside quotation marks unless they are part of the quotation.

> In seventh-grade English class most of us recited "The Raven";
> only three chose "Kubla Khan": Eddie, Julia, and Sam.

[The semicolon and colon are not part of the quoted material.]

> Read and summarize "Diets: Good and Fad."

[The colon is part of the quoted material.]

16a
" "

Place question marks, exclamation points, and dashes inside quotation marks if they apply to the quotation only and outside quotation marks if they apply to the whole sentence.

> Ted asked himself, "Did I forget the mustard?"

[Only the quotation is a question.]

> Did that sign say "Detour Ahead"?

[The sentence is a question.]

EXERCISE 2

Add quotation marks where they are needed in the following sentences. Capitalize any new sentences you create.

1. The professor said, Read the next chapter and answer the questions at the end.

2. I'm not sure I understand, said Henry. Will you repeat the directions?

3. Is your ticket marked Use only on Tuesday?

4. Jack said that all of the material would be ready soon.

5. After I write a paper, I ask myself these questions: Did I leave anything out? Did I explain my ideas clearly?

6. My community has signs that say please don't litter.

7. One of the questions in the Black history contest I entered was by whom was the shoe last invented?

8. I hate to disagree with my dictionary, but I believe a wife is more than, as it says, a married woman.

16b
Put quotation marks around the titles of short stories, songs, articles in magazines, parts of books, and short poems.

Titles of short materials are enclosed within quotation marks.

> "Variation Under Domestication" is the first chapter of Darwin's *Origin of the Species.*
> Please read Emily Dickinson's poem "I'm Nobody. Who Are You?"
> Woody Guthrie wrote "This Land Is Your Land."

Notice that the names of the things referred to are *not* separated from the rest of the sentence by a comma. Each sentence is punctuated as though the quotation marks were not there. The quotation marks tell the reader that the words they enclose are titles of a chapter in a book, a poem, and a song.

16c
Do not use quotation marks around common nicknames or technical terms.

WRONG	When Mr. Clinton was president of the United States, many people called him "Billy."
RIGHT	When Mr. Clinton was president of the United States, many people called him Billy.
WRONG	The "hard drive" and the "processor" are major parts of the computer.
RIGHT	The hard drive and the processor are major parts of the computer.

16d
Avoid using quotation marks to enclose words used in a special sense.

Good writers use well-chosen words and clear sentence structure to get the reader's attention rather than clutter their papers with quotation marks.

WEAK   Many people use the term "global warming" when they refer to changes in the earth's atmosphere.

BETTER   Global warming refers to the theory that the earth's atmosphere is becoming warmer as a result of the extensive use of fossil fuels.

16e
Do not put quotation marks around the title of your paper.

Since you are the author of the paragraphs and essays (longer papers) being written, do not enclose the titles of your papers within quotation marks.

YOUR TITLES	AUTHORS'/POETS' TITLES
A Difficult Decision	"The Road Not Taken"
My Favorite Pastime	"Cooking Seafood"

16e
" "

 CHECKLIST:

Use quotation marks:
1. around a writer's or speaker's exact words;
2. when quoting fewer than four lines from newspapers, books, and magazines;
3. around titles of short poems, stories, and songs; or
4. cautiously around words used in a special sense.

Do not use quotation marks:
1. for nicknames,

2. for technical terms,

3. for well-known expressions, or

4. around titles of your paragraphs and papers.

EXERCISE 3

Edit the following paragraph, correcting all errors in the use of quotation marks.

"The Blues: My Favorite Music"

People have sometimes asked me "what my favorite music is." I have had to reply honestly: "blues music." As a teenager, I grew up listening to the singing of Ma Rainey and Bessie Smith on records, and the songs St. Louis Blues and Beale Street Blues were very much a part of my teenage years. An article in the *New York Times* titled Billie Holliday: the Blues Lady reminded me of the pleasure I took and still take in hearing the great blues singers. When I listen to some of the rock songs my children enjoy today, I can't help asking them, "Wouldn't you rather hear a spirited rendition of Gut Bucket Blues.?"

Chapter 17

THE PERIOD AND OTHER MARKS

Use the period, the question mark,
the exclamation point, the colon,
the dash, the hyphen, parentheses,
brackets, and ellipsis marks
correctly in your writing.

17a

.?!!
:/–()

The period, the question mark, and the exclamation point are especially important because they signal the conclusion of a complete sentence.

STATEMENT	Parents of diligent students usually help pay college expenses.
QUESTION	Do parents of diligent students usually help pay college expenses?
EXCLAMATION	Parents of diligent students do help pay college expenses!

Just as pauses and changes in the tone of your voice convey meaning when you speak, end punctuation marks—periods, question marks, and exclamation points—convey meaning when you write.

17a
Use a period to end a statement, a command, a request, or an indirect question, and after most abbreviations.

17a-1
Use a period to end a statement, a command, or a request.

The following are a statement, a command, and a request. Each requires a period.

STATEMENT	Having an education is especially important today.
COMMAND	Get an education.
REQUEST	Please be sure to get an education.

The length of the sentences does not matter. Each sentence has a subject and a verb. The subject of the second and third sentences is you (understood).

17a-2
Use a period to end an indirect question.

An indirect question repeats what someone has asked without using the speaker's exact words. This type of sentence ends with a period.

WRONG	My sister asked her professor which English course to take next?
RIGHT	My sister asked her professor which English course to take next.
	[This sentence states a fact. It does not ask a question.]

17a-3
Use a period after most abbreviations.

An abbreviation (a short form of a word) ends with a period. Although you should usually use complete words when you write, some titles, degrees, ranks, and other words are usually abbreviated. Among the abbreviations commonly used are the following:

Mr.	A.M.	OR	a.m.
Mrs.	P.M.	OR	p.m.
Ms.	B.C.		

Dr.   A.D.
C.O.D.   R.S.V.P.   OR   r.s.v.p.
B.A.   Ph.D.

Abbreviations for names of large organizations, government agencies, and for some technical terms are usually written without periods.

NAACP   FBI
GOP   TV
YMCA   FM
NATO   AM
IBM   AT&T

 Caution: Acronyms (words formed from the initials of organizations, government agencies, and others, such as SAT, NATO, radar, and NOW) do not require periods.

See **19b** for additional information on the use of abbreviations.

17c
.!?!!
:!–!()

17b
Use a question mark to end a sentence that asks a direct question.

A question is usually formed by changing the word order in a sentence from *subject–verb* to *verb–subject* or *by using asking words*. The end punctuation is a question mark.

Have you an important dental appointment tomorrow?
Why is your dental appointment tomorrow important?

17c
Use an exclamation point at the end of a sentence that shows a strong feeling of surprise, excitement, or disbelief or that gives a strong command.

Sometimes you might want to express a strong feeling or surprise or to show that something is happening suddenly. Since you cannot use the tone of your voice to show your excitement, you use an exclamation point.

> This is a wonderful surprise!
> What a football game!
> We want Tiger! Yea, Tiger!
> Quick! Dial 911!

Exclamations are usually short, and they are not used often. When you use an exclamation point, be sure that the feelings you express are strong and that the surprise you feel is genuine.

17d
Use the colon correctly.

17d-1
Use the colon to call attention to something that follows such as an explanation, a series, a list, or a quotation.

> My husband and I enjoy listening to music, but we disagree on one important thing: its volume.
>
> [In this sentence the writer stresses the fact that she and her husband do not agree on the loudness of the music.]
>
> Toby, our golden retriever, serves us in several ways: protector, playmate, and beloved companion.
>
> [Here the colon is used to call attention to the various ways Toby serves.]
>
> Our football coach always ended the last practice before a big game with this directive: "Come back tomorrow, prepared to win."
>
> [Here the colon is used to call attention to a direct quotation.]

 Caution: Remember *not* to use a colon when the list of items follows a verb or when the list merely completes the sentence.

> WRONG   Among the most popular movies being featured this summer are: *The Perfect Storm* and *The Patriot.*
>
> RIGHT   Among the most popular movies being featured this summer are *The Perfect Storm* and *The Patriot.*

17d-2
Use a colon after the formal salutation in a business letter.

FORMAL SALUTATION	INFORMAL SALUTATION
Dear Sir:	Dear John,
Dear Doctor McKinnon:	Dear Jane,
Dear Madam:	Dear Dad,

17d-3
Use a colon to separate the figures that give hours and minutes, chapters and verses in the Bible, or volumes and pages in magazines.

WRONG   Remember that your classes on Tuesday start at 830 A.M.

RIGHT   Remember that your classes on Tuesday start at 8:30 A.M.

WRONG   Exodus 203 is the first of the Ten Commandments.

RIGHT   Exodus 20:3 is the first of the Ten Commandments.

WRONG   See *Time 15610* for details.

RIGHT   See *Time 156:10* for details.

Caution: A colon is used more frequently in formal writing than in informal writing. In addition, be careful not to confuse the colon and the semicolon. Their names and marks may seem to be similar; however, their purposes differ. The semicolon joins two sentences, and the colon calls attention to something following it. See **14e** for additional information.

17e
Use a dash to show a sudden or abrupt break in a sentence, to explain, and sometimes to add a comment.

The dash signifies a break in thought, puts emphasis on information that follows, makes a comment, or clarifies something. Avoid confusing the dash and the hyphen. In handwriting the dash is a line as long as two or three hyphens. On the computer the dash is made by striking the hyphen key twice.

17e
./?//
:/–/()

ABRUPT BREAK	When Betty comes home—maybe for Christmas—we will be delighted to see her.
IDENTIFICATION	Some people think that these three—Faulkner, Hemingway, and Millay—are among the best American writers.
COMMENT	Every four years from the first primary in February until the national election in November—much too long—Americans are overwhelmed by radio and television commercials seeking votes for candidates who hope to become president.

EXERCISE 1

Add any periods, question marks, colons, or dashes needed in the following sentences.

1. The title of the article is "Oprah Winfrey A Person I Admire."

2. Does your job start at 930 AM

3. What job did Thurgood Marshall have before becoming a justice in the Supreme Court

4. The farmers were expected to remember the idea in Leviticus 2022.

5. There are three common types of billiards eight-ball, nine-ball, and rotation.

6. A trip to the moon that was what children dreamed of in the 1960s and 1970s.

7. "Red Riding Hood" my favorite childhood story has passages that could be frightening to children.

8. The TV was not working when Dr Martinez wanted to watch the final episode of the popular show: *Survivor*.

9. There are three important steps for my music group writing the music and lyrics, choreographing the dance steps, and designing the wardrobe.

10. Cars used to be made in one color: black.

17f
Use parentheses to enclose certain words, numbers, or letters.

Parentheses are always used in pairs. Use parentheses to enclose numbers or letters that go with items in a series.

> A man whose behavior conforms to a high standard and who is usually (1) courteous, (2) trustworthy, and (3) respectful fits my definition of a gentleman.
> [By enumerating a gentleman's traits, you make it easy for your reader to understand.]

Use parentheses to enclose an explanation or a comment within a sentence. Periods and commas that are not part of the information in the parentheses should be placed outside the parentheses.

> When my husband does our weekly grocery shopping (which he really enjoys), he has a carefully prepared shopping list (which he usually ignores).
> [The writer is probably going to expand on the comments in the parentheses above.]

17g
/?!/
:/–/()

17g
Use brackets to enclose a word or words of comment or explanation within quotation marks or parentheses.

> Every day our instructor says, "Be sure that you develop only the ideas you put in the topic sentences of your paragraphs [as if we could forget], or the paragraphs will not be unified."
> I enjoy using new recipes if the directions are specific and complete (no "pinch of salt," "bake in a moderate oven until done" [my grandmother's directions], or "sweeten to taste").

EXERCISE 2

Add any colons, dashes, parentheses, or brackets needed in the following paragraph.

Complete sentences, correct punctuation, related ideas these things make a good paragraph. You can write good paragraphs if you follow these three steps (a) plan what you are going to write about, b get your ideas in order, c write the paragraph, d proofread and correct (this is a very important and frequently overlooked step, and e make a good final copy.

17b
Use a hyphen to join or divide words.

A hyphen has two main uses: to join two or more words together as one word and to divide a word into syllables so that part of the word fits at the end of a line.

17b-1
Use a hyphen to join parts of a compound word.

A compound word is two or more words that work together as one word.

a *get-together*	playing *make-believe*
the *play-offs*	a *tractor-trailer*

Many compound words, particularly adjectives, are joined by a hyphen.

a well-known writer	BUT	a writer who is well known
an out-of-date book		a book that is out of date
a long-horned grasshopper		a grasshopper that has long horns
a queen-size bed		a bed that is a queen size

17b-2
Use a hyphen to spell out compound numbers from twenty-one to ninety-nine.

thirty-three	seventy-seven
fifty-six	ninety-two

17b-3
Use a hyphen with fractional amounts.

one-fourth	one-quarter
three-eighths	two-thirds

17h-4
Use a hyphen to join self-, all-, and ex- to a word in order to make a single word.

self-control	all-American	ex-Navy
self-righteous	all-city	ex-spouse

17h-5
Use a hyphen to divide a word at the end of a line.

When using a long word that does not fit at the end of a line, consult a dictionary to see where the word can be divided. The dictionary puts dots in places where the word can be separated into syllables.

soph·o·more   Nor·we·gian   par·ti·tion

See **20b-1** for additional information on dividing words into syllables.

17h
sp

EXERCISE 3

Add hyphens as they are needed in the following sentences. Some sentences are correct.

1. All night study sessions soon became a way of life for many students.
2. I will be twenty one on Thursday.
3. My exhusband finally completed his on the job training.
4. One third of the students in French 111 have studied that language in high school.
5. Be sure not to drive faster than twenty five miles per hour near the school.
6. Most gas stations have self service pumps.
7. New wall to wall carpeting will make the dining room more attractive.
8. Perhaps some of the harshest punishment is self inflicted.
9. College days are over all too soon.
10. The English 101 students are learning to write well developed paragraphs.

17i
Use ellipsis marks (...) to show omission of a word or words from quotations.

Omission within the quotation is indicated by three spaced dots (ellipsis marks).

> **At Gettysburg many people heard Lincoln's inspiring words: "It is rather for us to be here dedicated to the great task remaining before us ... that government of the people, by the people, for the people shall not perish from the earth."**

Omission at the end of a quotation is indicated by ellipsis marks following the end punctuation of that sentence: a period, a question mark, or an exclamation point.

> **Goethe writes in *Apprenticeship:* "A teacher who can arouse a feeling for a single good action, for one single good poem, accomplishes more than he who fills our memory with rows on rows of natural objects. . . ."**

✔ CHECKLIST: Punctuation Marks

1. Periods end sentences expressing statements, requests, or mild commands.
2. Question marks end sentences that ask questions.
3. Exclamation points end sentences that show emotion or surprise, give strong commands, or make requests.
4. Colons call attention to something that follows; follow the salutation of formal letters; and separate hours from minutes, chapter from verse, and volumes from pages.
5. Dashes show an abrupt break in a sentence and provide areas for comments or emphasis.
6. Brackets enclose comments or explanations within quotations or parentheses.
7. Hyphens join two or more words to form one word and divide words into syllables.
8. An ellipsis indicates that a portion of the material being quoted is omitted.

Chapter 18
CAPITALS

Use capital letters correctly.

18a
Capitalize the first word of a sentence.

Show your reader exactly where each sentence begins by starting the first word of each sentence with a capital letter.

> Dictionaries provide synonyms to help explain the meaning of a word.
> When did the computer age begin?

18b
Capitalize proper names.

A proper name is the name of a specific person, place, or thing.

	GENERAL	SPECIFIC
PERSONS	man	Elmer Peabody
	woman	Jane Doe
	child	Billy
PLACES	city	Philadelphia
	store	Lord & Taylor
	school	Norcom High School

225

THINGS	car	Ford
	book	Bible
	day	Saturday
	camera	Kodak

18b-1
Capitalize proper names of persons.

Initials stand for names; therefore, initials are capitalized.

> FDR and LBJ are the initials of two twentieth-century presidents.
> Both Al Gore and G. W. Bush hoped to succeed W. J. Clinton as president.

Specific names of animals are also proper names and begin with capital letters.

> Many years ago Fisher-Price Toy Company made a dog named Snoopy.
> One of Disney's most popular creations is Dumbo, the little elephant with the big ears.

18b-2
Capitalize a title used before a name.

> In 1948 President Harry S. Truman defeated Governor Thomas Dewey of New York in the presidential election.
> Has Doctor Robey returned your research paper?
> Chief Petty Officer Lewis has been in the U.S. Navy twenty-five years.

A title not followed by a name is usually not capitalized.

> My favorite aunt has been traveling in Spain and Portugal this summer.
> What did your doctor say about your recent x-rays?
> The police chief explained the traffic situation to the Lions Club.

18b-3
Capitalize the personal pronoun *I*.

When you use the word *I*, you are talking about a very specific person: *yourself*. *I* is used in place of your own name, and *I* is always capitalized when it is used this way.

> I can't believe that I forgot to tell you what I did yesterday.

EXERCISE 1

Add capitals where they are needed in the following sentences.

1. Deborah Sampson was an orderly to major general Paterson.

2. Her dentist is dr. t. l. osmondson.

3. the tall police officer talked to mr. johnson.

4. they saw sam and haley leave the yard together.

5. Did you hear professor Dixon's lecture on toxic waste disposal?

6. when lieutenant halder opened the door, he saw five men wait-
    ing for him.

7. Did i miss all of the program?

18b-4
Capitalize the names of specific cities, states, countries, continents, and sections of the United States.

> Des Moines   California   Asia
> Argentina   the West   South America

Notice that words such as *city*, *state*, *country*, and *continent* are not capitalized unless they are part of the name of a particular city, state, country, or continent.

> New York City is the largest city in New York State.

18b-5
Capitalize the names of specific avenues, streets, and routes.

> Fifth Avenue   Beale Street   Route 66

Notice that words such as *avenue*, *street*, and *route* are not capital-ized unless they are part of the name of a particular avenue, street, or route.

> All the routes in the town have avenues or streets leading into them. Main Street leads to Route 94.

18b-6
Capitalize the names of specific buildings, mountains, parks, planets, and bodies of water.

> Pocono Mountains   Seashore State Park   Sherwood Forest
> Lake Ontario   Mars   Empire State Building

Notice that words such as *mountain, lake, park,* and *forest* are not capitalized unless they are part of the name of a particular mountain, lake, park, or forest.

The neighborhood picnic was held on Labor Day at the local lake.

EXERCISE 2

In the following sentences, capitalize the names of any specific places.

1. Serious fires ravaged areas of montana and idaho during the summer of 2000.

2. Local farmers exhibit their cattle and their produce at the Iowa state fair.

3. In 1804 President Jefferson commissioned Lewis and Clark to explore the west—land recently purchased from france.

4. The amazon river flows from the andes mountains to the atlantic ocean.

5. The largest land mass in the world is asia.

6. Estes park is located on the border of Rocky mountain national Park.

7. The stores and offices in many american cities and towns are located on Main street.

8. My sister and I watched the Olympic games that were held in australia.

18b-7

Capitalize the names of months, days of the week, and holidays.

February   Saturday   Labor Day

Notice that words such as *month, day, week,* and *holiday* are not capitalized unless they are part of the name of a particular month, day, week, or holiday.

A group of computer enthusiasts meet at TCC the second Saturday each month.

Christmas Day is always celebrated on December 25.

18b-8
Capitalize the names of government departments or agencies, schools, political parties, companies, and organizations.

the State Department	the American Accounting Association
the Orioles	the Internal Revenue Service
General Electric Corporation	Washington State University

18b-9
Capitalize the names of historical events and documents.

the Declaration of Independence   the American Revolution

18b-10
Capitalize words that refer to God or the Deity, religious denominations, and sacred books.

18b
—
cap

Words referring to God or the Deity
- Allah
- the Trinity
- the Messiah
- Jesus
- the Lord

Religions and members of religious groups
- Jewish
- Buddhist
- Moslem
- Protestant

Sacred books or writings
- the Bible
- the Koran
- the Old Testament
- the Talmud
- the Vedas

18b-11
Capitalize the names of specific peoples, their languages, and words that come from those names.

Serbs	African Americans
Chinese	courses in Chinese and English

Use either Blacks or blacks; use either Native Americans or native Americans.

EXERCISE 3

Add capital letters where they are needed in the following sentences.

1. Knox college will offer spanish on monday night.

2. Jeff did his christmas shopping at the bookstore on main street.

3. This country gained a large area of land by means of the louisiana purchase.

4. i went to kemper high school for two years.

5. We will study the talmud and the koran next year.

18c
Use correct capitalization in titles.

Capitalize the first, last, and important words in the titles of books, magazines, newspapers, plays, songs, poems, movies, TV programs, records, and tapes. Capitalize the second part of important hyphenated words. Do not capitalize short prepositions (*to*, *for*, and others), short coordinating conjunctions (*and*, *but*, *or*, and others), or the words *a*, *an*, and *the*.

> My father always watches *Washington Week in Review* on WHRO.
> Jane recently read Faulkner's novel *As I Lay Dying*.
> *Newsweek*, *Time*, and *U.S. News & World Report* are popular weekly magazines.
> Highways in North Carolina's Outer Banks are heavily traveled.
> *Othello* is my favorite Shakespearian play.

18d
Capitalize the first word of a quoted sentence.

> Katie said, "You can tell a great deal about people by the way they dress."

If the quotation is separated by an interrupter, only the first word of the sentence is capitalized.

> "Unless you eat your spinach," mothers often say, "you'll have no dessert."

18e
Do not use more capitals than you need.

18e-1
Do not capitalize the name of a high school or college course unless it is the name of a specific course or a language.

a history course	accounting	an English book
BUT	BUT	AND
History 102	Business 200	English 101

18e-2
Do not capitalize the names of seasons or directions.

Knowing that the sun sets in the *west* sometimes keeps us from getting lost.

For many people *summer* is the time for vacations.

18e-3
Do not capitalize the names of sports or games unless the name is a trademark.

SPORTS	GAMES WITH TRADEMARKS
football	*Monopoly*
baseball	*Rollerblade*
hockey	*Bridge*

18e-4
Do not capitalize the name of a disease unless it is named for a person or place, and then do not capitalize the word disease.

measles	Parkinson's disease
pneumonia	Hodgkin's disease
chicken pox	Addison's disease
shingles	

CHECKLIST: Deciding When to Use Capitals

Use the following reference list as a guide.

CAPITALIZED (SPECIFIC)	NOT CAPITALIZED (GENERAL)
Valley High School	my high school
the Democratic party	a political party
the Exchange Club	a club for civic leaders
Chase Bank Building	the bank building
the Medal of Honor	a medal for bravery
the All-Star game	a basketball game
the Richmond Coliseum	a sports arena
the Denver Broncos	a football team
History 312	a course in history
Emporia College	a college
the Spanish people	people of a country
the Middle Ages	an era in history
Pepsi-Cola	a cola drink
New York State	the state on the map
the East	an eastern country
the Blue Ridge Mountains	some mountains in Virginia
Labor Day	a day to honor laborers
Byrd Airport	an airport
Cousin Jimmy	a cousin
Golden Gate Bridge	a long bridge
Christmas in December	a day in winter
Springdale Acres	a retirement community
the South	the southern part of the United States

EXERCISE 4

Add capitals where needed in each of the following words or expressions.

1. math 113

2. theater 101

3. broadway avenue

4. california redwood trees

5. a chemistry exam

6. napa valley

7. yankees

8. a stroke

EXERCISE 5

Correct any errors in capitalization in the following sentences.

1. Clarence thomas and Sandra day O'connor are Associate justices of the U. S. supreme Court.

2. "I cannot tell a lie," i said, "because i know you saw me take the cookies."

3. Almost every day my Mother watches *the today show*.

4. All college students should take and pass math 111 and 112.

5. Willie Nelson made outlaw music famous with songs such as "Blue Eyes Crying In The Rain" and "Red-headed Stranger."

6. it was in Pennsylvania that president Lincoln delivered the Gettysburg Address.

7. Robert Frost, an american poet, wrote "the Road not Taken."

8. First discovered in Old Lyme, Connecticut, Lyme Disease results from the bite of a tick that lives on deer; however, that tick can also infect dogs.

18e
cap

Chapter 19

UNDERLINING, ABBREVIATIONS, AND NUMBERS

Use underlining, abbreviating, and number writing correctly.

19a
Underline or italicize titles of books, magazines, and newspapers; names of ships, trains, airplanes, and spacecraft; foreign words and phrases; and words used in a special sense.

Some words are *underlined* in handwritten or typed papers. If you use a computer or a word processor, you may choose to use *italic type*.

HANDWRITTEN	*Beth reported on an article she read in Scientific American.*
TYPEWRITTEN	Beth reported on an article she read in Scientific American.
ITALICIZED	Beth reported on an article she read in *Scientific American*.

19a-1
Underline or italicize specific names or titles of books, magazines, newspapers or periodicals, and the additional items listed below.

Following is a list of items whose specific titles can either be underlined or italicized:

BOOKS	*Chesapeake*	Chesapeake
MAGAZINES	*Time*	Time
NEWSPAPERS	the *New York Times*	the New York Times
PLAYS	*Hamlet*	Hamlet
FILMS	*The Perfect Storm*	The Perfect Storm
TELEVISION	*60 Minutes*	60 Minutes
RADIO	*All Things Considered*	All Things Considered
VIDEOS, CDS, AND CASSETTES	*Thelonious Monk: Criss-Cross*	Thelonious Monk: Criss-Cross
COMIC STRIPS	*Blondie*	Blondie
SOFTWARE	*Windows 98*	Windows 98
WORKS OF ART	the *Mona Lisa*	the Mona Lisa
SHIPS	*Queen Elizabeth II*	Queen Elizabeth II
TRAINS	*The Orient Express*	The Orient Express
AIRCRAFT	*The Spirit of St. Louis*	The Spirit of St. Louis
SPACECRAFT	*Challenger*	Challenger

19a
—
und

Do not underline titles of poems, stories, articles from newspapers or periodicals or chapters from books because they are only parts of published works. Use quotation marks instead. For more information on titles of short works, see **16b**.

> "The Lottery" is a short story in *Literature: Structure, Sound, and Sense.*

 Caution: Use neither underlining nor quotation marks for the following:

1. references to the Bible or its divisions (Genesis, Job),
2. references to legal documents (Last Will and Testament),
3. the titles you give to your paragraphs and themes (My First Job, My Friend Jessie).

19a-2
Underline or italicize foreign words or phrases.

In my favorite New York restaurant I always order <u>arroz con pollo</u>.
When she calls, Aunt Marie expects her children to answer *tout de suite*.

19a-3
Underline or italicize words, letters, and numbers spoken of as such. (See also 16d.)

The words *there* and *their* are pronounced the same.
In English the names of things become plural when *-s* is added.
The *j* that you wrote looks like an *i*.
Write carefully so your reader won't mistake your <u>3</u>'s for <u>8</u>'s.

19a-4
Do not underline or italicize words for emphasis or stress.

Use strong, specific words instead.

WEAK	The noise in the gym during the basketball game was *awful*.
	[Underlining is used for emphasis.]
BETTER	The noise in the gym during the basketball game not only hurt our ears but also shook the walls.
	[Underlining is not needed.]

EXERCISE 1

Underline words as needed in the following sentences.

1. All premedicine students should read the informative article on Hodgkin's disease in the New England Journal of Medicine.
2. The movie showing now at our theater is The Crew.
3. Gone with the Wind tells the story of the misfortunes of a Confederate family during and after the Civil War.
4. Longfellow's "The Children's Hour" is in the Anthology of New England Poetry.
5. Picasso's Guernica is a famous mural showing the horrors of war.
6. Write carefully so that your reader can distinguish between your l's and h's.

7. Sometimes John refers to his wife as la belle dame.
8. Place a dot over every i and cross every t.
9. The discussion group went to the museum in Raleigh to view a reproduction of Rodin's The Thinker.
10. Have you ever completed a crossword puzzle printed in the New York Times?

19b
Use the abbreviations or shortened versions of names and titles correctly.

Some abbreviations are accepted in all kinds of writing, but usually it is better to spell out the words. Periods follow most abbreviations.

19b-1
Use the abbreviations *Mr.*, *Mrs.*, *Ms.*, *Dr.*, and *St.* before proper names.

Mr. James Thompson	Mrs. Jane Williams
Ms. Anne Bigelow	St. Nicholas
Dr. Juan Ramos	Dr. James Mitchell

Spell out *doctor* and *saint* when they are not followed by proper names.

Yesterday my sister had her first appointment with the new doctor.
November 1, a day to honor all the saints, follows Halloween.

19b-2
Use the abbreviations *Prof.*, *Rep.*, *Sen.*, *Rev.*, and *Capt.* before full names. Do not use them before last names alone.

WRONG	Sen. Kennedy	Rev. Bruton	Capt. Swint
RIGHT	Senator Kennedy	Reverend Bruton	Captain Swint

19b-3
Abbreviate titles and degrees if they appear after proper names. Use commas to separate abbreviations from the given names.

William Lassiter, Jr.	Jacob Levin, Sr.	Honora Diaz, M.A.
Terry Patmore, Ph.D.	L. J. Bisesse, D.D.	Robert Jordan, M.D.
Jason Keene, D.V.M.	Mark Mitchell, C.P.A.	Sally Kear, M.S.

19b-4
Abbreviate words used with dates and numbers.

> A.D. 1776   44 B.C.   A.M. or a.m.   P.M. or p.m.   No. or no.

> Julius Caesar was assassinated in 44 B.C.
> I prefer to use No. 2 pencils when I'm working on crossword puzzles.

19b-5
Abbreviate the names of organizations and government agencies, as well as expressions that are commonly referred to by their initials.

Abbreviate capitalized words in the names of organizations and agencies and use capital letters for common words and expressions usually referred to by their initials, such as TV and CD. Do not use periods with these abbreviations.

NATO	North Atlantic Treaty Organization	NBA	National Basketball Association
GOP	Grand Old Party (Republican)	AMA	American Medical Association
FBI	Federal Bureau of Investigation	NFL	National Football League
IRS	Internal Revenue Service	PC	personal computer
NRA	National Rifle Association	AIDS	Acquired Immuno-deficiency Syndrome
TV	television		

For additional information about using periods with abbreviations, see **17a**.

19b-6
Abbreviate *D.C.* and *U.S.* unless they are used alone.

> Washington, D.C.   BUT   District of Columbia

> The capital of the United States is Washington, D.C.
> Residents of the District of Columbia have neither representatives nor senators.

> U.S. Supreme Court   BUT   the United States

> The U.S. Supreme Court is composed of a chief justice and eight associate justices.
> Three of my cousins are citizens of both the United States and Ireland.

19b-7
Avoid incorrect abbreviations.

Spell out the following words:

MONTHS AND DAYS	June	Tuesday
STATES AND COUNTRIES	Nebraska	Italy
HOLIDAYS	Christmas	NOT Xmas
UNITS OF MEASUREMENT	five pounds	six feet
COURSES OF STUDY	biology	science
FIRST NAMES	George	NOT Geo.
AVENUES, STREETS, AND RIVERS	High Street	
BOOK CHAPTER AND VOLUME	Chapter 14	Volume 3

19c
Spell out most numbers that can be expressed in one or two words. Use a hyphen with compound numbers from twenty-one to ninety-nine.

19c
—
num

Only *eighty-five* tickets were sold for the play, although the theater has *two hundred* seats.

Use numerals for large numbers that need more than two words to express.

The estimated population is 1,255,900.

19c-1
Use numerals in addresses and zip codes.

Joan and her family live at 12 Ruskin Court, Peoria, IL 60601.
I moved to 1232 Twenty-first Street, Sioux City, IA 61101.

19c-2
Use numerals correctly.

Use numerals for the following:

DECIMALS AND PERCENTAGES	9 percent, 10.5 percent
PAGES AND DIVISIONS OF BOOKS	page 8, Chapter 1
TELEVISION STATIONS	Channel 4
ROAD NUMBERS	Interstate 664
ROOM NUMBERS	room 110

TIME OF DAY	5 P.M.
DATES	April 21, 1995 OR 21 April 1995
AMOUNTS OF MONEY USED WITH DOLLAR SIGN	$25.50

19c-3
Spell out a number at the beginning of a sentence, or rewrite the sentence.

WRONG   7:30 p.m. is the time for dinner.
RIGHT   Seven-thirty is the time for dinner.
                        OR
            Dinner will begin at 7:30 p.m.

WRONG   117 students are in the class.
RIGHT   There are 117 students in the class.

 CHECKLIST: When to Underline and When to Use Italics, Abbreviations, Number Words, and Hyphens

1. Underline or italicize titles of books, magazines, and newspapers; names of ships, trains, airplanes, and spacecraft; words used in a special way; and foreign words and phrases.
2. Use abbreviations for titles before proper names, for words with dates and numbers, for names of government agencies and business organizations, and for titles and degrees that come after proper names.
3. Spell out numbers that can be expressed in one or two words; use a hyphen with compound numbers from twenty-one to ninety-nine.

EXERCISE 2

In the following sentences, circle the correct form in parentheses.

1. Did you hear (Sen., Senator) Barnes last night on Channel (Three, 3) at (ten P.M., 10 P.M.)?

2. (Prof., Professor) Martinez lives on Maple (Ave., Avenue).

3. Political analysts often say, "As (Me., Maine) goes, so goes the nation."

4. He poured some water (and, &) sugar over (2, two) pounds of fruit and hoped for the best.

5. Why is it that now that (Mr, Mr.) Johnson has his (PHD, Ph.D.), he doesn't seem to have much better sense than he had before?

6. Review Chapter (6, six) and list (5, five) physical properties of oxygen described in your (chem., chemistry) text.

7. (2, Two) members of the (AARP, American Association of Retired Persons) attended the conference on aging in Washington (D.C., District of Columbia).

8. Did you really pay ($52.95, fifty-two dollars and ninety-five cents) for that (ridiculous, *ridiculous*) Jog-a-Dog machine?

9. (40%, Forty percent) of my time is spent preparing for classes.

10. Representatives of the (United States, U.S.) took part in the Olympic Games in Australia during (Sept., September) 2000.

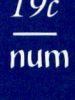

19c
num

Chapter 20

THE DICTIONARY
AND SPELLING

Use the dictionary as a resource for
improving your pronunciation, spelling,
and vocabulary-building skills, as well as
for gaining additional information.

20a
Learn to use the dictionary.

A dictionary is a valuable reference book which holds much more information than how to spell or define a word. To use it easily, however, you might need to review the procedure for locating a word when you want information about it.

Locating a word in the dictionary requires using the alphabet to find the page listing the *entry*, which is a word followed by information about it. Dictionary pages are divided into columns. The guide word located at the top left is the first entry on the page. The guide word at the top right is the last entry on the page.

In order to locate *ensign*, find the page with guide words between which *ensign* is located alphabetically. Here the words are *en masse* and *ensoul*.

NOTE: Because all dictionaries are not the same, the guide words in your dictionary probably differ.

En masse is the word at   *Ensoul* is the word at the
the top on the left.   top on the right.

The entry *ensign* is on this page.

All entries arranged alphabetically between *en masse* and *ensoul* are on this page.

EXERCISE 1

In this exercise the words on the left are the guide words on a dictionary page, and the words on the right are the entries. From the entries, select and underline the one you would find on the page having the cited guide words. The first one has been completed.

GUIDE WORDS	ENTRIES
1. beacon .... bearing	bay, bread, <u>beaker</u>, beat
2. calmly ..... cameo	calm, calf, camel, calorie
3. textbook ... that	thank, theater, tear, thigh
4. empty ..... enchantment	empire, enamel, en-, endeavor

20b
Learn the kinds of information given in a dictionary.

After you have found a word in the dictionary, you can find additional information: word division, pronunciation, part of speech, history of the word, and in some dictionaries synonyms, antonyms, and word labels.

Different kinds of information are identified in the following sample dictionary entry:

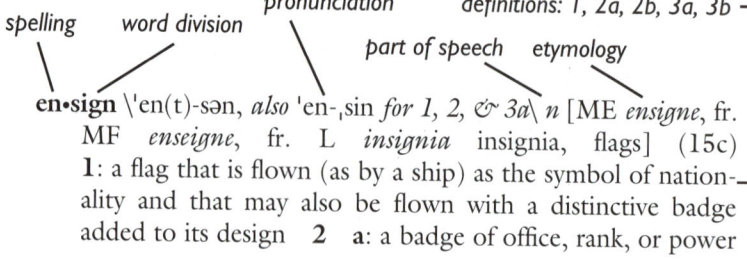

en•sign \'en(t)-sən, *also* 'en-ˌsin *for 1, 2, & 3a*\ *n* [ME *ensigne*, fr. MF *enseigne*, fr. L *insignia* insignia, flags] (15c) **1**: a flag that is flown (as by a ship) as the symbol of nationality and that may also be flown with a distinctive badge added to its design   **2**   **a**: a badge of office, rank, or power

b: EMBLEM, SIGN   **3**   **a**: an infantry officer of what was formerly the lowest commissioned rank   **b**: a commissioned officer in the navy or coast guard ranking above a chief warrant officer and below a lieutenant junior grade

EXERCISE 2

Using the entry for *ensign* as your source of information, answer the following questions.

1. What part of speech is *ensign*?
2. What is definition 2b for *ensign*?
3. Which definition identifies *ensign* as a flag?
4. Explain the meaning of *ensign* to the Navy and the Coast Guard.

20b-1
Use a dictionary to learn to divide a word into syllables.

Identifying the syllables in a word is helpful for both spelling and pronounciation. The dictionary uses a dot (•) to show where to divide the word if it is too long to fit at the end of the line. Although you should avoid dividing words, you can do so at a place indicated by a dot.

20b
dict

> iden•ti•fy•ing   spell•ing   pro•nun•ci•a•tion   dic•tio•nar•y

Do not confuse a dot (•) with a hyphen (-) in a dictionary entry. The hyphen is used when you *write* the word; a dot is not.

PRINTED IN THE DICTIONARY	HANDWRITTEN
ko•a•la self-as•sured	*Koala self-assured*

EXERCISE 3

Use a dictionary to divide the following words into syllables.

1. illustrate _____
2. primarily _____
3. cylinder _____
4. sensational _____
5. determination _____
6. psychoanalysis _____

20b-2
Use a dictionary to learn the pronunciation and part of speech of a word.

In addition to using the dictionary for spelling, dividing a word into syllables, and finding definitions, you can learn its pronunciation and part of speech (noun, verb, pronoun, adverb, adjective, etc.) as well.

The dictionary entry at the beginning of **20b** is labeled to show the usual locations of information about pronunciation and part of speech of a word.

EXERCISE 4

Using information from a dictionary, complete the following chart. The first item has been completed.

	ENTRY	PRONUNCIATION	PART OF SPEECH
1.	stimulant	'stim-y-lant	noun
2.	equivocal		
3.	yacht		

EXERCISE 5

Use a dictionary to determine the part of speech of each of the following words.

1.	roof	4.	assassin	7.	arrange	10.	dry
2.	allow	5.	happily	8.	however	11.	and
3.	allowance	6.	opposite	9.	gulch	12.	thereat

20b-3
Use a dictionary to learn how and when to use a word.

Many dictionaries include suggestions about which words to use and which to avoid in your writing. Although all dictionaries do not use the same labels for these words, the following four are frequently listed.

INFORMAL: The word or its meaning is used in everyday speech or writing; however, it is not used in formal writing.

> **tren•dy** (tren′•de) *adj.,* informal: of or in accordance with the latest fad.

SLANG: The word or its meaning is used only in very informal speech.

    cool (kool) *adj.* slang: excellent, first rate.

REGIONAL: The word or its meaning is used in informal speech of a particular region or group.

    fix•ing (fiks•in) *v.* regional or dialect: getting ready to do something.

SUBSTANDARD: The word or its meaning is not acceptable in general standard English speech or writing.

    ain't (ant) substandard contraction of am not, is not, have not.

NOTE: If no label is applied to words in a dictionary that uses labels, the words are considered **standard** or **formal**. These are the words to use in writing.

EXERCISE 6

With the help of a dictionary which uses labels, find the following words. Then, write the word, its label, and its definition.

1. gyp
2. hisself
3. nowheres
4. nuts
5. hang out
6. lots

20c
———
dict

20c
Use a dictionary to spell words correctly.

If you are not certain about verb forms, endings of words, or irregularities of spelling, confirm or correct the spelling by using a dictionary. Especially in a paperback dictionary, you may need to look for a word *at the end of a dictionary entry*. For example, if you looked for *informality* as an entry, you would not find it because it is part of the entry for *informal*. Check the part of speech (*n, v, adj,* and so on) of any similar words at the end of the entry to help decide which word to use.

    in•for•mal (in•fôr′•ml), *adj.* 1. not formal; not in the regular or prescribed manner. 2. done without ceremony. 3. used in everyday common talk, but not used in formal talking or writing.—**in•for•mal•i•ty**, *n.*—**in•for•mal•ly**, *adv.*

A dictionary will help you to spell verb forms correctly because the main forms of the verb are given if there is any irregularity in spelling. The forms are usually near the beginning of an entry. These forms of the verb are called the *principal parts*. (See **7a**, **7b**, and **7d**.) The order of these principal parts is shown in the following labeled example:

past   past participle   present participle

run (run), *v.*, **ran**, **run**, **running**, 1. move the legs quickly; go faster than walking.

Some dictionaries may give this type of information at the end of the entry.

2. go hurriedly; hasten. 3. flee.   —**ran**, **run**, **running**.

If the past and past participle forms are the same, only one verb form will be listed for both past and past participle.

bring (bring), *v.*, **brought**, **bringing**

Some dictionaries may not list regular (-*ed*) past and past participle forms. See Chapter 7 for additional help in spelling verb forms.

20d
Learn some simple spelling rules.

To write acceptable papers, you must spell correctly. If you have trouble with spelling, the words that give you the most trouble are probably not particularly long or unusual but actually short and familiar—so familiar that you do not think it is necessary to look them up in a dictionary. But use a dictionary whenever you are in doubt about the spelling of a word. There are some rules you can use to help you remember the spelling of some of the familiar words that might cause you trouble.

20d-1
Change the *y* at the end of a word to *i* before you add an ending, except when you add the ending -*ing*.

ugly + ness = ugliness	funny + est = funniest
study + es = studies	party + es = parties
study + ed = studied	party + ed = partied
study + ing = studying	party + ing = partying

EXCEPTION: When *y* is preceded by a vowel, do not change *y* to *i*.

enjoy + able = enjoyable	employ + er = employer
enjoy + s = enjoys	employ + s = employs
enjoy + ed = enjoyed	employ + ed = employed

EXERCISE 7

Add the endings indicated to the following words and write the words correctly with the added endings.

1. happy + ness
2. marry + ing
3. easy + est
4. employ + able
5. worry + es
6. marry + ed
7. duty + ful
8. carry + ed
9. lovely + er
10. obey + ing
11. greedy + est
12. fry + ed

20d-2
Write *i* before *e*,

field	grief	belief
relieve	niece	friend

except after *c*

ceiling	deceive	receipt
receive	conceit	conceive

or when sounded like $\bar{a}$, as in neighbor and weigh.

EXCEPTIONS:

seize	neither	height
weird	either	foreign

These are not the only exceptions to this rule. Look in your dictionary if you are not sure about the spelling of a word.

20d
sp

EXERCISE 8

Fill in the blanks with *ie* or *ei* to complete the following words.

1. p _____ ce
2. repr _____ ve
3. b _____ ge
4. dec _____ t

5. w _____ ght   8. rel _____ f
6. perc _____ ve   9. ch _____ f
7. s _____ ge   10. bel _____ ve

20d-3
Learn the different ways to make words plural.

You usually add -s to a singular noun to make it plural.

$$\text{fence} + s = \text{fences} \qquad \text{chair} + s = \text{chairs}$$

If a singular noun ends in s, *ch*, *sh*, or *x*, add -es to make the word plural.

$$\begin{aligned}
&\text{class} + es = \text{classes} &&\text{brush} + es = \text{brushes}\\
&\text{church} + es = \text{churches} &&\text{box} + es = \text{boxes}
\end{aligned}$$

If a singular noun ends in *y* preceded by a consonant, change the *y* to *i* and add -es to make the word plural.

$$\begin{aligned}
&\text{candy} + es = \text{candies}\\
&\text{party} + es = \text{parties}
\end{aligned}$$

If a singular noun ends in *y* preceded by a vowel, keep the *y* and add -s to make the word plural.

$$\begin{aligned}
&\text{toy} + s = \text{toys}\\
&\text{key} + s = \text{keys}
\end{aligned}$$

If a singular noun ends in *fe*, change *fe* to *ve* and add -s to make the word plural.

$$\begin{aligned}
&\text{life} + s = \text{lives}\\
&\text{knife} + s = \text{knives}
\end{aligned}$$

EXCEPTIONS:
$$\begin{aligned}
&\text{safe} + s = \text{safes}\\
&\text{café} + s = \text{cafés}
\end{aligned}$$

If a singular noun ends in *f*, change the *f* to *v* and add -es to make the word plural.

$$\begin{aligned}
&\text{half} + es = \text{halves}\\
&\text{leaf} + es = \text{leaves}
\end{aligned}$$

EXCEPTIONS:

belief + s = beliefs
dwarf + s = dwarfs
OR
dwarf + es = dwarves

Add *-es* to some singular nouns that end in *o* to make them plural.

hero + es = heroes
potato + es = potatoes

NOTE: Not all singular nouns that end in *o* take *-es* to become plural. Look in a dictionary if you are not sure about the plural form of a word.

EXCEPTION: Add *-s* to the first word of singular combination words to make them plural.

mother-in-law + s = mothers-in-law
head of state + s = heads of state

The spelling of some singular nouns changes without the addition of *-s* to form a plural.

woman = women
child = children

Some singular nouns do not change at all in the plural.

A deer jumped into the clearing.
I saw three deer beside the road.

20d
___
sp

EXERCISE 9

Make the following singular nouns plural.

1.	lobby	5.	valley	9.	industry	13.	foot
2.	noise	6.	match	10.	business	14.	child
3.	man	7.	video	11.	tomato	15.	belief
4.	pass	8.	son-in-law	12.	fox	16.	sheep

20d-4

Learn the difference between words ending in *ent* and *ence* and between words ending in *ant* and *ance*.

Some words may sound the same when you say them quickly, but they do not mean the same thing.

ADJECTIVES	ADJECTIVES USED WITH THE NOUNS THEY DESCRIBE
different	That is a *different* idea.
important	This is an *important* letter.
convenient	That is a *convenient* restaurant.
patient	He is a *patient* teacher.
present	All students are *present* today.
silent	*P* is a *silent* letter in psychology.

NOUNS	NOUNS USED BY THEMSELVES
difference	That is the *difference*.
importance	This letter has *importance*.
convenience	A dishwasher is a kitchen *convenience*.
patience	He has little *patience*.
patients	The emergency room was full of *patients*.
presents	Put the *presents* under the tree.
presence	I sensed the *presence* of my father in the room.
silence	My aunt always says, "*Silence* is golden."

WRONG   Another different between these two restaurants is the hours they are open.

RIGHT   Another *difference* between these two restaurants is the hours they are open.

WRONG   Don has more patient that I have.

RIGHT   Don has more *patience* than I have.

If you are in doubt about the way to spell the form of the word you need, it is best to find the word in a dictionary. For example, a dictionary shows that *evident* and *evidence* are two different words.

ev•i•dence (ev ə dent[t]s) *n:* an outward sign; something that furnishes proof.

ev•i•dent (ev ə dent) *adj:* clear to the vision or understanding.

EXERCISE 10

Correct the following sentences by changing the spelling of any word forms that are spelled incorrectly.

1. The children thought they sensed the present of a being from another planet.

2. The detective has found no evident to support his suspicions.

3. A nurse's aide has to be patience.

4. Suddenly there was silent in the room.

5. The new shopping center in the middle of town is the most convenience place to shop.

20d-5
Double the final consonant of a word before adding an ending.

This should be done if:

1. the ending begins with a vowel.
2. the word ends in a single consonant.
3. the final consonant is preceded by a *single* vowel.

    stop + ed = stopped
    (*p* is doubled because it is a final
    consonant, preceded by a single vowel, *o*)
    stoop + ed = stooped
    (*p* is not doubled because it is preceded by a double vowel, *oo*)

 Caution: If a word has more than one syllable, the rule in 20d-5 applies only if the last syllable is stressed.

    begin + ing = begin*n*ing (*n* is doubled because *-gin* is stressed)
    happen + ing = happe*n*ing (*n* is not doubled because *-pen* is not stressed)

20d
___
sp

EXERCISE 11

Add the endings indicated to the following words, and write the resulting words correctly.

EXAMPLE hum -ed *hummed* _____

1. grin + ing _____

2. mail + ed _____

3. wet + est _____

4. chop + ing _____

5. soon + er _____

EXERCISE 12

Add the endings indicated to the following words, and write the resulting words correctly.

1. listen + ing _____
2. refer + ed _____
3. put + ing _____
4. remember + ing _____
5. expel + ed _____

EXERCISE 13

Put a check mark after each word which is spelled correctly.

1. runing _____   running _____
2. greeted _____   gretted _____
3. prefered _____   preferred _____
4. answered _____   answerred _____
5. controled _____   controlled _____

20d-6

Drop the final unpronounced *e* of a word before adding an ending beginning with a vowel, but keep the *e* if the ending begins with a consonant.

hope + ing = hoping	have + ing = having
tide + al = tidal	manage + ing = managing
image + ist = imagist	dispose + al = disposal
hope + ful = hopeful	rude + ness = rudeness
live + ly = lively	polite + ness = politeness

EXERCISE 14

Carefully following the spelling rule in **20d-6**, add one of the endings *-ing*, *-ly*, *-al*, *-ness*, or *-ful* to each of the following words.

1. dine

2. write

3. brave

4. course

5. late	6. sure
7. force	8. stale
9. forget	10. accurate

20e
Count the syllables in the words you write to avoid omitting letters or writing extra letters.

Every syllable has a vowel sound. Usually you can avoid misspelling words by counting their syllables.

REMINDER: **Count the Vowel Sounds**

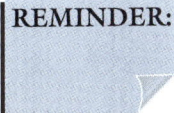

Count the vowel sounds rather than the number of vowels:

su•per	two vowel sounds and two vowels
cool	one vowel sound but two vowels
in•ter•est	three vowel sounds and three vowels
quite	one vowel sound but three vowels
qui•et	three vowels and two vowel sounds

20e
—
sp

NOTE: Developing spelling skills depends on effort. Besides those discussed above, other methods you might want to try include studying from personal spelling lists and developing techniques for improving your memory.

You can compile a list of frequently misspelled words used in each of your classes and learn their spelling.

You can also develop techniques for improving your memory such as this one:
Notice the spelling of fami*liar* and simi*lar*, and don't make a *liar* out of similar.

20f
Use a spellcheck program cautiously.

If you have access to a word processor with a spellcheck program, this program may help you spell difficult words quickly. You must remember, however, that such a program cannot help you with problem words like *their* and *there*, and it will not help you correct typing mistakes like writing *form* for *from*. You cannot count on any program to correct all your spelling errors. You must always proofread carefully, using the dictionary when necessary.

 CHECKLIST: When to Use the Dictionary

Dictionary: Learn to locate entries by using *guide words*. Become familiar with the kinds of information in a dictionary: dividing words into syllables; pronunciation and spelling; parts of speech; word labels; and definitions.

Spelling: Use the dictionary to find spelling; word endings; roles of vowels and consonants; problem words; and pronunciation.

Chapter 21

USING THE
RIGHT WORD

Use words correctly.

The words you choose help give your reader a good or a bad reaction to what you write. It is important to use the words you mean to use and to use the best words you can think of or find in a dictionary.

21a
Use the words you mean to use.

You can ruin a perfectly good sentence by using the wrong word. If you are not positive about the meaning of a word, consult a good dictionary and thesaurus. Remember that it is better to use a word that sounds too simple than to use a word that does not exist or is used incorrectly.

 Caution: Most word processing programs now have built-in spelling checkers and thesaurus help. However, it is important to remember that a spelling checker tells you only whether a word in question is a correctly spelled word. It does not tell you whether you have used a word accurately. A word processing thesaurus is also a very useful tool. However, because an electronic thesaurus is so easy to use, you may find that you rely on it too often. Remember to consult your own common sense and memory first.

WRONG   My friends and I conversate every night.
         [*Conversate* does not exist.]
RIGHT   My friends and I converse every night.

WRONG   The smell of dirty socks and underwear was stiffening.
RIGHT   The smell of dirty socks and underwear was stifling.

WRONG   It was something we just had an urge to do on the spare of the moment.
RIGHT   It was something we just had an urge to do on the spur of the moment.

WRONG   Juan and Anthony cheered for their team as the game prolonged.
RIGHT   Juan and Anthony cheered for their team as the game continued.

EXERCISE 1

Correct the words that are used incorrectly in the following sentences.

1. The conflict arouses when Mr. Hatch comes to get Mr. Helton for killing his brother.

2. Dee was embarrassed of her home and family members.

3. Single parenting exists tremendously in our society today.

4. In effect, it struck down all statues that were based on the decision.

5. The symptoms of this disease are not only symptoms, but they attribute to making it worse than it already was.

6. They overwork in an attempt to escape the unpleasant feelings that come up in their unconscious.

7. General Motors is the biggest car manufacture in the world.

8. Sometimes I forget that I am human but—guest what—I am.

9. This memory lost is the second of Mr. Merrill's encounters with conflict with himself.

10. Most recently, mini-dramas have revolved from our nation's focus on irresponsible dating.

11. Her hair, yellow as the sun, lingers to her stomach.

21b
Use clear and specific words.

Sometimes a word is used correctly, but it is not the best word that could be used. The best word is the one that gives the reader a vivid picture of what you mean to say. Which of the following examples give you a clearer picture of what the writer is saying—those in the left column or those in the right column?

a fat man	a three-hundred-pound man with three chins and a barrel-shaped belly
an old car	a 1982 Buick with faded, chipping paint, clacking engine, and bald tires
a tired woman	my snoring sister, Carmen, whose eyelids flutter and droop while she pretends to be listening to me

Of course, the examples on the right are livelier and create word pictures for the reader. Your papers will be better if you choose words that give your readers a clear picture of what you want to tell them. Consider the following sentences:

21b
——
ex

VAGUE   I like Amanda because she has a nice personality.
CLEAR   I like Amanda because she laughs at my jokes and doesn't get angry—even when I tell her I will be late picking her up.

VAGUE   My room is very cheerful.
CLEAR   My room has plenty of sunlight, a rug in a warm, red shade, overstuffed yellow chairs, and a welcome sign hanging over the door.

VAGUE   My room is very messy.
CLEAR   My room is filled with old, moldy, ant-infested take-out food cartons, smelly clothes, and piles of forgotten papers.

VAGUE   Some people buy all kinds of ridiculous things for their pets.

CLEAR   Some people buy pet products like gold jewelry, evening gowns, rain coats, top hats and tails, pajamas, diapers, wigs, false eyelashes, eyeglasses, nail polish, pet potties, and air-conditioned pet houses.

EXERCISE 2

Rewrite the following paragraph, replacing the vague italicized words with clear and specific words and details. You may find a dictionary and a thesaurus useful here.

Usually people daydream about *agreeable things*. In a daydream they can visit *the past* or place themselves in *the future*. Daydreaming makes possible *the impossible*. It allows people to rid themselves of *unhappy feelings*. Daydreaming offers a release from *the cares of society*.

21c
Use appropriate words.

When you write a paper, you should use appropriate language. That means you should present ideas that you know your reader will clearly understand. Certain kinds of language are not appropriate for good formal writing because they may confuse the reader.

21c-1
Avoid slang and informal language.

Some words that you might use when talking with friends are not acceptable in formal writing. Try to avoid words or expressions like the following:

awesome	phat	
dissed	blew them away	like, you know
gotta book	I'm outta here.	Duuude!
Wow!	bummed out	joking on

21c-2
Avoid clichés and trite expressions.

Clichés, or trite expressions, have been used so many times that they do not contribute anything clear or distinct to your paper. If anything, they annoy and bore your reader and keep you from expressing yourself effectively. The following are some common clichés:

taking the bull by the horns   better safe than sorry
last but not least   better late than never
beating around the bush   pretty as a picture
a sight for sore eyes   a drop in the bucket
putting your best foot forward   under the weather

EXERCISE 3

The following sentences contain slang, clichés or trite expressions. Rewrite the sentences, eliminating all inappropriate words, clauses, or phrases.

1. You can thank your lucky stars that you didn't burn the candle at both ends last night.
2. The little woman has become thin as a rail since she has gone on her miracle diet.
3. I have to say in no uncertain terms that getting ahead in life is easier said than done.
4. To add insult to injury, my blind date turned out to be as ugly as sin.
5. I fell head over heels in love with a man who was clumsy as an ox and old as the hills.
6. Last but not least, strike while the iron is hot.
7. Don't ask Angela to put her life on hold.
8. He goes, "I'm not happy," and then I go, "I'm not happy either."
9. It was hotter than a firecracker at our graduation ceremony.
10. When I returned home after curfew, my mother went off without giving me a fair shake.
11. We just sat in the den and vegged out in front of the television.
12. I almost croaked when I heard that my old boyfriend was in town.
13. This class stinks.
14. I heard that John is in the slammer.
15. I could scarf down three pizzas all by myself.
16. That test was a piece of cake.
17. Let's nuke some popcorn.
18. She's history.
19. Fred gave us a hairy ride home from the party.
20. My credit cards are all maxed out.

21c
ex

21c-3
Avoid overusing regional expressions.

The following are some examples of regional expressions:

> Reynoldo used to could play the piano very well.
> LaShaun has to red up her room before she goes outside to play.
> Did you cut off the lights?
> Yolanda has to leave out of the party early.
> It was so humid, Sunna and I nearly fell out.
> Milo has wicked cool hair.
> Priscilla is toats crushing on Matthew Broderick.
> Depending on where he is in the United States, Ben can order a hoagie, a submarine, a grinder, or a po'boy.
> Depending on where Sook is, she can order a soda, a pop, or a seltzer.

If you don't understand some of these expressions, you are beginning to realize why you should avoid using them in formal writing. Some people will not know what you mean because they live in regions of the country where these words or phrases are not used.

21c-4
Avoid jargon.

Jargon is language associated with certain fields such as technology, business, education, or government. Usually, people use jargon because they think it is the accepted language of their profession, but many times the people who use jargon could say the same thing by getting to the point simply.

JARGON	The group that interviewed Samantha wanted to know if she would be a team player.
PURE EXPRESSION	The group that interviewed Samantha wanted to know if she would get along well in the new company.
JARGON	Our online sales department is there to serve you 24/7.
PURE EXPRESSION	Our online sales department never closes.
JARGON	Our boss wants these new plans ASAP.
PURE EXPRESSION	Our boss wants these new plans immediately.

JARGON	Alonzo tried to implement the plan.
PURE EXPRESSION	Alonzo tried to carry out the plan.
JARGON	The teaching of composition is undergoing a paradigm shift.
PURE EXPRESSION	The teaching of composition now focuses on new principles.

EXERCISE 4

The following sentences contain slang, informal expressions, regional expressions, clichés, and jargon. Rewrite them in clear, correct, formal English.

1. My son-in-law Ozzie really has an attitude.
2. I'm really into collecting baseball cards and Beanie Babies, but I need to get on with my life.
3. We don't have time to mess with that problem.
4. Some spectators at football games just walk around and chill with their friends.
5. Somewhere Fred fell by the wayside.
6. Cut off the lights before vacating the facility.
7. We will need to access the data and get more input before we can know how this change will impact our decisions.
8. We have heard that the largest employer in our town is downsizing.
9. Elaine is an incurable micromanager.
10. You are wasting Internet bandwidth if you attach silly image and joke files to your e-mail.
11. I need someone to carry me to the store because I don't drive.

21c
—
ex

21c-5
Avoid mixed metaphors.

A metaphor is an implied comparison such as, "Joe, my former friend, is slime." Sometimes, when two of these implied comparisons are used together, the result is unintentionally confusing or even humorous. Avoid sentences such as the following:

Joe, my former friend, is slime, so he is always in hot water.
Before he saw the light at the end of the tunnel, Jason decided to throw in the towel.
The pot of gold at the end of the rainbow turned out to be a wolf in sheep's clothing.

21c-6
Avoid sexist language.

You should not suggest a preference for males by using a masculine pronoun when you are really referring to anyone—man or woman. Therefore, it is wise to be careful to avoid *he*, *his*, or *him* unless you are referring specifically to a male. Such usage troubles many readers in a time when we accept the equality of the sexes. Whenever possible, use the plural or eliminate the pronoun completely when it is not clear whether you are referring to a man or a woman.

INSTEAD OF	Everyone should do his best to fight crime.
WRITE	People should do their best to fight crime.

OR

Everyone should try to fight crime.

You should also avoid suggesting by the words you choose that certain professions or activities (law, medicine, fishing) are primarily masculine and others (nursing, babysitting) are primarily feminine.

INSTEAD OF	WRITE
male nurse	nurse
policeman	police officer
chairman	chair
steward or stewardess	flight attendant
mailman	mail carrier
A good typist takes her time.	Good typists take their time.
A good doctor keeps his office organized.	A good doctor keeps an organized office.

EXERCISE 5

Rewrite the following paragraph, eliminating all sexist language.

One of the characteristics of a good engineer is that he takes care of all his responsibilities in an efficient way. He must complete his research and develop his designs neatly so that his secretary can do her typing without having to consult him or to ask for assistance from the office manager, who has his own job to do. Finally, a meticulous engineer should make certain that all the information he uses in the preparation of a plan is filed securely so that a cleaning lady does not accidentally destroy any of his important material.

21d
Learn how to use these problem words.

The following is a list of some confusing words that have caused students problems in writing. Be sure that you know how these words should be used.

a	is used before a consonant sound
an	is used before a vowel sound
	a beer, *a* cork, *a* habit, *a* unit
	an alligator, *an* elevator, *an* hour
accept	means to "receive"
except	means "not included"
	I *accept* your apology.
	Everyone *except* my St. Bernard was invited to the cookout.
advice	is a noun meaning "counsel"
advise	is a verb meaning "to offer counsel"
	If you *advise* someone, give good *advice*.
affect	means "to influence" It is a verb.
effect	usually means "result" In this form, it is a noun. However, sometimes it can be a verb meaning "bring about."
	Hearing the French national anthem on D-Day *affected* my grandfather deeply.
	Who knows what the *effect* of a nuclear war would be?
	The new drug could *effect* a cure.
a lot	is not spelled *alot*
already	means "before now" or "by this time"
all ready	means "completely prepared"
	The crowd is *already* assembled.
	We are *all ready* to go.
always	means "all the time"
all ways	means "every way"
	Judy is not *always* prepared for class.
	I try to be helpful in *all ways*.

amount	means "a sum or total of things"
number	means "people or things that can be counted individually"
	You can buy those items for a small *amount* of money.
	Let me know the *number* of oysters you need.
as, as though, as if	introduce clauses
like	introduces prepositional phrases
	The word *like* is often used incorrectly instead of *as*, *as though*, or *as if* in everyday speech. However, in formal writing, follow standard rules.
	He acts *as though* he is angry.
	He looks *like* you.
at	See **to, at**.
between	refers to two people or things
among	refers to more than two people or things
	A woman shouldn't have to choose *between* marriage and a career.
	The will divides his money *among* several heirs.
borrow	means "to get, with the intention of returning"
lend	means "to let someone have something you expect to get back"
	I *borrowed* some money from my brother.
	Lisa didn't want to *lend* me any of her clothes.
bought	means "purchased"
brought	means "caused to come here"
	Liz *bought* a lottery ticket.
	I *brought* along my knitting.
bring	means "to cause to come here"
take	means "to cause to go there"
	Bring that photograph album to me.
	Take that ugly vase into the other room.
by	in time expressions means "not later than a certain time"
until	means "up to a certain time"
	I will be at your house *by* noon.
	I will be at your house *until* noon.

conscience	means "someone's idea of right and wrong"
conscious	means "aware"
	She has a guilty *conscience*.
	I am *conscious* of what you are saying.

effect	See **affect, effect.**
except	See **accept, except.**

every day	is a noun expression suggesting repeated action
everyday	is an adjective and requires a noun
	I work *every day*.
	These are my *everyday* activities.

every one	means "each of a particular group"
everyone	means "all people"
	Every one of the children wants to go.
	Everyone is here for the game.

fewer	means "not as many" It is a plural word and refers to things that can be counted
less	means "not as much" It is a singular word referring to a quantity.
	I have *fewer* problems than I had ten years ago.
	I have *less* money than I had ten years ago.

foot	is singular
feet	is plural
	The stool is less than a *foot* tall.
	I am five *feet* tall.
	When the measurement comes before the person or thing it describes, however, use the word *foot*.
	This is a ten-*foot* ladder.

21d
---
ex

from	Do not use *off* or *off of* when you mean *from*.
off	The meanings are often similar, but *off* usually means "from the top of."
	WRONG Jim copied off my paper.
	RIGHT Jim copied *from* my paper.

hole	See **whole, hole, hold.**

in	means "located within"
into	means "toward the inside" of a place
	We were all gathered *in* my aunt's room.
	Joe just walked *into* my aunt's room.

imply   means "to suggest without actually saying" A speaker or a
writer implies.

infer   means "to arrive at a conclusion because of evidence
presented" A listener or a reader infers.
The teacher *inferred* from the essay that the student was *implying* that she was afraid of the dark.

its   means "belonging to it"

it's   means "it is" or "it has"
Virtue is *its* own reward.
It's a small price to pay for being beautiful.
It's been that store's policy to give cash refunds.

lead   is a metal It is also a verb meaning "to conduct."

led   is the past tense of the verb *to lead*
He is going to *lead* the research on *lead* poisoning.
My float *led* the parade last Easter.

learn   means "to gain knowledge"

teach   means "to pass on knowledge"
I *learned* how to surface-dive from my brother.
Let me *teach* you how to stay awake in class.

leave   means "to go away from"

let   means "to allow to"
I am *leaving* my past life behind.
I will *let* him have my answer soon.

lend   See **borrow, lend.**

less   See **fewer, less.**

mind   means "intelligence" or "pay attention to"

mine   means "belonging to me"
Exercise your *mind* as well as your body.
Mind your parents.
This umbrella is *mine.*

like   See **as, as though, as if, like.**

loose   means "not tight" or "unfastened"

lose   means "to allow to get away" or "to misplace"
Susie seems to have a *loose* tooth.
It's sad to *lose* an old friend.

number	See **amount, number**.
off	See **from, off**.
passed	means "went by"
past	means "former times" or "belonging to former times"
	The parade *passed* through the town.
	It is often comforting to remember the *past*.
principal	is an adjective or noun meaning "first or most important"
principle	is a noun meaning "essential rule"
	She is the *principal* of my school.
	Michael is the *principal* player on his high school basketball team.
	Act according to a high moral *principle*.
quiet	means "not noisy"
quit	means "to leave" or "stop"
quite	means "very"
	I am going to *quit* my job.
	The room was *quite quiet*.
take	See **bring, take**.
teach	See **learn, teach**.
than	is used in a comparison
then	can mean "at that time"
	Superman is supposed to be faster *than* a speeding bullet.
	Wait awhile; Lou will *then* be free to help you.
that	See **who, which, that**.
their	means "belonging to them"
there	means "in that place" and sometimes introduces the subject of a sentence
they're	means "they are"
	Let them have *their* way.
	There are many reasons for avoiding those rock concerts.
	They're here! *They're* here!
these	is a plural pronoun
this	is a singular pronoun
	This driver is transporting *these* boxes.

21d
ex

to	means "toward" or "in the direction of" It also appears before the verb in expressions like *to want* and *to have*.
too	means "also" or "more than enough"
two	means "one plus one"

Margaret hates *to* go *to* the dentist.
My brother Samuel hates *to* go *to* the dentist *too*.
I tried *two* or three times *to* teach Lisa.

to	means "toward" or "in the direction of"
at	means "near" or "in the location of"

WRONG   They arrived to our house.

RIGHT   They arrived *at* our house.

OR

They came *to* our house.

weather	refers to the atmosphere
whether	introduces choices

How is the *weather*? I wonder *whether* it will rain.

were	is the past of *are*
where	asks about location

We *were* there yesterday.
Where is the bank?

who	refers to people
which	refers to things
that	can refer to people or things

Betsy Ross is the woman *who* made the first American flag.
"The Swimmer" is the story *which* I prefer.
This is the wrench *that* I need for the job.

who's	means "who is" or "who has"
whose	means "belonging to what person"

Who's at the door?
Whose jellybeans are these?

whole	means "entire"
hole	means "opening"
hold	means "keep"

I can't believe I ate the *whole* pie!
Every doughnut has a *hole*.
I won't believe I have the money until I *hold* it in my hand.

your   means "belonging to you"
you're   means "you are"
        Take *your* seat.
        I think that *you're* mistaken.

EXERCISE 6

Write *to*, *too*, or *two* in each of the blanks in the following sentences.

1. Americans drive cars that burn _____
    much gasoline.
2. I was _____ tired _____
    understand what I was doing.
3. The nail was _____ inches _____long.
4. I was _____ proud _____
    admit that I wasn't ready to be on my own.
5. My father's sweater was _____ big for me.
6. Tom was _____ afraid _____ stay
    home alone.

EXERCISE 7

Write *a* or *an* in each of the blanks in the following sentences.

1. Mr. Rodriguez is known as _____ honest man.
2. My cousin Edna attends _____ university in Ohio.
3. My boyfriend is twenty-seven; I never thought I could fall in
    love with _____ older man.
4. _____ twenty-minute drive took _____ hour and _____half.
5. Eve wanted to get _____ job in _____ office.

EXERCISE 8

Write *their*, *there*, or *they're* in each of the blanks in the following
sentences.

1. _____ own land was rich farmland.
2. _____ going to be late if they don't hurry.

21d
ex

3. I'll never learn all _____ is to learn about that subject.

4. George had never been _____ before.

5. _____ are many stresses that can bring on a heart attack.

EXERCISE 9

Underline the correct word in parentheses in the following sentences.

1. I went (in, into) the kitchen and saw my brother frying bacon.
2. When the firefighters arrived (at, to) our house, they wanted to know where the fire was.
3. One day when I walk (in, into) my brother's room, I'll be able to do it without stepping on anything.
4. If you can get (to, at) the store by 10:30, you won't find it crowded.
5. It looks (like, as if) everyone is already (at, to) the ball park.

EXERCISE 10

This paragraph was written by a student who had trouble recognizing plural words. Proofread the paragraph, correcting any errors in the use of singular and plural nouns or in the use of *this* and *these*.

One of America's biggest problem is the dumping of chemical wastes. These problem grows worse as time passes. In designated areas chemical waste is dumped and buried. It has recently been found, however, that these chemical do not go away. Many of them interact with one another and bubble and boil back to the surface, releasing toxic gases. Many seep down into underground water supplies. This is a very dangerous situations. Many community have felt the effects of these situations by experiencing birth defect and mutations in the new generations.

EXERCISE 11

In the following sentences, if any of the italicized words is incorrectly used, change it to *who, which,* or *that.*

1. He is the only man *that* I have ever loved.

2. Pick up the pliers *which* are on the workbench.

3. The attendant *which* parked your car doesn't seem to be around right now.

4. Andrei Gromyko was a Russian politician *who* survived many changes of government in this century.

5. In many restaurants there seem to be too many servers *which* aren't even willing to bring you a cup of coffee.

EXERCISE 12

Underline the correct word in parentheses in the following sentences.

1. (Who's, Whose) clothing did Elaine borrow this week?
2. It's easy to tell (whose, who's) put too much squash on his plate.
3. When my mother and father argue, it's not always easy to tell (who's, whose) right.
4. My grandmother worries about (who's, whose) in the park at night.
5. Just as we started to relax, the sergeant called out, "(Whose, Who's) gear is piled on the floor?"

21d

ex

EXERCISE 13

Using the list in **21d**, correct any incorrect problem words in the following sentences. Write *C* next to any sentence that is already correct.

1. My father said, "Just let go of the clutch and your off."

2. One recent diet made this claim: "Loose five pounds in one week, and still eat whatever you want."

3. Just past the door is a black bookcase.

4. My father is afraid to learn any of us to drive.

5. Mr. Purdy's talk to his students inferred that they had all passed the course.

6. People who have the blues a lot usually have other emotional problems.

7. Before zip codes were in effect, clerks had to look up all the names of small towns.

8. Lucy is willing to except the job even though it has less benefits than her old one.

9. I wanted to borrow a chain saw off my uncle, but he did not want to lend it to me.

10. Bring those books to the city library before you have to pay a fine.

11. The answers to the difficult questions are always hidden into the back of the manual.

12. There's no point in rushing; your all ready late.

13. Darryl is an handsome, six-feet-tall man.

14. The election comes down to a choice among two very good candidates.

15. It takes less people then you might think to make a good basketball team.

16. She spilled a large amount of pennies on the floor.

17. Alisa brought many snacks at the grocery store.

18. Because Joseph wasn't quiet ready for his brother to find him, he was very quite.

19. Please leave me go or I will never get to work on time.

CHECKLIST: Remembering How to Use Words Correctly

Ask yourself these questions:

1. Have I said exactly what I meant to say?
2. Are my words specific and vivid?
3. Have I used appropriate words, avoiding:
   —slang and informal language?
   —clichés and trite expressions?
   —regional expressions?
   —jargon?
   —mixed metaphors?
   —sexist language?
4. Have I used problem words correctly?

21d

ex

Chapter 22
Too Few Words

Do not leave out necessary words.

Many times readers can understand what you mean to say even if you occasionally leave out a word in a sentence, but it is not a good idea to omit words. Most people omit words in their writing because they are careless, because they have developed the habit of leaving out certain words in writing, because English is their second language, or because they often omit these words in speech and this habit has been transferred to their writing. Careful proofreading will help with this problem.

22a
Do not leave out short words like the, and, he, she, it, his, her, of, on, *or* that.

WRONG   It was my letter convinced my sister to come and see what was going on.

RIGHT   It was my letter *that* convinced my sister to come and see what was going on.

WRONG   My birthday, I had a party with my friends.

RIGHT   *On* my birthday, I had a party with my friends.

Remember to include *of* in expressions like *kind of, type of, sort of,* and *a couple of.*

278

WRONG	He is the type person you don't want to have as an enemy.
RIGHT	He is the type *of* person you don't want to have as an enemy.

If you are giving directions, do not omit the words *it, a,* and *the.* You may see such omissions in cookbooks and technical manuals, which try to save space, but you should include these words in your papers.

WRONG	Take from bowl second half of dough and roll same way you rolled first piece.
RIGHT	Take from *the* bowl *the* second half of *the* dough, and roll *it in the* same way you rolled *the* first piece.
WRONG	Measure four-by-four carefully, marking places for slots with carpenter's pencil.
RIGHT	Measure *the* four-by-four carefully, marking *the* places for *the* slots with *a* carpenter's pencil.

22b
Do not leave out short verbs like is, are, was, were, has, *or* have.

WRONG	This a description of my brother.
RIGHT	This *is* a description of my brother.
WRONG	Your hair dryer is the hottest I ever felt.
RIGHT	Your hair dryer is the hottest I *have* ever felt.

22c

∧

22c
Do not leave out words when you are asking questions.

When you are speaking with friends, it is all right to leave out some words when asking questions. However, when you write these same questions, do not leave out words like *Are you* and *Do you.*

WRONG	Understand?
RIGHT	*Do you* understand?
WRONG	Going to the party at Duane's house?
RIGHT	*Are you* going to the party at Duane's house?

22d
When you compare two people or two things, do not leave out any words that would make your comparison clear.

WRONG   Use our product. You'll feel cleaner than your soap.
[You can't compare a person and a soap.]

RIGHT   Use our product. You'll feel cleaner than *you would using* your soap.

22e
When you use so *in a comparison, be sure the comparison is complete.*

WRONG   I was so tired.

RIGHT   I was so tired *that I fell asleep immediately.*

EXERCISE 1

Insert any words that are needed to complete the meaning of the following sentences. Complete all incomplete comparisons.

1. Nosy neighbors can tell you what happening in your neighborhood.

2. The first thing came into my mind was that Bob hadn't come over my house for a long time.

3. Here is how to do shopping in less time.

4. Aunt Josephine and Uncle Leon will visit our family for a couple days.

5. During the traffic jams, some people got out their cars.

6. My sister and her husband been late for our family reunion every year.

7. People gamble more on big sports events like the Super Bowl.

8. Joey is the type man you wouldn't trust with much of your money.

9. I think my sister's singing is better than my mother.

10. Place ingredients on kitchen counter.

EXERCISE 2

Edit the following paragraph, inserting any words or expressions that the student left out.

My baby brother can ruin any date. When a date comes my house, my brother always pulling and kicking him. Once my date takes seat, here comes my baby brother, jumping up his lap and trying to attract his attention. Even though I try pull him away, in a few minutes there is he again, pulling at my date's clothing. Finally, tired of whole thing, my date leaves early. I then try to talk my brother, but, as usual, he not listening. He so stubborn.

 ## CHECKLIST: Including All Necessary Words

Ask yourself these questions:

1. Have I included all necessary short words like *the, and, he, she, it, his, her, of, on,* and *that*?
2. Have I included all necessary short verbs like *is, are, was, were, has,* and *have*?
3. Have I included all the words I need in my question sentences?
4. Have I included all words that I need to make my comparisons clear?

Chapter 23

TOO MANY WORDS

Leave out any words that repeat something
you have already said or that serve no
purpose in your sentence.

23a
Do not use the same word too often in a single sentence or short paragraph.

Sometimes it is difficult to think of a word that has the same meaning as the one you have just used. Finding a new word is usually worth the effort, though, if you can thus avoid repeating yourself needlessly. Usually a little thought will suggest a better way to say something.

REPETITIOUS	Mr. Barnes was chosen to coach the Tigers because he was well qualified for coaching the team. [There is no need to repeat the idea that Mr. Barnes is a coach.]
BETTER	Mr. Barnes was chosen to coach the Tigers because he was well qualified *for the job.*
REPETITIOUS	The section to be plated has to be roughed in order to be plated. [There is no need to repeat that the section is to be plated.]
BETTER	The section to be plated has to be roughed *first.*

23b
Avoid other forms of wordiness.

23b-1
Do not repeat an idea that does not have to be repeated.

REPETITIOUS	Moving your fingers on the frets of the guitar will give you the desired sounds you want. [*Desired sounds* and *sounds you want* mean the same thing. Only one of the expressions is needed.]
BETTER	Moving your fingers on the frets of the guitar will give you the desired sounds.
REPETITIOUS	Return the book back to the library. [*Return* means *to take back.* Omit the word *back.*]
BETTER	Return the book to the library.

23b-2
Avoid using expressions that are repetitious.

REPETITIOUS	BETTER
ink pen	pen
school teacher	teacher
the modern world of today	the modern world
at this point in time	now
continue on	continue
true facts	facts
overexaggerate	exaggerate
redouble our efforts	double our efforts
each and every	every

23b-3
Do not repeat the subject by using *he, she, it,* or *they* right after it.

REPETITIOUS	The coach, he is just there to help the quarterback decide what plays to run. [*He* repeats the subject *coach.* It is not needed.]
BETTER	The coach is just there to help the quarterback decide what plays to run.

23b
¶

23b-4
Avoid using *at* in a *where is something* expression.

At is incorrect because it repeats the idea of location expressed in the word *where*.

> WRONG Where is the library at?
> RIGHT Where is the library?

23b-5
Do not use a pronoun or an adverb to repeat an idea that you have already expressed in the sentence.

> WRONG I was worried about the exam that I hadn't studied for it.
>
> [You have already identified the exam you were worried about. The pronoun *it* is unnecessary.]
>
> WRONG This is the building where the CIA offices are located there.
>
> [You have told the reader where the offices are located. You do not need the adverb *there*.]

23b-6
Avoid using *then* to introduce a main clause when the dependent clause that comes before it already suggests that the two clauses are closely related.

> REPETITIOUS If you are not careful using a rotary motor, then you may get a serious injury.
>
> BETTER If you are not careful using a rotary motor, you may get a serious injury.

EXERCISE 1

Rewrite the following sentences, eliminating any unnecessary words.

1. Farm Fresh offers employees many good benefits.
2. When I practiced my speech, some of the contents of my speech were twisted, which caused distortion in the development of my speech.

3. Through the years bikes have been improved and made better.
4. Many violent films are rated R because of their violence.
5. Rembrandt, he was the greatest art painter of all time.
6. Do not hold or depress the tongue down.
7. The subject of the place of women in combat has been argued back and forth.
8. In my opinion, I feel television is playing an important role in our modern society.
9. Champ can catch a ball in his mouth and return it back to you.
10. Where is the registrar's office at?
11. I always obey my feelings and emotions.
12. The significance of the title "The Guest" is very important.

23c
Use a simple, direct style.

Sometimes student writers think that they will sound intelligent and educated if they use elaborate words and write complicated sentences.   Although good writers use a variety of sentence lengths and styles, they know that the best style is usually the simplest one. After you have written something, take the time to delete unnecessary words and reword sentences to make your work straightforward and clear. Ask yourself whether every word or group of words is really necessary to the meaning of a sentence.

23c
rep

Here are some sentences that are wordy. How could they be simplified?

WORDY   My sister dressed to assume the appearance of Goldilocks.
[*To assume the appearance of* is a long-winded way of saying *as.*]

BETTER   My sister dressed as Goldilocks.

WORDY   College prepares you for the field you may be entering, or if you aren't planning to work, it still helps you talk about things in a conversation that is interesting to you and other people.
[This could be said in fewer words.]

BETTER   College prepares you for an occupation and makes you a good conversationalist.

OVERWRITTEN   It hasn't escaped my notice that your counte-
nance exhibits a somewhat crestfallen de-
meanor.

BETTER   I notice that you seem sad.

OVERWRITTEN   Be cognizant of the inherent ramifications before
ascertaining which course of action will be
most propitious.

BETTER   Consider the consequences before making an
important decision.

EXERCISE 2

Eliminate wordiness and overwriting in the following sentences.
Rewrite any sentences where it is necessary.

1. Put the jack in a position where it will lift the car in a way so
   that you can change the tire.

2. To me, I believe that the jet plane has changed the entire
   course of existence in this modern world in which we now live.

3. The roles of males and females can be reversed in many and
   varying situations on a daily basis throughout the world.

4. The snow began to reach a higher level on the ground on
   which it lay.

5. When I was in high school, I never studied enough to accumu-
   late the knowledge of the many and varied important things
   I needed to know.

6. Community colleges offer classes geared toward the older student who only has a limited amount of time to go to school
   and start back into the working field.

7. My experience involving secretarial duties qualifies me for the
   position of secretary.

8. Pursuant to the matter you broached in the epistle of Thursday
   last, the discrepancy between the requested remittance and that
   which you were led to expect has been rectified.

9. The body soap and shampoo are used for washing the baby's
   body and hair.

EXERCISE 3

Eliminate all unnecessary repetition and wordiness in the following passages by writing the essential ideas in one or two sentences.

(a) Many people find commercials on TV very vexing because they interrupt the programs. Some programs have commercial breaks eight to ten times every half hour. A viewer watching pay TV is not distracted by continual advertising urging him to buy a special cleaner or hear about the heartbreak of hemorrhoids. Quite a few people have a limited time to watch TV. A large part of this time is spent watching commercials. If they had pay TV, they could watch more programs without the wasted time of commercials.

(b) One of the most difficult adjustments any individual has to make is learning how to get along with others. People have individual differences in appearance, personality, and personal habits. Knowing that people are all different in the above-mentioned ways and aspects makes a person feel confused about how to adjust to others. There are several essential behavior patterns that all people have in common. It is each person's job to look for these patterns in order to understand and adjust to others.

23c
w

 CHECKLIST: Eliminating Unnecessary Words

Ask yourself these questions:

1. Have I avoided using the same word too often in a single sentence or short paragraph?
2. Have I avoided other forms of wordiness?
3. Have I written in a simple, direct style?

Chapter 24
THE WRITING PROCESS

Follow the steps of the writing process:
discovering, organizing, drafting,
revising, editing, and formatting.

Whether you are writing a single paragraph or a full-length essay, you will do your best work if you think of the creation of a piece of writing in terms of six stages: discovering, organizing, drafting, revising, editing, and formatting. If you feel overwhelmed at the thought that so many steps are involved in the writing of a single paragraph, let alone a multiparagraph essay, try to remember two things: (1) the shorter the piece of writing, the less time you will spend on each stage, and (2) all professional writers go through these same stages. This is simply the way that good writing gets written, so trust the process to help you produce work that you can be proud of.

Stage 1—Discovering

24a
Discover your ideas.

Before you begin to express your ideas in sentences you imagine will appear in the finished product, you need to discover the ideas that you want to work with. *Discover* is a good term to associate with the first stage of the writing process because, like a treasure hunt, this stage involves exploring, unearthing, and recovering what is already buried somewhere in your mind—that is, what you already know about a topic. You can try several activities to help discover what you already know.

24a-1
Keep a journal.

Record your thoughts in a spiral-bound notebook or composition book which serves as your journal (or keep a computer file for this purpose). Do not use the pages of this journal for anything else. Unlike diary entries, which often record only the owner's activities, journal entries record the owner's thoughts, opinions, and feelings. Both diaries and journals are considered by their owners as places to record private thoughts, off limits to anyone else, including instructors. Because a journal is a private place to "think on paper," you will not feel self-conscious as you write in it. Consequently, you will tell the truth, discovering what you really think and feel as you write. You can record either bits of ideas which you want to explore later or long passages which seem to pour out of you because the time is right. Likewise, you can either set aside a time each day to write whatever comes to mind or respond to journal prompts (topics) your instructor has given you. Remember that journal entries are private writings intended to be read by no one except you; therefore, you are free to misspell words, ignore rules of punctuation, and say things you might not even mean the next day. The point is to access thoughts that might not ordinarily occupy your mind.

EXERCISE 1

To collect ideas for writing, complete the following exercises.

1. Write a journal entry in which you explore any idea that is in your head at the moment you begin to write.
2. Write a journal entry in which you respond to one of the following subjects: *high school, neighbors, a fear you have, your mother, your father, your goals, what makes you sad,* or *what makes you happy.*
3. Make a list of ten subject prompts (topics you might want to explore in your journal). Choose one and write a journal entry about it.

4. Choose one word from each of the following three columns. Then link the three words in such a way that they remind you of something you think or have experienced. Write a journal entry about that thought or experience. (For instance, "a parent" + "can be" + "frustrating" might lead to the idea that taking care of one's aging parents can be both frustrating and rewarding.)

1	2	3
work	taking care of	frustrating
a sport	relating to	boring
shopping	relaxing	fun
children	can be	confusing
vacations	changes	rewarding
a pet	types	easy
waiting	uses	crazy
a parent	punishing	hard
shoppers	sizes	tiring

24a-2
Try freewriting.

Another way to discover your ideas is to freewrite. Freewriting involves writing nonstop for a specific length of time, usually from five to ten minutes. The important thing to remember when you freewrite is that during the time you have committed yourself to freewrite, you should not allow yourself to stop putting words on a page, even if the words are sometimes off the topic. The point of freewriting is mainly to jump-start your memory and language-making skills. The hardest part of freewriting is keeping your hand or fingers (if you are typing) going for a specific number of minutes. Remember that like journal writing, freewriting is intended for your eyes only, so feel free to make mistakes and to express opinions you might change ten minutes later. The following is an example of freewriting on the topic "My Family."

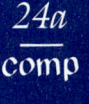

24a
—
comp

> My family . . . well, there's Dad, Mom, my brother Jack, and me. What can I say about them? Dad fishes all the time when he's not at work—always in the early morning. He's fished all his life for relaxation and . . . one time he said that sometimes he didn't even care if he caught fish—he just liked sitting in his boat in the

middle of a lake listening to the trees grow. Guess he likes the silence. My mom likes silence too when she relaxes. I can see her on the couch every chance she gets with her nose in a book. No TV—no loud music. Not Jack—he relaxes by listening to music as loud as he can get it when nobody's home. He uses earphones the rest of the time. I like to do both—read and listen to loud music—depending on my mood. I also like to work on my car, or even just clean it—just me and my Honda—wash, wax, clean the interior. Looks like I'm beginning to focus on the ways people in my family relax. What do they have in common? Liking to shut out the rest of the world through silence or loud music. What can I say about that?

As you can see, freewriting is loose and relaxed. The freewriter pays no attention to spelling, punctuation, wording, sentence structure, or anything else that will be tended to in the later stages of the writing process. The freewriter is merely discovering ideas about the topic, as well as angles from which the topic might be explored. Notice that in the freewriting example above, the writer quickly realized she was beginning to focus the general topic "My Family" on the more specific topic "How the Members of My Family Relax." She also discovered that even though members of her family like to do different things, all the activities have something in common: shutting out the rest of the world. Now the freewriter may even decide to freewrite again on the narrowed topic as she tries to discover something about the psychological value of music, reading, and working on cars. The point is that freewriting is one way to discover what you already know.

24a-3
Try brainstorming.

Another way to discover your ideas is to brainstorm. Brainstorming involves writing down ideas about a subject as they come to you. Because in the discovery stage you are searching for ideas, not their full expression, your brainstorming page will contain words or phrases rather than complete sentences. Also, some brainstormers purposely ignore the lines on the paper and avoid listing ideas because they don't want to organize their ideas too early, that is, before they have uncovered all of the ideas. The following is an example of brainstorming on the topic "My Family":

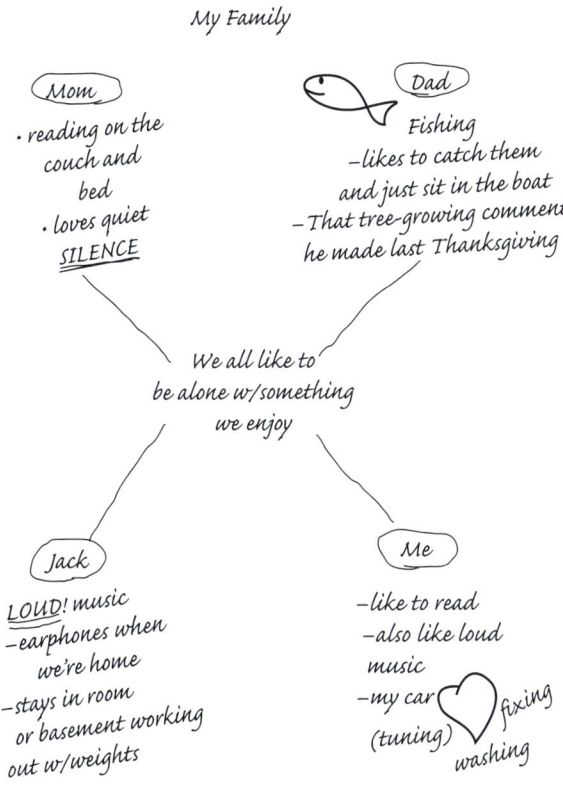

My Family

Mom
· reading on the couch and bed
· loves quiet SILENCE

Dad
Fishing
– likes to catch them and just sit in the boat
– That tree-growing comment he made last Thanksgiving

We all like to be alone w/something we enjoy

Jack
LOUD! music
– earphones when we're home
– stays in room or basement working out w/weights

Me
– like to read
– also like loud music
– my car (tuning) fixing washing

As you can see, brainstorming, unlike freewriting, often just lists ideas and avoids trying to express them in very many words. Also unlike freewriting, brainstorming does not require the writer to write without stopping. However, even drawing the fish may have helped to keep the brainstormer's mind in gear.

24a-4
Try questions.

Still another way to discover your ideas is to ask questions. These questions, sometimes referred to as *5W's* and an *H*, are similar to the questions reporters are supposed to ask when preparing a story. The questions are *who, what, when, where, why,* and *how.* Here is an example of questions applied to the topic "My Family."

WHO?   My family—Dad, Mom, Jack, Me
WHAT?   What we do for fun and relaxation

WHEN?   When we're not working, on weekends, at night, etc.
WHERE?   Depends—Dad (lake, river), Mom (couch, bed), Jack (his room, basement), me (room, basement)
WHY?   To get rid of stress, to feel pleasure, sense of accomplishment (Dad catching fish, me having a clean, well-running car)
HOW?   Similarities—We do all these things alone. Think about differences.

As you can see, answering these five questions ensures that you have important information to work with even if you don't end up using it all. The questions also help you focus on aspects of the topic which need more exploration (for instance, the similarities and differences among the ways these family members relax).

24a-5
Try clustering.

Another way to discover ideas is to cluster. To use the cluster method of discovery, place your topic in the center of a piece of paper and draw a box around it. Next, surround the box with words which this topic suggests to you. Circle each of these words and then surround each of them with ideas which come to you. Here is an example of clustering on the topic "My Family":

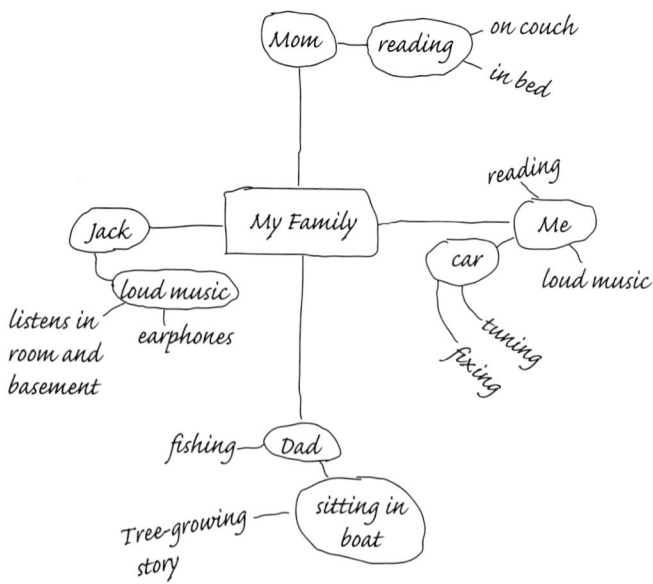

As you can see, clustering, like the other methods of discovery, helps you to see what you already know and sometimes even to focus on aspects of the topic you would like to think more about. All the discovery methods which make up the first stage of writing will help you not only find out what you already know but also determine what you need to think more about.

24b
Discover your topic, purpose, audience, and tone.

In most writing classes, you will be asked not only to come up with your own topic for writing but also to focus more sharply on a topic your instructor gives you. Both types of writing assignments require that you collect as many ideas as possible about a subject and limit your discussion to only one aspect of the subject. Limiting your subject will cause your material to be more specific and ultimately more memorable and interesting. For instance, it would be impossible to write a specific, interesting essay of around 500 words discussing how to play basketball. Can you imagine trying to explain the rules of the game, the scoring system, the types of fouls, the requirements of each position, time-outs, and so on in 500 words? However, an excellent 500-word essay could be written on tips for making successful foul shots. After you have successfully limited your topic, you can further focus your topic by thinking about the purpose, audience, and tone.

24b-1
Choose a workable topic.

If your instructor allows you to choose your own topic for an assignment, you should choose a topic you know something about and find interesting. You should also choose a topic which can be developed in an interesting, specific way, given the word limit of the assignment.

EXERCISE 2

Make a list in which you include three of your hobbies, three of your career goals, three of your favorite sports, two personality traits of

24b
comp

your best friend, three of your favorite restaurants, three times in your life when you have been especially happy, and three principles by which you live.

When you complete this assignment, you will have a pool of twenty topics you know something about. The next time your instructor tells you that you can write about anything, perhaps you can choose something from this list.

EXERCISE 3

Each of the following topics would be too broad for an essay of around 500 words. Using the example as a guide, rewrite each topic so that it is more specific.

EXAMPLE Hurricanes [Topic]

The Damage Hurricane Opal Did to My Parents' Home [More specific]

1. Sports
2. Party Guests
3. The Outer Banks
4. Cats
5. Airplanes
6. Presidents of the United States
7. Marriage

24b-2
Identify the purpose of your paper.

Every piece of writing you produce will fall into one of four categories, depending on its purpose. It will describe, tell a story, explain something, or persuade the reader to agree with you. It is important for you to know which of these categories a piece you write falls into because the purpose of your writing will determine your organization. For instance, let's say that your instructor gives you the general topic of housework and that it is up to you to focus the topic more specifically and then write a paper. In the following chart, notice that the topic of housework can be focused in many different ways according to purpose. Also notice that the order of information differs according to purpose.

GENERAL TOPIC: HOUSEWORK

PURPOSE	TOPIC	TYPE OF ORGANIZATION
To describe	A Description of the Apron My Grandmother Made Me	General characteristics to specific details: color, shape, texture, pattern
To tell a story	The Fateful Day I Tried to Clean the Oven	What happened first, next, and so on
To explain	How to Clean the Oven (process)	First step, second step, and so on
	The Way My Husband Cleans the Kitchen Versus the Way I Clean It (comparison/contrast)	The first basis for contrast (how he unloads the dishwasher/how I do it), the second basis for contrast (how he cleans off the counters/how I do it), and so on
	What is Spring Cleaning? (definition)	The first characteristic of spring cleaning, the second characteristic, how it differs from ordinary cleaning, and so on
	How Cleaning My House Has Affected My Health (cause/effect)	The mental strain, the physical strain, the drain on my free time, and so on
	Three Types of Housework (classification)	Heavy cleaning, light cleaning, maintenance cleaning
To persuade	Why Men and Women Should Share Housework	First reason, second reason, and so on

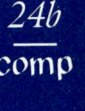

24b
―
comp

24b-3

Identify your audience. Use the appropriate tone.

Knowing your audience—that is, the people who will read your writing—is as important as focusing your topic and knowing your purpose. Two aspects of your audience are important to consider as you choose your words: educational level and the degree of formality the audience expects from you. For instance, if you are writing about a technical subject such as the installation of cables aboard a ship, you will need to define many of your terms if your readers are not familiar with the process. In contrast, if you are a physician writing a report to other physicians, you do not need to define most of the medical terms.

Not only should you consider the educational level of your audience, but you should also consider the level of formality your audience expects of you. For instance, it would be acceptable to use the phrase *a dude I know* in a letter to your friend but not in a letter to your supervisor. It might be appropriate to say *One can always spot a fool in the marketplace* in a college essay but not in a letter to your friend (unless your friend also likes and uses formal language). For additional information on the way a dictionary can help you tell whether a word is considered formal, informal, slang, dialect, or substandard, see **20b-1**.

EXERCISE 4

In the blanks provided, write *A* if the word choice creates the appropriate tone for the type of writing in parentheses; write *NA* if the word choice is not appropriate.

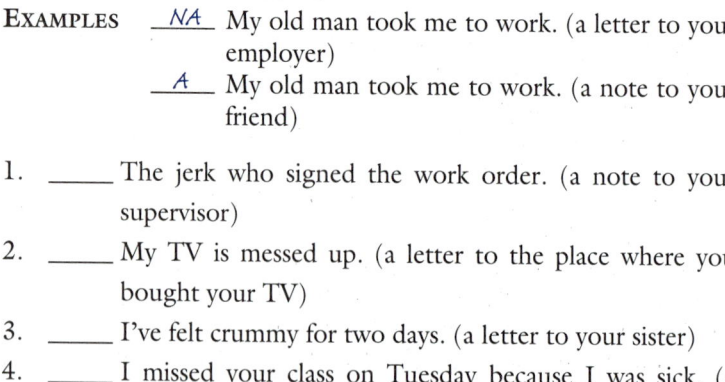

EXAMPLES   _NA_ My old man took me to work. (a letter to your employer)

    _A_ My old man took me to work. (a note to your friend)

1. _____ The jerk who signed the work order. (a note to your supervisor)

2. _____ My TV is messed up. (a letter to the place where you bought your TV)

3. _____ I've felt crummy for two days. (a letter to your sister)

4. _____ I missed your class on Tuesday because I was sick. (a note to your instructor)

EXERCISE 5

Study the following essay about how to avoid housework; then answer the questions that follow. As you read, you will notice that although the tone is formal, discussing housework generally does not lend itself to formal language. Think about why the writer may have chosen formal language anyway.

A Primer:
How to Avoid Housework—
Or, I'll Do It Next Weekend, Honey

At the risk of sounding chauvinistic, I will say that God did not intend for the human male to perform the menial duties around the house collectively termed housework. Examples of housework to be avoided, especially during the major sports season (January 1–December 31), are making the bed, ironing, doing the laundry, and cleaning the kitchen. The male does have some chores to perform such as taking out the garbage and mowing the lawn, but even these typically male tasks can be avoided. The female of the species, however, suffers from the delusion that housework should be shared. To help my fellow males in their quest to avoid housework, I have developed the AVOID technique for putting off until later what might be done never.

A. Step one is assurance. This is the first and perhaps the most critical step in avoiding housework. Assurance involves persuading your wife, girlfriend, significant other, and so on that the task in question will be completed a) at the commercial; b) at the half; c) right after this inning; d) next week.

It is obviously to your advantage to delay performing the task as long as possible. One thing you should never say is "I don't want to" or "why me?" Responses like these only make the female determined that you *will* do the job and it will be done right then!

V. Step two in the AVOID technique is never volunteer. Once you have volunteered to do anything, no matter how small, a female immediately jumps to the conclusion that you have decided to cooperate. Rest assured she will expect cooperation in the future.

O. "O" is for obstacles. When confronted by a household task, consider all the reasons why that job just can't be done. If faced with the unpleasant task of having to do the laundry, simply state, "There's no hot water" or "We're out of laundry soap." Bring up any possible obstacle to a task, no matter how trivial it may seem.

24b
comp

I. "I" is for incompetence. If trapped into performing housework, manage to make it appear that you are incapable of doing the job. The female involved will frequently take over the task. She might even say things like, "Give me that. Can't you do anything right?" or, my favorite, "If I want a job done right, I guess I'll just have to do it myself!"

D. If all else fails, when you get the feeling your spouse is about to come up with some innovative chore that will ruin your weekend, simply duck out, disappear, or ditch that place. Do it fast.

Remember **AVOID**: **A**ssurance; **V**olunteer (never); **O**bstacles; **I**ncompetence; **D**isappear, and say goodbye to household duties forever!

1. What is the purpose of the essay? A. To give directions B. To tell a story C. To classify types of housework D. To give directions in an entertaining way
2. Who is the writer's intended audience? A. Women B. Men
3. What clues in the essay tell you who is the intended audience?
4. List three phrases which cause the tone of the essay to be formal.
5. Housework is not usually discussed in formal terms. Why do you think the writer chose to do so anyway?

Stage 2—Organizing

24c
Sharpen your focus with a clear, specific topic and a rough outline.

24c-1
Sharpen your focus with a clear, specific topic.

After you have chosen a general topic you want to write about, it is time to sharpen it. Let's say that when you did Exercise 1, number 4, you chose "shoppers" + "types" + "easy." From there you focused on the idea that anyone can observe different types of shoppers. Now it is time to sharpen that idea by limiting the shoppers to a specific place because shoppers may behave differently in different types of places. Also, it is time to determine your purpose so that you will know how to organize your material. After some consideration, you decide that you want to write about different types of shoppers at a shopping mall and that the purpose of your writing will be to classify them.

Now that you have a sense of the topic and purpose of your essay, it is time to discover what you already know about types of shoppers through journaling, brainstorming, clustering, or asking questions. Let's say that you used brainstorming to uncover this information about shoppers and that you have crossed out the material which doesn't relate to your topic:

Mall Shoppers

~~*Spending too much money*~~

~~*-shoplifting-*~~

-*people who only shop at*
Christmas, Easter, etc.

Some people aren't really
shopping but just tag
along — husbands
children
window
shop *sisters, etc.*
browse, don't buy

The Pros — shopping
down to a science-
– best parking places
–Know all clerks by name

People running in
and out — one item
only (*batteries, a*
particular book)

~~*I hate to shop!*~~

24c
comp

24c-2
Sharpen your focus by organizing your material.

Now that you have discovered the types of shoppers you will write about, and because the purpose of your paper is to classify them, you know that you will discuss first one type and then the next. At this stage of your writing, many instructors will suggest that you work with only a very rough outline. Unlike a formal outline, which uses Roman numerals to designate sections of your essay, a rough outline is made up of informal notes to yourself about the order of your material. A rough outline about types of shoppers at a shopping mall might look something like this:

> —veteran shoppers
> —in-and-out shoppers
> —seasonal shoppers
> —nonshoppers
> > —spouses and relatives
> > —lookers

A formal outline, which your instructor might require at this stage, would look like this:

> I   Veteran shoppers
> II. In-and-out shoppers
> III. Seasonal shoppers
> IV. Nonshoppers
> > A. Spouses and relatives of shoppers
> > B. Just lookers

Since you know that essays which classify (a type of explaining) discuss one type at a time, you now know what your organization will be. Chapters **25** and **26** will give you more information about organizing and developing single paragraphs and full-length essays, but the following guidelines will help you as you think about the organizing stage of the writing process:

1. Remember that working outlines can be changed. Be willing to discard a point in your outline if it doesn't seem to lead anywhere as you write your first draft.
2. Try to arrange your points with your reader in mind. Perhaps you will want to save the most interesting, most important, most humorous, or most powerful point for last since it will be

the last thing the reader has in mind as your paper comes to a conclusion.

3. If you feel you do not have enough points to begin writing, try returning to the discovery stage of your writing in order to uncover more ideas.

Stage 3—Drafting

24d
Write the first draft.

The most important thing you should remember about the first draft of your paper is that it is not the final draft. The first draft is just a first try, an attempt to see what your thoughts look like when you try to express them on paper. Therefore, you should approach writing your first draft in much the same way you approach writing in your journal, without worrying about spelling or punctuation. Remember that you are trying to express your ideas, this time in complete sentences. If you stop to look up the spelling of a word or a comma rule, you might lose a thought that might have turned out to be the best point in your paper. During the drafting stage, you might discover many things about your topic which will require you to spend more time on the first draft than you had planned. For instance, you might learn that it takes you more time than you thought it would to compose sentences about your topic because it is difficult to discuss. You might learn that you don't know as much as you thought you did about your topic and need to gather more information. Finally, you might learn that you need to change your organization for a more effective presentation. Here is a list of guidelines that will help you write a useful first draft:

24d
comp

1. If you are writing your draft by hand, skip every other line and leave wide margins so that you can jot down ideas for further development as they come to you.
2. If you are using a word processor, double-space and print the draft so that you can add comments in pencil or pen.
3. If time permits, put your first draft aside for a day or two. Getting some distance from a draft is an excellent way to see its weaknesses with a fresh mind.

4.   Remember that the first draft is never the finished product. It is merely a roughly organized attempt to put your thoughts on paper about a topic for the first time.

Stage 4—Revising

24e
Revise your paper.

Revising your paper is not the same as editing or proofreading it. Unlike editing, which involves looking for mistakes, *revising* means changing your material by adding to, taking out, or rearranging what you wrote in your first draft. The following checklist will help you revise your paper so that it will be the best paper you can write.

✔ CHECKLIST: Revising

1. Is your paper too short? If so, add another point to develop the main idea. Also, try adding material which will make your paper more interesting. For instance, try adding a sentence in each paragraph which begins with *For example*.
2. Look at your introduction. Have you begun with any sentences to gain your reader's interest in your subject before stating the main point of your paper? If you haven't, then do so. Depending on your subject, you might tell a little story, ask some questions, discuss a problem, or offer a quotation—all of which somehow lead to your main point.
3. Look at your conclusion. Do you merely restate your main point? If so, try summarizing all the points you used to discuss your main point. Also, refer to some idea you mentioned in your introduction as you tried to catch your reader's attention. If you do this, your essay will seem to have come full circle, leaving your reader feeling satisfied that your discussion is finished.
4. Take out any sentences which do not really add to your main point. It is easy to get off the subject when you are writing a

first draft because it is the first time you will have tried to express your ideas in sentences. During the revision process, most writers find that they need to eliminate some things they have written in the first draft.

5. Does your paper seem dull, something that even you wouldn't read if you didn't have to? If so, add details, examples, and illustrations to bring to life your general ideas. When you do, your writing will be much more interesting.

6. Look at every paragraph which is not the introduction or the conclusion. Does each one begin with a sentence stating the main point of the paragraph? If not, add one. Does each paragraph end with a sentence which summarizes the paragraph's main point? If not, add concluding sentences.

7. Can you combine any short paragraphs (those under four sentences) which discuss the same point? If you do combine them, begin the new paragraph with a sentence strongly stating the main point of the paragraph.

8. Do you have any exceptionally long paragraphs? If you do, consider breaking them down into shorter paragraphs, each of which begins with a strong statement of its main point.

9. If you have used any terms which your reader may not know, define them.

10. Look at the order of sentences in your paragraphs. If you can rearrange any of the sentences so that your reader can understand your points better, do so.

The following is the first draft of a paper titled "Types of People at a Shopping Mall," with suggestions for revision shown in the margin. Study this draft carefully, noting the suggestions. Then read the revised version which follows. You can easily see how much the paper has been improved with revision.

24e
org

First Draft

Types of People at a Shopping Mall

Shopping malls are a reflection of the people they serve. Anyone who observes the people who frequent shopping malls will see that there are many categories of shoppers.

Why? Make clearer.

What are they?
Improve thesis.

The first group contains the veteran shoppers. These people usually have a certain gleam in their eyes. *Why?* They know the best time to shop. They are on a first-name basis with all the store managers. *Use more details.* Be warned! If you desire to join this exclusive group, you must be willing to make shopping a way of life. It will take three or four trips a week for many years to become a veteran shopper.

The next group of shoppers consists of very fast movers, so you have to keep your eyes peeled to spot them.

Development needed—what are fast movers like?

The third main group in a mall is the seasonal shoppers. These shoppers usually select Friday night or Saturday to shop. The fact that all seasonal shoppers have this same idea explains why they always complain about the crowded malls.

awkwardly put. Who are they? Clarify. Explain: Are Friday and Saturday shoppers seasonal shoppers?

There is also a small group of people who are present during business hours. Some of these people are the spouses or relatives of the serious shoppers. They sit patiently on the benches and watch all the people scurry to and fro. Still other types are there just to browse and pass the time. They love the excitement of the mall and enjoy window shopping.

Who are they?

Why are they at the mall?

Shopping malls are an American institution. Different people with diverse tastes can come to one shopping area and find all their needs answered.

Improve focus in conclusion.

Revised Draft

Types of People at a Shopping Mall

THESIS →
STATEMENT

Since the introduction of the suburbs, shopping malls, which sprang up in response to the needs of those suburbs, have become an extension and a reflection of the people they serve. Anyone who observes the people who frequent shopping malls will see that they fall into four main categories: the veteran shoppers, the in-and-out shoppers, the seasonal shoppers, and the nonshoppers.

POINT 1 → The first group contains the veteran shoppers. These people usually have a certain gleam in their eyes. This gleam comes from knowing exactly where everything is in the mall and having a mental price list for every item in each store. They know the best times to shop, the good parking spots, and the name of every experienced salesclerk. They are on a first-name basis with all the store managers, and their checks are accepted without a credit check. Be warned! If you desire to join this exclusive group, you must be willing to make shopping a way of life. It will take three or four trips a week for many years to become a veteran shopper.

POINT 2 → The next group of shoppers consists of very fast movers, so you have to keep your eyes peeled to spot them. These in-and-out shoppers go to the mall knowing exactly what they want and plan on shopping in the shortest time possible. There is no time for browsing when you accompany an in-and-out shopper.

POINT 3 → In the third main group an observer may find the seasonal shoppers. These people show up only during the main holidays like Christmas or Easter. You can pick them out by the harried expressions on their faces. Around Christmas an air of forced gaiety is added, and you can imagine them saying to themselves: "I'm going to have a good time Christmas shopping, even if it kills me." These shoppers usually select Friday night or Saturday to shop. The fact that all seasonal shoppers have this same idea explains why they always complain about the crowded malls.

POINT 4 → There is also a small group of people, known as non-shoppers, who are present during business hours. Some of these people are the spouses or relatives of the serious shoppers. They are there because nothing was on television, or they were the ones who had to drive. They sit patiently on the benches and watch all the people scurry to and fro. Still other types of nonshoppers are just there to browse and pass the time. They love the excitement of the mall and enjoy window shopping.

24e
org

Shopping malls are an American institution. Different people with diverse tastes can come to one shopping area and find all their needs answered. Shopping malls are great places to engage in the sport of people watching, and a careful observer will soon identify four distinct types of shoppers at almost any shopping mall.

EXERCISE 6

The following is the first draft of a paper which defines the torque wrench. Using at least five points from the checklist in **24e**, write ideas about how the writer can revise the paper.

A Definition of a Torque Wrench

According to *Webster's International Dictionary*, a torque wrench is "a wrench that measures and indicates the amount of turning and twisting force applied in tightening a nut or bolt." Here are a few examples of how it looks, where it is used, and how it operates.

A torque wrench at first glance looks very simple, but careful scrutiny reveals that it is an intricate tool. It is about two feet in length. It is made of chrome-plated alloy steel. At one end is a rubber handle, and at the other end is a ratchet head. Somewhere between the ratchet head and the handle is a scale calibrated in foot-pounds.

A torque wrench is used to tighten nuts and bolts to a specified torque. It is very important that a mechanic tighten every nut and bolt on an engine to the manufacturer's specification. Even though in some cases nuts and bolts are sufficiently tight, this should not be the case when it comes to connecting the engine's head to its block. If it is not done correctly, water will leak from the water jackets into the combustion chamber. A torque wrench operates much the same way as an ordinary wrench. However, there are two added features. The ratchet head on the torque wrench allows the mechanic to tighten nuts and bolts in an area of limited space. The use of an ordinary wrench forces the mechanic to remove it from the nut or bolt head several times before the nut or bolt is tightened. Because the ratchet head allows movement only in one direction at a time, a simple back and forth movement of the hand will suffice.

Stage 5—Editing

24f
Edit and proofread your paper.

Unlike revising, which involves adding, taking away, or rearranging information, *editing* involves making changes to your paper on three levels: the word level, the sentence level, and the punctuation level. If you have written a paper which is due at the end of the class period during which you began it, you will not have much time for editing. Even so, you should always save at least five minutes at the end of the period to catch and correct any mistakes you can. Most instructors, however, also make writing assignments which you can work on over several days, thus giving you plenty of time for revision and editing. Once you have made these changes, it is time to proofread your paper to see if you have overlooked any errors.

24f-1
Edit your paper at the word level.

1. Spell each word correctly. If you have any doubts about the spelling of a word, look it up in a dictionary.
2. Make sure each word conveys the appropriate tone to your intended audience. Remember that slang and informal language are usually not appropriate when you are writing on the job or for a college class.
3. Make sure you have put the final *-s* or *-ed* on words as needed. For instance, check to see that you have written "two boy*s*," not "two boy"; "he make*s*," not "he make"; and "I finish*ed* yesterday," not "I finish yesterday."
4. Capitalize all proper nouns and the appropriate words in the title, as explained in Chapter **18**.
5. If you have used pronouns like *they* and *it*, make sure they refer to something specific in the same sentence or in the sentence before it.

24f-2
Edit your paper at the sentence level.

1. Combine two short sentences next to each other with words like *and* or *but* if the points in each sentence are equal in importance.

24f

edit

2. Combine sentences next to each other if there is a relationship between them in time (using words like *when, after,* and *before*) or cause and effect (using words like *because* and *since*) or if the point in one sentence merely adds to the point in the one next to it (using words like *who, which, if,* and *although*).

3. If you have written a sentence fragment, try combining it with the sentence before or after it.

4. If you have written two sentences together, with no punctuation between them, separate them with a semicolon or put a period after the first one and capitalize the first word of the second sentence.

5. If you have written two sentences together, with only a comma to separate them, change the comma to a semicolon or put a period after the first one and capitalize the first word of the second sentence.

6. If many of your sentences begin with their subjects, rewrite the beginnings of some of them for the sake of sentence variety. For instance, try to begin some of your sentences with prepositional phrases and some with *because* or *since.*

24f-3
Edit your paper at the punctuation level.

1. Make sure you have used apostrophes with possessive nouns and contractions.

2. Enclose in quotation marks or italicize titles according to the rules explained in Chapters **16** and **19**.

3. Make sure your questions end with question marks, not with periods.

4. Make sure your semicolons are easy to distinguish from commas.

24f-4
Make up your own editing checklist.

After you have written several papers, you will have some idea of the kinds of mistakes you make most frequently. At this point, you can make up a personalized checklist to guide you through the editing and proofreading stages of writing. Using such a list will help you catch specific errors which you have probably been making out of habit.

EXERCISE 7

The following is a personal checklist made by the student who wrote the paragraph titled "The Shotputer." Using this checklist, edit the student's paragraph. Be sure to correct any other errors you see as well.

____√____ misspellings   ____√____ left-out words
____√____ comma splices   ____√____ verb tenses
____√____ capitals   ____√____ commas

The Shotputer

He stands there, a massive body of muscle and bone, with a solid Iron ball in his hand awaiting his turn to prove his strength. His shoes were tore while his shoelaces have been tied in several knots to insure strength of the shoe. The overstretched and unmatched socks protrude from the top of his ragged old shoes. He seems like an earthquake when he moves, all the massive muscles in his calfs and thighs contract and expand dramatically. His blue shorts hug his thighs so tight that their are several tears in them. The marks on his abdomen form eight separate rectangles which work together when he moves his arm. Just above his abdomen a floresent orange cut-off shirt covers his massive chest. His shoulders, which are the size of a cannonball hold his 25-inch biceps to his prefect body. Anyone watching him has to notice his huge veined neck the size of a tree and his red weather-beaten face as he gets ready for his turn.

24g
Try editing on the computer.

If you have access to a computer and word-processing software, you will find that a few basic commands will allow you to write and edit your papers easily and accurately. You will be able to change wording, omit points, or add information at any position in the paper without having to rewrite sentences you plan to use in the final draft. When you discover how easy it is to make corrections using the computer, you will overcome any hesitation about using it. Even if you do not have highly developed typing skills, you can use the computer to produce carefully organized and edited papers.

Starting with the rough draft, you can simply add to or revise the original without having to print several drafts of your paper. However, it can be useful to print a hard copy of the rough draft to use as a guide as you improve your ideas. In fact, having a printed (hard) copy of each stage of the writing process can help you see how each new draft improves upon the last. Because it is so easy to revise using the computer, you will probably find yourself especially willing to revise heavily until you are satisfied with your work.

The final editing stage is the point at which you will appreciate the computer most. Discovering how easy it is to correct errors in spelling and grammar will keep you from feeling frustrated when you find errors which you have overlooked. For most writers, finding errors in a typed draft is easier than finding them in a handwritten one.

Most word-processing programs offer useful features like grammar check and spellcheck. While these features can help you find errors, it is wise to keep in mind their limitations. For instance, grammar check sometimes fails to underscore certain errors because it has not been programmed to detect them. Likewise, it sometimes underscores passages which contain no errors because it is not capable of predicting the full intent of your sentence. Spellcheck, too, has limitations. For instance, it will not underscore words which are used incorrectly even if they are spelled right (like *there/their/they're, bought/brought,* or *whether/weather*). Therefore, if your instructor permits you to use these features, view them as an aid to editing, but not as the last word. Remember that you must look for errors everywhere, not just in the places grammar check and spellcheck have underscored.

24h
Proofread your paper.

Although you will have corrected most of your errors as you have edited your paper, it is always wise to proofread your paper one last time before formatting it. Because writers are so familiar with their papers by the time they proofread them, it is sometimes hard for them to see all of their own errors. The following are some proofreading techniques which can help you find your own errors:

1.   Proofread your paper backward. Starting with the last word in the last sentence, work your way backward, word by word, until you reach the word which begins your paper. This way you will be sure to look at each word carefully without getting

caught up in the flow of your ideas. This is a good technique for finding errors at the word level.

2. Put a pencil or your finger (if you are using a computer) on each word and say it aloud. Again, whether you are proofreading backward or forward, this technique will keep your mind focused on each word rather than on the flow of ideas. This technique is also useful if you tend to leave out words like *the* or *is.*

3. After you have looked at each word, proofread at the sentence level. Read each sentence carefully, looking especially for sentence fragments, comma splices, and run-together sentences. Again, starting at the end of your paper and working backward helps you to see your sentences in isolation, standing on their own without the distraction of sentences before and after them.

EXERCISE 8

Edit the following paragraphs as you would your own, inserting changes where necessary.

The Disadvantage of the Pass–Fail Grading System

There is many disadvantage of the pass–fail grading system in college. For one thing it require only a little effort from the student. Instead of learning. A student is concern with only passing a subject and just go through the motions of education. Another disadvantage is the the pass–fail system discourage a student progress, a student who would ordinarily try to do well in their courses are trying only to pass them these students become underachievers and they learn less than their ability will allow. Competition is reduce to the lowest level—between those who past and those who do not. It is also argue that the pass–fail system reduce the prestige of a college education. And that the college degree become less valuable, the better argument seem to be that this system has no motivation. A good student is not recognize, but he seen as one of many passing student, there is no motivation to excell. The importance of motivation in college reflect a person need to grow and change. Under the pass–fail grading system. A student don't have this moitvation and will suffer as a result.

A needed Neighborhood Improvement

My neighborhood is pretty normal. It's not overly fancy or deprived. It is pretty much an ordinary area, much like you would see

24h
—
edit

in a t.v. show like "Home Improvement." There is one thing, however about my neighborhood that really tends to get on my nerves. This one thing is the garabage service. It only picks up once a week. So by the end of the week you have any where from 6 to 10 garbage bags piled up outside your house. This not only smells badly, but it attracts stray dogs. If they would pick up trash just one more day a week, I believe my neighborhood would be a cleaner and healthier place for every one.

The Sounds of a Race Track

When I close my eyes. I hear the sounds of a race track. It is surprising how many different sounds you can hear. There are the sounds of two stroke engines screaming through the tight corners and hitting the jumps. Then the sounds of four stroke engines thumping through the woods. Sounds of Rachets, Wrenches and Screwdrivers tightning bolts and turning screws. Sometimes there are some terrible sounds like bikes colliding or bikes hiting fences or trees. The one sound you never hear is the sound of silence.

Stage 6—Formatting

24i
Format your paper.

After you have edited and proofread your paper, it is time to format it. (To *format* means to put the paper into its final form.) Unless your instructor tells you otherwise, use these guidelines to format the final draft which you will submit to your instructor.

24i-1
Format your handwritten final draft.

1. Use standard-sized, white, lined notebook paper, not paper torn from a spiral-bound notebook.
2. Write in blue or black ink only.
3. Write your name, the instructor's name, the class name, and the date in the upper-left corner of the first page.
4. Center your title on the first line.
5. Skip a line after your title and begin your paper.

6. Indent each paragraph about an inch (or five spaces) from the left margin.

7. Leave margins of about an inch on the right side of each paper and at the bottom.

8. Skip every other line as you write.

9. Do not write on the backs of the pages.

10. Number each page after the first using Arabic numbers (2, 3, 4, etc.). Place the page number in the upper-right corner of each page.

11. If you need to divide a word at the end of a line, look it up in the dictionary to see how it is divided.

12. Make sure your capital letters look different from your lowercase letters.

13. Use solid dots, not circles, for periods and dotted *i*'s. Cross all *t*'s.

24i-2

Format your typed or computer-printed final draft.

1. Use heavy-weight, white, 8½-by-11 paper.

2. Use 10- or 12-point type and a font which resembles typewriter type, such as Times New Roman. Do not use fonts which are fancy and difficult to read.

3. Set margins of one inch on all sides of the page.

4. Type your name, the instructor's name, the class name, and the date in the upper-left corner of the first page.

5. Center your title, double space, and then begin typing your paper.

6. Indent each paragraph five spaces from the left margin.

7. Double-space your paper.

8. Number each page after the first using Arabic numbers (2, 3, 4, etc.). Place the page number in the upper-right corner of each page.

9. Before you submit your paper, tear off any pin-feed strips, separate your pages, and staple or clip them together.

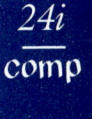

24i-3

Proofread your paper one last time after it has been formatted.

Although you are probably really tired of your paper by the time you have prepared your final draft, it is wise to proofread it one last time before submitting it to your instructor. This is especially true if you have handwritten the final draft, and even more so if you were in a hurry to finish the paper and turn it in. When writers rush through the final draft, they sometimes make mistakes like leaving out words or leaving off *s*'s and *ed*'s. Do yourself a favor and protect your careful, hard work by proofreading one last time.

Chapter 25

THE PARAGRAPH-
LENGTH PAPER

Write clear, well-developed paragraph-length
papers about one idea or topic.

Sometimes, you may find it easier to first practice the writing
process by writing a single paragraph because a paragraph is the
most basic collection of sentences.

A paragraph is easy to find on a page because its first word is
indented from the left margin. The length of a paragraph depends
on where you find it. Some paragraphs in history textbooks, for
instance, are much longer than paragraphs in newspapers. The
length of your practice paragraphs will depend on the topic you
are writing about because some topics are more complicated than
others are and take more words to develop. Therefore, your paragraph probably will consist of five to twelve sentences, or about
75 to 200 words. Most of your paragraphs will look like the following one:

Sports Superstitions

Superstitions play a significant role in the lives of some of today's
athletes. For instance, some players must follow the same routine
because they think their teams will lose if they don't. Some players

in major league baseball put the same sock on the same foot before every game. Not only that, but some put their shoes and socks on in the same order every time. Still others refuse to wash their "lucky" jerseys during a winning streak because they are afraid they will jinx the streak. Other superstitions involve pepping up the team. For instance, some teams chant the same cheers together before every game. Another example is the practice of team members wearing caps inside out. These are known as rally caps and remind the team that all is not lost and that they may still come back to win. Finally, some players go to extremes to avoid bad omens. If a player cracks his bat, it is not a good sign. Others think it is a bad omen to talk about a winning streak. Many superstitions exist in sports.

As you can see, this paragraph is about one topic. A paragraph has unity if it is about one topic. This paragraph is also clear. A paragraph is coherent if it is clear to its readers. Finally, this paragraph is well developed. In other words, the author has provided enough details and examples to get the point across. Perhaps it will help if you see that this paragraph has a definite structure, or skeleton. The following information clearly shows the skeleton of the paragraph.

Title: Sports Superstitions

Topic Sentence: Superstitions play a significant role in the lives of some of today's athletes.

Main Point 1: Routines
  Example 1: Putting same sock on same foot
  Example 2: Putting shoes and socks on in same order
  Example 3: Wearing dirty clothes

Main Point 2: Pepping up the team
  Example 1: Wearing rally caps
  Example 2: Chanting cheers

Main Point 3: Avoiding bad omens
  Example 1: Not cracking a bat
  Example 2: Not talking about a winning streak

25a
Make sure that your paragraph has unity.

It is important that readers be able to follow the main idea and direction of your paragraph. Here are some things you can do to help them.

25a-1
Unify your paragraph by staying on the subject.

The following paragraph has some unity problems because it does not stay on track with one topic.

> (1) Working in an emergency room at a hospital gives a person many opportunities to experience bad days, but my worst day came recently after a heavy rain and sleet storm. (2) On the other hand, just last week I had three pleasant days in a row. (3) On that day our emergency room was overrun by drivers who were unused to the slick streets, little old ladies who had slipped on the ice, police officers who were hauling in the previously mentioned drivers, and a physician (only one) who was bleary-eyed and sneezing. (4) The hospital staff physicians are poorly paid and don't seem to care about the patients. (5) With a few more days like that one, I will be a good candidate for geriatric nursing. (6) I hope I can get off early on Friday.

In this case, the first sentence seems to state the main idea of the paragraph. However, some of the rest of the sentences only add confusion because they do not help to prove the point that that particular day was the student's worst day of work in a hospital emergency room. Sentences 2, 4, 5, and 6 add words, but really just get in the way. The writer should remove the sentences which do not add details that prove the point; then, possibly, he or she can develop the actual point with additional important details about that bad day.

25a
¶

25a-2
Unify your paragraph with a good topic sentence.

Knowing your focus and purpose for writing will help you write your topic sentence. This sentence tells the reader what you are going to say, or what you have said, in the rest of your paragraph. It makes a statement that you will need to develop with examples and details.

1. A good topic sentence is actually a sentence stating the point the writer is making about a topic. It is not just a topic.

   NOT A TOPIC SENTENCE   Superstitions in Sports

2. A good topic sentence is not an announcement.

   WEAK   In this paper, I will tell about superstitions in sports.

3. A good topic sentence indicates what the whole paragraph is about. The following is not a good topic sentence for the sample paragraph at the beginning of this chapter.

   WEAK   I like to watch sports on television.
           [Even though this may be true, it does not reflect the focus of the paragraph.]

4. A good topic sentence does not promise more than a writer can possibly develop in one paragraph.

   TOO BROAD   All sports are important to every young person in America today.
                [This cannot even be covered in an entire book, let alone a single paragraph.]

5. A good topic sentence does not say less than it needs to say to control the entire paragraph.

   TOO NARROW   Sometimes, players wear dirty clothes.
                 [This is not a good topic sentence because only part of the paragraph is about wearing dirty clothes.]

6. A good topic sentence unifies the paragraph by making the point clear.

   BETTER   Superstitions play a significant role in the lives of some of today's athletes.

The following are some topic sentences that suggest what the writer's purpose is:

1. to describe

   My bedroom is the messiest room in my house.
   Sarah always wears the latest styles.

2. to narrate

   Last Monday I forgot everything I was supposed to do.

3. to instruct

   If you want to make a foul shot almost every time, there are three easy steps to remember.

4. to compare or contrast

   A baseball and a basketball are different in appearance and in purpose.

5. to classify

   The most dangerous drivers on the roads are those who talk on cell phones, those who change lanes repeatedly, and those who go through red lights.

6. to define

   Daydreaming is a practice that temporarily removes the dreamer from the real world.

7. to analyze or explain

   My neighborhood could be improved by the addition of several streetlights.

8. to argue or persuade

   A disadvantage of the work-release program is that it gives a known criminal the opportunity to commit another crime.

25a
¶

EXERCISE 1

Noting the focus and purpose of the following topic sentence, eliminate any details listed below it that would get in the way of the unity of a paragraph.

My favorite season is Christmas.

It is the time of year for great happiness, joy, and fellowship.
It is the time of year to visit with friends and family.
These visits cause much tension and disappointment.
It is the time of year to engage in exciting activities.
There are many parties.
The exhaustion we experience from attending these events
    causes illness.
Sometimes the weather is very bad.
The lights on homes are beautiful.
The food offered is wonderful.
We gain weight.

25b
Make sure that your paragraph is coherent.

The following paragraph has some coherence problems because it does not move smoothly and clearly from beginning to end.

Two Dentists to Avoid

(1) Two common types of dentists that you should try to avoid are the strangler and the joker. (2) The strangler was probably a Marine sergeant at one time. (3) The joker smiles at you from across the room and tells you stories while you are in the dentist's chair. (4) The joker makes bad jokes about your teeth if you are not keeping them clean. (5) If you have to choose between the strangler and the joker, maybe you should wait until a new dentist moves into your neighborhood. (6) The strangler yanks your head back really hard when he wants to see your teeth. (7) He uses a tongue depressor so hard that your tongue feels paralyzed.

Can you figure out why it is so hard to follow the thoughts of the author of the paragraph above? For one thing, the sentences are out of logical order. Perhaps the paragraph would be more coherent if the order of the sentences were 1, 2, 6, 7, 3, 4, and 5. Of course, there is still something wrong with this paragraph. Read it aloud. It seems choppy, doesn't it? Adding transitional words and expressions and even combining some sentences would help to move the paragraph smoothly from beginning to end. One possible improvement follows.

Two Dentists to Avoid

Two common types of dentists that you should try to avoid are the strangler and the joker. The strangler was probably a Marine sergeant at one time because he uses force to yank your head back really hard when he wants to see your teeth. Also, he is so rough with a tongue depressor that your tongue feels paralyzed. Not much better is the joker, who smiles at you from across the room and tells you stories while you are in the dentist's chair. He also makes bad jokes about your teeth if you are not keeping them clean. If you have to choose between the strangler and the joker, maybe you should wait until a new dentist moves into your neighborhood.

25b-1
Select a general pattern of development.

Coherence, or clarity, can be achieved in many ways. First, decide what general pattern you want to use to present your ideas. Either move from a topic sentence to particular ideas or examples, or move from particular ideas or examples to a topic sentence. Your topic sentence can be placed at the beginning of your paragraph, at the end of your paragraph, or sometimes within your paragraph. The location you choose depends on a number of things, including whether you want to reveal your topic immediately or whether you want to first present details which convince your readers that what you are writing is true, or logical. Examine the two examples that follow.

(a) Blowing a really impressive bubble from a wad of gum requires the proper technique. Hold the gum flat against the back of your closed front teeth. Use your tongue to spread it so that it covers the entire front one-fourth of your mouth. While starting to exhale slowly, begin pushing the gum between your teeth and lips. Continue to blow steadily, using your lips to round the bubble as it emerges. Not only do your lips form the bubble's shape, but they become the base of the bubble itself. This enables you to keep the size of the bubble under control. After all, you can only form a bubble as big as the wad just before it comes loose from your mouth. Be sure to keep away from drafts, for your bubble is extremely susceptible to breezes at this point.

(b) When I lived in my native country, I usually went on a picnic with some friends on the weekends. On one clear Saturday morning

25b
¶

we decided to pass our weekend in a village which was situated ten miles from Saigon. After twenty minutes of driving we came to the village. The atmosphere was tranquil. The fresh air of the morning made us feel elated. The rays of the sun went through the leaves of the trees and colored the scene with a fresh light-yellow color. The village was almost entirely occupied by fruit gardens and rice fields. Houses were scattered throughout the village, and we were greeted by an old couple sitting under the porch of one house, watching the children playing in the yard. Some bamboo trees rose above the village. On that day, as on every other day, people brought their products to the market to sell and men carried farming implements to their fields. It was so quiet that we could hear the song of the crickets coming from the bushes. This peaceful atmosphere made us forget that we were living in a country at war.

25b-2

Select a specific pattern of development.

Two common specific patterns are space order and time order, both of which can either begin or end with the topic sentence.

The space-order method is frequently used in a description of a person or a place. Space order begins at one point and moves logically toward another—from one side to another or from top to bottom, or from bottom to top. The direction you choose really depends on your subject. If you are describing a room, you may lead your reader from the entrance and then logically through space, stopping to describe important details, in order, within the room. If you are describing a person, you will use space order from top to bottom or bottom to top, but you will not describe from one side to another because that might include only the elbow area of your subject. You will not mention every detail—only those which support your topic sentence.

Here is a description of a person. Can you see that it follows a top-to-bottom order? Do you see that the topic sentence is at the end, and that it indicates that the paragraph has presented Officer Dooley's "crisp, tidy appearance"? These details are presented in a logical space order, but the paragraph only includes the "crisp, tidy" details. It does not mention any smudge that Officer Dooley may have on his cheek.

The immaculate, neatly pressed uniform fitted well on Officer Dooley's small, but solid, almost rocklike frame. His cap, smartly squared on top of his head, covered his close-cropped red hair yet added an intangible flair to the fresh, rosy-cheeked Irish face that looked back at him from the mirror. With a glance downward, he picked up the holster he had placed on the bench beside him and buckled it on with that peculiar movement of ease and carefulness that he had acquired over the years. He then took a look at his gleaming black shoes and, seeing his face reflected in the glossy shine, could not suppress a momentary flush of pride in his crisp, tidy appearance as he prepared for another day of serving and protecting the people of Boston.

Use a time-order method when you want to tell about a series of events or relate the steps to follow in a series of instructions. Use it in a narrative paragraph when you want to tell what happened from the first to the last event.

In the following paragraph of narration, the writer begins with an observation about the meaning of an experience and then uses time order to illustrate that meaning. You will find that the writer does not use any details which do not prove that scuba diving is exciting. For instance, the writer does not include information about a long, exhausting walk to the water's edge just because it happened first. In fact, it would get in the way of the "exciting" feeling the writer wants to get across to the reader.

As a child I watched the television show "Sea Hunt" and imagined myself scuba diving, but it took my first diving experience in Guantanamo Bay, Cuba, to show me how exciting this sport could be. As I prepared for my first dive, I was filled with anticipation mixed with fear. Once I actually entered the water, my first sensation was amazement at the silence that surrounded me. After touching some plants and sea creatures, I was fascinated by their texture. The most exhilarating part of the experience was hitching a ride on the back of a very large, but friendly, sea turtle. He swam through the water, allowing me to hold on to his shell. When he tired of showing me the ocean sights, he dove down at a very steep angle, indicating that my ride was over. I got out of the water, feeling that I had finally accomplished a lifelong dream. The ocean is a beautiful place to visit, and I recommend scuba diving as a wonderful means of experiencing all that it holds.

25b

¶

25b-3
Repeat key words.

One way to help your reader see the main idea of your paragraph is to repeat key words that will emphasize this idea. Suppose you are writing about the importance of Franklin D. Roosevelt as an American hero. You can do as the author of the following paragraph does. He refers first to Roosevelt's efforts to restore confidence in the "American people" and repeats the word "American" or variations on this word by describing Roosevelt's importance to the "American worker," his faith in "America's future," and his summoning of "America's courage." After establishing the value of this president to his country, he also uses words like "friend" and "protector" which emphasize the picture he has already created of this man. The writer also uses Roosevelt's own repetition of a key word in a line from a famous speech, "The only thing we have to fear is fear itself."

Notice that pronouns can also repeat important ideas. In the last sentence of the paragraph on Roosevelt, for example, the writer uses "this combination of faith and trust" to emphasize the idea that Roosevelt was regarded as a friend and protector by the American people.

During his famous fireside chats, Franklin D. Roosevelt lit a flame of new hope in the midst of a great depression when he promised a "new deal." He became president at a time when many workers were unemployed, people had no money for food, and many families had lost their homes because they could not pay the mortgages. As a result, *the American people* had lost confidence in their ability to control their own destiny and were afraid of what might happen next. In his inaugural address, President Roosevelt called for faith in *America's future*, saying, "The only thing we have to *fear* is *fear* itself." After summoning *America's courage*, he established several work programs designed to provide jobs that would not only put food on the table but also restore personal dignity and self-confidence to the *average American worker*. Millions of people came to regard Roosevelt as a *friend* and *protector* of the common man, and this combination of faith and trust was the key to his success in politics.

 Caution: Repetition of key words can be very helpful, but be careful not to overdo it. If repetition becomes distracting to your readers, you will lose them rather than convince them.

25b-4
Use parallel structure to emphasize your meaning.

Correct use of parallel structure can make paragraphs effective. This technique is also illustrated in the paragraph in **25b-3** to stress that Roosevelt appeared at the right time in history. In three parallel expressions, the writer tells us that Roosevelt became president at a time when "many workers were unemployed, people had no money for food, and many families had lost their homes." He also uses a "not only but also" format to stress Roosevelt's accomplishments. He talks about his work programs that created jobs "that would *not only* put food on the table *but also* restore personal dignity and self-confidence to the average American worker."

You can use this same technique by repeating the structure of sentences within a paragraph to emphasize a point. Many people remember the effectiveness of this technique in the famous words of John F. Kennedy: "*Ask* not *what your country can do for you. Ask what you can do for your country*" or in the repeated use of "I have a dream" in the most famous speech of Martin Luther King, Jr. You may not want to use parallel structure in every paper, but it can help you, where appropriate, to emphasize an important idea.

25b-5
Use transitional words to help the reader move smoothly from one detail to the next.

Another way to provide paragraph coherence is to use transitional words between details that support your main idea. For example, in a paragraph comparing and contrasting two people or ideas, you might use words like *in the same way, likewise, but, however*, or *yet*. If you are moving from a general statement to particular examples, you might introduce your details or examples with words like *for example* or *for instance*. Notice that in the paragraph on Roosevelt, the writer uses the words *as a result* to show what caused the lack of confidence of Americans before Roosevelt's presidency. Transitional words are also important in a paragraph that uses time order so that the reader can move easily from what happens first to what happens last.

The details in the following paragraph are arranged from first to last, so most of the transitional words make it clear what time something happens (*first, after, now*, and so on).

25b

¶

How to Groom Your Cat

TOPIC →
SENTENCE

To groom your cat properly, you must follow a definite procedure very carefully. *First,* plan the procedure before your cat knows you intend to groom it. *This procedure* should include gathering the necessary tools—such as comb, brush, and baby powder—and getting your cat's attention, maybe by playing with its favorite toy. *After* you've gathered the tools and lured your cat to a likely spot, the kitchen table, *for example,* you're ready to begin. *Now,* holding your cat firmly at the shoulders with one hand, begin brushing its coat with your other hand. *When* you come to a tangle that won't come out with the brush, use the comb to get rid of it. *Once* you have removed all the tangles, sprinkle a little baby powder into your cat's fur and brush through it again to make its coat look fluffy and clean. *Now* your cat should be ready to win a blue ribbon at any cat show.

REMINDER: Using Transitional Words

Transitional words serve the following purposes:

to show time (*first, before, after, now*)
to show space (*behind, next to, in front of*)
to compare or contrast (*like, as, unlike, however, similarly*)
to limit or suggest an example (*if, unless, in particular, for example, for instance, such as*)
to add or emphasize (*also, too, besides, another, again, in fact, undoubtedly, surely, certainly, of course*)
to show cause or result (*because, for, thus, so, as a result*)

There are many other transitional words and many other purposes for them, but no matter what specific uses they have, they all guide your readers from one detail or example to another. They help you develop your topic sentence effectively.

EXERCISE 2

Improve the following paragraph by adding transitional expressions to make the ideas flow smoothly. Combine sentences when it is necessary.

Captain Kirk from the show *Star Trek* is my favorite television hero. He commands a great ship, the *Enterprise*. Captain Kirk faces tremendous responsibilities. He has strange encounters with carnivores and human-hating aliens. He explores strange new worlds and civilizations. His crew depends on him for his superb leadership. This is the part of his character I identify with the most. His relationship with his First Officer, Spock, is one of brotherhood. Spock is from a different world. Kirk's dynamic character allows him to be friends with someone remarkably different from him. I hope I can use Kirk's reason and intuition to solve problems in my own life.

25b-6
Complete your paragraph.

Sometimes when you are finishing a paragraph in a hurry, you forget that must make a final impression on your reader. Be sure that your paragraph seems complete. The following paragraph tells how to write a paragraph.

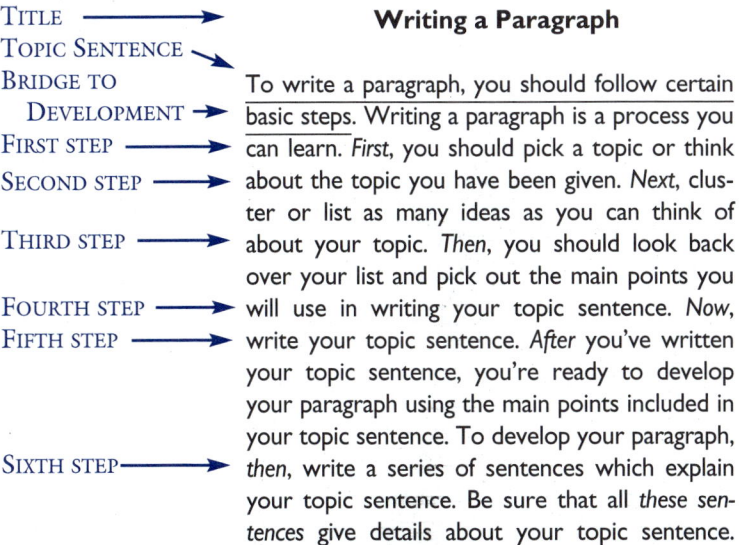

TITLE ⟶	**Writing a Paragraph**
TOPIC SENTENCE ⟍	
BRIDGE TO	To write a paragraph, you should follow certain
DEVELOPMENT ➔	basic steps. Writing a paragraph is a process you
FIRST STEP ⟶	can learn. *First,* you should pick a topic or think
SECOND STEP ⟶	about the topic you have been given. *Next,* cluster or list as many ideas as you can think of
THIRD STEP ⟶	about your topic. *Then,* you should look back over your list and pick out the main points you
FOURTH STEP ⟶	will use in writing your topic sentence. *Now,*
FIFTH STEP ⟶	write your topic sentence. *After* you've written your topic sentence, you're ready to develop your paragraph using the main points included in your topic sentence. To develop your paragraph,
SIXTH STEP⟶	*then,* write a series of sentences which explain your topic sentence. Be sure that all *these sentences* give details about your topic sentence.

25b

¶

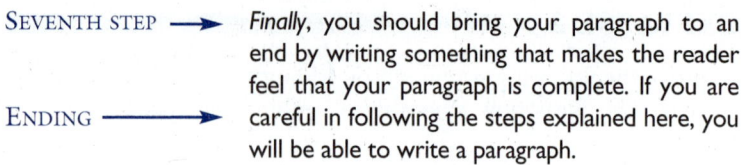

SEVENTH STEP ⟶   *Finally,* you should bring your paragraph to an
end by writing something that makes the reader
feel that your paragraph is complete. If you are
ENDING ⟶   careful in following the steps explained here, you
will be able to write a paragraph.

25c
Make sure that your paragraph is well developed.

The following paragraph has some development problems because
it does not provide enough information and examples:

The Community Recreation Center

When I recently returned to the community recreation center I
had enjoyed as a child, I saw that it had really changed. The playground was a mess. People who use a place shouldn't neglect it like
that. I felt very sad about how the center had been abused, and I left it
as soon as possible.

Of course, the reader can only guess how the recreation center
had changed. What does the writer mean by "a mess"? The student
should have developed the paragraph further, in space order, by including details and examples. For instance, he or she could have
added "Crumbling rust coated the old see-saw handles, swing
chains, and merry-go-round seats. Then I noticed that paint was
chipping off the outside of the neglected, rotting, wooden building.
When I entered the building, I could see that the lobby and gym
were dark, but dust particles were floating around the only tiny
beams of light coming through the mud-coated windows. The
once-shiny gym floor now showed only scuff marks, take-out food
wrappers, and dented, partially full soda cans." You get the idea.
Can you think of any more details? Use your imagination. Good
development in a paragraph adds interesting information and clarifies your purpose for writing.

EXERCISE 3

Imagine that you are getting ready to write paragraphs using each
of the following topic sentences. List three specific details that you
could use to develop each of those paragraphs.

EXAMPLE   My friend Mary is very trustworthy.

    a. I can lend her my car and know that she will return it promptly.

    b. I can tell her a secret about my finances, and she will not tell anyone else.

    c. When she tells me that she will meet me in the library to help me study, I know that she will be there.

1. My mother is the most generous person I know.
2. On May 11, 1999, I was involved in a freak accident.
3. In order to paper a wall successfully, you must master three skills.
4. The general store in my old neighborhood doesn't look much different from the way it looked twenty years ago.
5. The best definition of laziness is an illustration of what the word means in action.
6. I enjoy playing football because it is a very physical game.

25c-1
Model Paragraphs

Sometimes, it helps to have models of different types of paragraphs when you are trying to learn what is expected of you as a student writer. Of course, you may look back at the sample paragraphs already included in this chapter.

The paragraph about Office Dooley in Section **25b-2** is a very good description of a person, and the one about Viet Nam in Section **25b-1** clearly describes the atmosphere of peace that the writer felt, even during the time of war. The paragraph about blowing bubbles in Section **25b-1** is a very effective presentation of instructions.

Examine the following additional model paragraphs for more ideas.

25c

¶

Narration

The maintenance department at my workplace provided me with a very frightening experience. As an apprentice, I must encounter many hazardous situations. One day, I had an assignment to repair an inoperable brake cylinder on a bridge crane. The assignment itself was rather simple, although the preparation and physical labor were very involved. The brake cylinder was located in a very tight spot. Through the years, many of the cranes have been modified to add support, thus adding obstacles for the worker. Because of these modifications, my path to the brake cylinder was blocked by one of the new structural supports. I took it upon myself to climb into an unauthorized area with exposed electrical wires containing thousands of watts of electricity. As I stepped over the support, I realized my body was about to hit the exposed wire. My heart dropped to the floor as I turned white as a ghost at the thought of being electrocuted because of my negligence. This terrible experience taught me a valuable lesson in following important safety procedures.

Directions

(a) For some people it is easy to fall asleep, but it is the waking up that creates a problem. To get a person to wake up, you may want to try three methods: create noise, shake the person, and create a pungent odor. First try making noise. Usually, calling the sleeper by name will awaken him, but if calling doesn't work, slamming a door or running the vacuum cleaner can be effective. If you are still unsuccessful, try shaking the person or pulling the pillow out from under his head. If none of these techniques work, cook something the sleeper is bound to notice, or burn what you are cooking. No matter how deep a sleep the person is in, his nose is bound to react to this method. One of these steps will usually work, but if, for some reason, the person is still not awake, you should just give up and take a nap too.

(b) Loading a pig for market can be the most frustrating job on earth, but done right, it can be something you'll never forget. You first need a pickup truck with four plywood walls around the bed to keep the pig from getting out. Next you need a ramp with sides around it. The ramp must have two openings, front and back. With these important tools you are ready to get started. Back the truck up until it touches the ramp, the other end of which is in the pig yard. Then open the tailgate on the truck. Next, get yourself an old mop stick, pick yourself out a hog, and give chase. Whatever you do, do not get the pig tired or he'll fight back. Try luring him by trotting or walking behind him in the direction of the ramp. Once he is in the ramp, bait him into the truck with some hog eatin's. Then, close the tailgate and wipe the mud and pig droppings off your feet. If it's summer, water him down before you leave to keep him from overheating. Now get into the truck and get on your way.

Comparison/Contrast

One difference between the water skier and the snow skier is the amount of physical exertion each uses. Although the water skier is being pulled, he usually has to lean back on his skis and hold on to the towrope. This process enables him to have a smooth run across the water. Because of this position on the skis, he uses many leg, arm, and back muscles to maintain his balance. Thus, the skier can tire easily due to the strenuous effort. The snow skier, however, usually positions himself slightly forward on his skis. His boots, which are clamped to his skis, help to support leg and ankle muscles that he must use to maintain good body control. His ski poles also help him to keep his balance. The snow skier simply doesn't use as many or the same kind of muscles as the water skier. Therefore, he can set his own pace and speed, and ski for longer and further distances and periods than the water skier.

Classification

All snorers can be annoying to other people, but the whistler, the lip blower, and the nose snorter are the worst. They can set your nerves on edge and push your patience to the limit. Whistlers are constant in their nightly harassment. They take loud, deep breaths that sound as though they are sucking up all the air in the room, and they release that air in the form of long, high-pitched whistles. Lip blowers, who are more annoying than whistlers, use their mouths for exhaling. The noise created when they exhale sounds like a small motorboat slowly running out of fuel. This is one boat you would love to sink. Sleepers who snore with a snorting noise are the most irritating. When they inhale air through their noses, they sound like pigs feeding at the trough. All three of these snorers have been known to break up marriages, cause fights, and even disturb sanity. The whistler, the lip blower, and the nose snorter are the most irritating snorers, but the nose snorter heads the list.

Definition

Women have always been denied the forthright expression of even healthy and realistic anger. They may show anger in defense of a child but must never take up their own cause. To express anger—especially openly, directly, or loudly—makes a woman unfeminine and unattractive. When a woman is called aggressive, this accusation may repel other women, frighten men, and send the woman herself into despair. Women are the nurturers, the soothers, the peacemakers, and the steadiers of rocked boats. All our definitions of femininity have perpetuated the myth that the truly feminine woman is devoid of anger.

Analysis (also sometimes called Cause–Effect or Reasons)

I for one do not mind housework. In fact, I am very particular about a clean house. I like everything in its place and a place for everything. Although most people frown at washing dishes or cleaning the bathroom, these two household tasks don't bother me at all. Ironing is another story. I equate ironing with hard, unnecessarily cruel labor. I will put off ironing until I just have to do it, prolonging the agony. Whether it's the heat from the iron or the cement-like wrinkles in the 100% cotton shirts that I detest most, I'm not sure. That up-and-down, back-and-forward motion can drive me bananas. I hate collars and cuffs the most. Or do I hate pleats the most? Whichever it is, give me liberty or give me death, but don't give me an iron. If I were to win the big lottery, I would not hire a maid, cook, or driver. I'd hire an ironer.

 ## CHECKLIST: Remembering How to Write Effective Paragraphs

Ask yourself these questions:

1. Is my paragraph unified?
2. Is my paragraph coherent?
3. Is my paragraph well developed?

Writing Suggestions: Paragraphs

1.   Almost everyone has experienced the frustration of losing something, and possibly the joy of finding something. Write about such an experience explaining what you lost or found, how you felt about this, when and where it happened, and the result.

2.   Choose someone who is a special friend and analyze what makes this person such a good friend. You may write about a relative as long as you focus on how he or she is also a friend. Write a paper that gives examples of the qualities that make him or her such a special friend.

3.   We all have favorite foods, sometimes for a lifetime and sometimes for a brief period of our lives. Describe a favorite dish or food which you enjoy now or enjoyed in the past. Include when you first ate it as well as the memories which are associated with it.

4.   Explain with specific reasons why you like or why you dislike a particular time of the year. Do not try to take both sides in your single paragraph. Include such aspects as weather conditions, any associated holidays, clothing worn, activities, relevant aspects of nature, and any people with whom you associate at this time.

5.   Have you ever found that a smell, such as of perfume, fresh-cut grass, or a certain food, can bring back very vivid memories? Write of a particular scent and the associations, either good or bad, that it brings to mind.

6.   Most people at some point in life experience the joys and frustrations of owning a pet. Describe a special pet which you, or someone you know, have now or had in the past. Include some examples of the pet's unique personality. Or, if you wish, describe your ideal pet or one which you hope to have in the future.

7.   What a satisfaction it can be to choose a perfect gift for someone special. It could be clothing, jewelry, or even something intangible such as a trip or a favor. Describe a time in which you felt you succeeded in giving a gift which truly touched someone you care about. Or describe a perfect gift which you received and what it meant to you.

25c

¶

8.   When famous people are interviewed, they are sometimes asked what song or movie title they feel represents their life or an aspect of their personality. Choose a title which you feel represents in some way your philosophy of life and explain it. Choices can range from serious to lighthearted.

9.   Travel back in time to your childhood and search your memory for a day that stands out. Write of an experience that taught you something or which affected your character or view of the world.

10. Use time order to write a narrative paragraph about a frightening experience. Write about this experience in time order, but include only those details that deal with the frightening aspect.

11. Use space order to write a paragraph-length description of a room or another place that makes you happy. Does it make you happy because it is cozy, chaotic, or colorful? Try to decide just what it is that makes you like that place. Then, moving your reader in logical order through space, describe it, including only those details that develop your point.

Chapter 26

THE FULL-LENGTH PAPER

Learn to write a good full-length
essay of at least three paragraphs.

You have learned to write a clearly-developed paragraph, a group of
sentences about one subject. Now you can learn to write a full-
length essay, a group of paragraphs about one subject. Both a paragraph and a full-length essay have a beginning, a middle, and an
end (that is, an introduction, a body, and a conclusion). Likewise,
both a paragraph and a full-length essay contain a sentence which
states the main idea. A paragraph's main idea sentence is called a
topic sentence, while a full-length essay's main idea sentence is
called a thesis statement. A paragraph and an essay differ, however,
in (1) the number of sentences in the introduction and conclusion
and (2) the degree to which the main idea is developed. The following is a simple chart to help you see the relationship between
the parts of a single paragraph and a full-length essay.

GENERAL PARTS	PARAGRAPH PARTS	FULL-LENGTH ESSAY PARTS
Beginning	A topic sentence (one sentence stating the main idea of the paragraph)	Several introductory sentences leading up to the thesis statement + the thesis statement (one sentence stating the main idea of the essay)

339

GENERAL PARTS	PARAGRAPH PARTS	FULL-LENGTH ESSAY PARTS
Middle	Sentences which develop the main idea of the paragraph through examples and illustrations	Paragraphs which develop the main points of the thesis statement (Each paragraph in the middle, or body, of the essay will contain the paragraph parts explained in this chart.)
End	A concluding sentence	A concluding paragraph which summarizes the main points of the thesis statement and restates the thesis statement in words slightly different from its original wording

The following are a paragraph and a full-length essay on the same topic: "Life at Sea—Yesterday and Today." Notice that while the paragraph is not nearly as developed as the full-length essay, they share the same structure: a beginning, middle, and end.

Paragraph

Life at Sea—Yesterday and Today

TOPIC SENTENCE   Life at sea today differs from life at sea two hundred years ago in four areas: food, living conditions, working conditions, and discipline. First, a typical sailor's diet aboard ship differs from that of his counterpart two hundred years ago. Today's sailor can look forward to meals planned for quality, nutrition, and variety while his counterpart's normal fare was salted meat stored in barrels and hard sea biscuits. Second, the living conditions of today's sailor differ drastically from those of his counterpart. While today's sailor enjoys spacious bunks and adequate locker space, a sailor two hundred years ago would have slept wherever he found a soft plank, often near his battle station.

BODY (MIDDLE)

BODY (MIDDLE) (CONT.)

Third, the working conditions differ greatly. Today's sailor may work a normal eight-hour day with adequate time for rest and relaxation while his counterpart worked constantly, never being allowed more than eight hours' sleep every thirty-two hours. Finally, discipline at sea has undergone many changes. When today's sailor is disciplined, he is usually fined, reduced in position, or jailed, depending on the nature of the offense. Yesterday's sailor, however, endured the harsh punishment of flogging, being beaten with the "cat" (the tackle used to hoist the anchor). While a routine minor offense would require twelve lashes, the number would increase according to the severity of the offense.

CONCLUSION

It is easy to see that life was more difficult for a sailor two hundred years ago than it is now.

Full-Length Essay

Life at Sea—Yesterday and Today

INTRODUCTION

THESIS → STATEMENT

From the viewpoint of a sailor of two hundred years ago, going to sea was like being jailed, with the added risk of drowning. Even today life at sea is a challenge, but a comparison of daily living conditions two hundred years ago and today shows that many conditions of life at sea have changed tremendously.

TOPIC → SENTENCE OF FIRST PARAGRAPH

Food is just one aspect of sea life which has changed over the years. Two hundred years ago when a ship went to sea, a typical sailor would not expect to see land again for some time. Ships were small, men were crowded together, and there was limited storage space, so the only foods that could be taken were those that stored easily and would not spoil readily. The normal fare was salted meat in barrels, hard sea biscuits that usually became worm-infested long before the cruise was over, and water that became so green and slimy in a short time that a sailor drank it only when necessary. A rare captain might provide some cheese or raisins, but since the cost of outfitting the ship came out of his pocket, extra rations were rare. Today when ships go to sea, sailors can look forward to an unlimited variety of foods and beverages. Meals are planned for quality, quantity, and proper nutrition. Usually little is spared to satisfy the crew, and although they may occasionally gripe, they may never in their lives receive better meals.

TOPIC → SENTENCE OF SECOND PARAGRAPH

Living conditions are another aspect of life at sea which has changed. It has only been in recent years that berthing of sailors aboard ship has even been considered. In early days a man slept wherever he could find a soft plank. In many cases, on warships, men were required to sleep near their battle stations. Men were not allowed to live ashore because of the high desertion rate, but they were allowed to have their wives aboard ship while in port. Many a lad was sired alongside a ship's cannon, giving rise to the old saying "son of a gun." Today, living conditions are a major morale factor, and sailors enjoy spacious bunks, adequate locker space, and additional recreation areas. In some cases, the crew are lucky enough to have wardrooms to live in.

TOPIC → SENTENCE OF THIRD PARAGRAPH

Besides these changes in living conditions, there have been major changes in working conditions at sea. In the days of sail it was considered too risky to allow idle hands. In consequence, a work day would last from sunrise to sunset. Men were divided into port and starboard watches. This routine allowed a man four hours' sleep out of his first thirty-two hours and eight hours' sleep out of his second thirty-two hours. Imagine living this routine for months at sea! This does not even consider the fact that all hands were required for such evolutions as changing sail. Nowadays, a sailor may work a normal eight-hour day with adequate time for recreation and relaxation. On merchant vessels there is often overtime pay for extra hours. Unhappily, the navy has not reached this point yet.

TOPIC →   <u>Finally, there have been changes in the forms</u>
SENTENCE OF   <u>of discipline used at sea.</u> Life at sea creates its own
FOURTH   unique community, which requires rules that a
PARAGRAPH   landlubber may not comprehend. In the navy of
two hundred years ago, the slightest infraction
usually called for harsh punishment. The usual
form of punishment was flogging with a "cat" (the
tackle used to hoist the anchor). A routine minor
offense would require twelve lashes, and the number would increase with the severity of the offense. The worst punishment was usually a deceptive disguise for sure death—a dozen through the
fleet. In this punishment a man was given a dozen
lashes, but he was tied in a boat and rowed to each
ship in port where crews were called out to wit-
ness punishment. Multiply these twelve lashes by
fifty ships in port! Discipline is still a problem, and
sailors still must face the mast, but gone are the
whippings and the cruelty of bygone days. Sailors
nowadays are fined, reduced in position, or jailed
for serious offenses, but they have all the rights of
every citizen and can appeal any cases. Justice at
sea is very similar to justice in any of our courts.

CONCLUSION   It is easy to see that life was much more difficult
for the sailor of two hundred years ago than it is
now. Despite the difficulties, life at sea has always
been an irresistible challenge.

26a
Plan your essay.

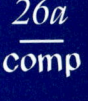

26a
——
comp

Planning a full-length essay requires more time than planning a
paragraph does. However, the steps of the writing process are the
same: discovering, organizing, drafting, revising, editing, and formatting. Before you begin to write a full-length essay, refer to
Chapter **24** to review each stage of the writing process and especially, in the planning stage, to review ways to discover what you already know about a topic and then to focus it with a good thesis
statement. To collect ideas for writing, try at least two of the discovery methods discussed in Chapter **24**: journaling, freewriting,
brainstorming, clustering, and 5 *W's* and an *H*. Next, study the ma-

terial you have produced to discover your purpose and main idea. Sometimes a thesis statement will arise from the main points you discover. The point is to keep studying your raw material until you become sure of your thesis statement, purpose, probable organization, audience, and tone, all of which are discussed in Chapter **24**.

26b
Write a good thesis statement.

Being able to write a good thesis statement requires that you understand both what it is and what it is not. First, a thesis statement is a complete sentence, not a sentence fragment. Second, it is a general statement, a position toward the subject, which you need and intend to support (or prove) in the body of your paper; it is not the statement of a fact. In addition to being a general statement in the form of a complete sentence, a good thesis statement often contains a list of the developing principles—that is, the major points each developing paragraph will explore. To understand further the qualities of a good topic sentence, study the following examples.

WRONG   How to avoid auto theft.
[This is a sentence fragment. It could serve as a title, but not as a thesis statement.]

WEAK   This paper will explain how to avoid auto theft.
[This announces the purpose of the paper. It does not provide a generalization or a position toward auto theft which the writer plans to explore or support.]

WEAK   I avoided auto theft by putting an alarm system in my car.
[This is a statement of fact, not a generalization.]

WEAK   Auto theft can be avoided by locking the car doors.
[Only part of the paper will be about locking car doors; therefore, the focus of the sentence is too narrow.]

WEAK   Auto theft is very common.
[This does not reflect the focus of the paper: ways to avoid auto theft. However, it might make a good introductory remark leading up to the thesis.]

BETTER   You are not as likely to have your car stolen if you heed the following advice.

[Your reader knows not only your topic, auto theft, but also your purpose, to explain how to avoid it.]

EVEN BETTER   You are not as likely to have your car stolen if you lock all car doors, park in a safe place, and use protective devices.

[Now the reader knows not only your topic and purpose but also the points you will use to develop your thesis statement.]

EXERCISE 1

The following are general subjects that might be assigned for full-length papers. The purpose for each is given. Taking the general subject and the purpose of each, narrow and focus the topic, decide what kind of audience you want to write for, and write a thesis statement. Refer to the chart in **24b-2** to help create a thesis from a subject and purpose.

EXAMPLE   Subject: automobiles
Purpose: to explain
Topic: A Comparison of Bias-Ply and Radial-Ply Tires
Audience: the consumer
Thesis: Bias-ply tires differ from radial-ply tires in three important ways: the manner in which the cords are placed in the plies, the difference in their wear characteristics, and the difference in safety provided by each type.

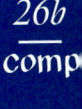

26b
―
comp

1. Subject: pets
Purpose: to give directions
Topic:
Audience:
Thesis:

2. Subject: gifts
Purpose: to explain
Topic:
Audience:
Thesis:

3. Subject: trips
    Purpose: to tell what happened
    Topic:
    Audience:
    Thesis:

4. Subject: heroes
    Purpose: to explain
    Topic:
    Audience:
    Thesis:

EXERCISE 2

Study the following list of sentences. If the sentence would make a good thesis statement, write *YES* beside it; if it would not, write *NO* as well as the reason it is a poor thesis statement.

1. My last trip to Dallas was enjoyable because of the company I kept, the food I ate, and the places I visited.

2. I went to Dallas in August.

3. How to change a baby's diaper.

4. The purpose of this paper is to explain how to change a baby's diaper.

5. Changing a baby's diaper is easy if you have the proper materials and a lot of patience.

6. I changed my baby sister's diaper last night.

26c
Write a formal outline to predict the organization of your paper.

After you have discovered your ideas and sharpened the point you want to make into a good thesis statement, you should create a formal outline. If you have thought carefully about the way you want to arrange the points you will discuss as you develop your thesis statement, your outline probably will not change as you go through the drafting, revising, editing, and proofreading stages of the writing process. However, writers sometimes find that as they draft and revise their papers, they need to add, take out, or rearrange material. Doing so, of course, means they will need to rewrite the outline so that it reflects the content of the final draft. A formal outline (or even an informal one) at first predicts and finally reflects the content and organization of a full-length paper. The following is a skeleton model of a formal outline which describes the main parts of a full-length essay: the introductory material leading up to the thesis statement, the thesis statement, the main points developing the thesis, the subpoints developing the main points, and the points supporting the subpoints. Notice that the main headings are indicated by Roman numerals (I, II, III), the subheadings by capital letters (A, B, C), and the supporting details by Arabic numbers (1, 2, 3). Also notice that the outline is blocked in such a way that the Roman numerals, capital letters, and Arabic numbers are followed by periods and are exactly under others of their kind.

Thesis statement
Introduction
  I. Main heading
    A. Subheading
    B. Subheading
      1. Supporting point
      2. Supporting point
  II. Main heading
  III. Main heading
    A. Subheading
    B. Subheading
Conclusion

26c-1
Learn to construct a sentence outline.

The following is a formal sentence outline which reflects the organization of the paper "Life at Sea—Today and Yesterday" at the beginning of this chapter. Notice that the introductory sentence and thesis statement make up the first paragraph (the introduction or beginning) of the paper. The Roman numerals describe the content of the developing paragraphs (the body or middle). The conclusion contains the main idea of the last paragraph (the conclusion or end). Note that the outline contains only one of the concluding sentences, not all of them. Likewise, if the introductory section leading up to the thesis sentence contains more than one sentence, the outline lists only one of them.

Life at Sea—Yesterday and Today

Thesis statement: Even today life at sea is a challenge, but a comparison of daily living conditions two hundred years ago and today shows that many conditions of life at sea have changed tremendously.

Introduction: From the viewpoint of a sailor of two hundred years ago, going to sea was like being jailed, with the added risk of drowning.

   I. Food is just one aspect of sea life which has changed over the years.
     A. Only food that could be stored was used in earlier times.
     B. There are fewer limitations on food today.
  II. Living conditions are another aspect of life at sea which has changed.
     A. Room for berthing was not considered then.
     B. Berthing is a major consideration today.
 III. Besides these changes in living conditions, there have been major changes in working conditions at sea.
     A. Working hours were very long.
       1. The daily routine allowed little sleep.
       2. The watches were long.
     B. Working conditions are better today.
       1. Sailors work eight-hour days.
       2. Watches are not as long.
 IV. Finally, there have been changes in the forms of discipline used at sea.
     A. Punishment seemed unfair and harsh.
     B. Today discipline is fairer.

Conclusion: Despite the difficulties, life at sea has always been an irresistible challenge.

26c-2
Learn to make a good topic outline

Some writers prefer to construct topic outlines rather than sentence outlines. As you can see in the following example, topic outlines use words or phrases instead of complete sentences in their entries.

Life at Sea—Yesterday and Today

Thesis Statement: Even today life at sea is a challenge, but a comparison of daily living two hundred years ago and today shows that many conditions of life at sea have changed tremendously.

Introduction: From the viewpoint of the sailor of two hundred years ago, going to sea was like being jailed, with the added risk of drowning.

I. Food rations at sea
   A. Kinds of food then
   B. Kinds of food today
II. Living conditions at sea
   A. Room for berthing not considered then
   B. Berthing major consideration today
III. Working conditions at sea
   A. Working conditions then
      1. Daily routine
      2. Watches
   B. Working conditions today
      1. Daily routine
      2. Watches
IV. Discipline at sea
   A. Harshness of earlier punishment
   B. Fairness of discipline today

Conclusion: Despite the difficulties, life at sea has always been an irresistible challenge.

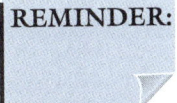 **REMINDER:**   Writing Outlines

26c
___
org

Topic and sentence outlines are equally effective. Unless your instructor directs you otherwise, choose the form you like best. Remember, though, the following guidelines:

1. Each entry in a topic outline is capitalized; however, there is no period after each entry.
2. You must commit to either a topic or a sentence outline and never mix the two. That is, there should never be a complete

sentence in the body (the part with Roman numerals) of a topic outline or a sentence fragment in the body of a sentence outline.

3. If you write a topic outline, your headings should be parallel in form. For instance, if you use a noun phrase in one heading, you should use noun phrases in other headings related to it.

CONFUSING   IV. Discipline
          A. Harsh punishment [noun phrase]
          B. Is easier and fairer today [verb phrase]

BETTER   IV. Discipline
          A. Harshness of earlier punishment
            [noun phrase]
          B. Fairness of discipline today [noun phrase]

4. Make sure your headings do not overlap. Each heading should explore a point which is different from the others.

OVERLAPPING   IV. There have been changes in the forms of discipline used at sea.
          A. Punishment was unfair and hard.
          B. A minor offense would require several lashes.

NO OVERLAPPING   IV. There have been changes in the forms of discipline used at sea.
          A. Punishment was unfair and hard.
          B. Today's discipline is fairer.

5. Do not use a I without at least a II, an A without at least a B, or a 1 without at least a 2.

EXERCISE 3

Study the following outline. Then list seven things which are wrong with it. Use the five guidelines above to help you locate the errors.

The Advantages of a Community College Education

Introductory Sentence: Each year, more and more high school graduates are choosing to attend community colleges instead of four-year institutions.

Thesis Statement: Attending a community college has several advantages in terms of cost, class size, and availability of the professors.

I. Cost
    a. Tuition
    b. Student activity fees.
II. Classes are small.
    A. Lecture classes
        B. Labs
III. Availability of professors
    A. Office hours
    B. Phone conferences
        1. During office hours

Conclusion: Because of cost, class size, and availability of professors, attending a community college for the first two years of a baccalaureate degree is a wise choice.

26d
In a full-length paper, develop each paragraph adequately.

With the exception of the introductory and concluding paragraphs, each paragraph of a full-length paper should be shaped like a mini-essay: It should have a beginning, a middle, and an end. Because of these three requirements, a paragraph should contain no fewer than three sentences. In fact, a really well-developed paragraph will usually have more than three sentences because it should contain examples and illustrations as well as the topic sentence and concluding sentence. The following is the beginning of an essay titled "Why Refrigerators Should Be Cleaned Once a Year." Note how choppy and ultimately confusing the writing sounds because the paragraphs are too short.

26d
org

Why Refrigerators Should
Be Cleaned Once a Year

Many changes have lightened a homemaker's tasks over the past several years, but one inescapable chore remains.

It is my position that all refrigerators should have an annual cleaning.

One of the reasons for this radical stand is the inner space factor. Remember this around the holiday season.

There will be no room for the special culinary delights synonymous with the season if there are forty plastic containers jammed into the fridge.

There is yet another problem posed by the overstuffed refrigerator. A new supply of liquid refreshment will be without a cool . . .

The following is the same paper, divided into complete paragraphs. The writer begins a new paragraph only when a new point is introduced. Study this revised version of the paper, noting the ways in which the paragraphs have been nicely developed through examples.

Why Refrigerators Should Be Cleaned Once a Year

THESIS →
STATEMENT

Many changes have lightened a homemaker's tasks over the past several years, but one inescapable chore remains. It is my position that all refrigerators should have an annual cleaning.

FIRST
REASON

One of the reasons for this radical stand is the inner space factor. Remember this around the holiday season. There will be no room for the special culinary delights synonymous with the season if there are forty plastic containers jammed into the fridge. There is yet another problem posed by the overstuffed refrigerator. A new supply of liquid refreshment will be without a cool home if the half-full jars of pickles are not thrown to the great god of garbage.

SECOND
REASON

Another reason for cleaning the refrigerator is known as family pressure. Eventually, your spouse will get tired of trying to find the leftover pork chop when there are twenty tinfoil-wrapped objects, none of which is labeled for content. The children become quite unreasonable when told that the chocolate syrup is "somewhere in the back" when they cannot find the middle, much less the back. The final blow comes when your mother comes over and tries to help by getting her own milk for her coffee. The despairing cry of "How can you find anything in here?" is a sure-fire method of making you feel guilty.

THIRD REASON   There is a third reason for attempting to clean out the refrigerator: the threat from everyone to call the Health Department. You are reminded that it is illegal to grow mold and fungus without a medical laboratory license. A mumbled mention of being a "threat to public health" makes you realize that a thorough cleaning may be necessary.

CONCLUSION   Finally, bowing to the inevitable, you break out the Arm & Hammer baking soda and get the job done. "That," you can say, "is it—until the next year."

26e
Write an effective introduction to your paper.

In a single paragraph or a paragraph-length paper, the topic sentence (the main idea of the paragraph) often comes first and serves by itself as the introduction. In a full-length essay, however, the thesis statement (the main idea of the entire essay) does not serve by itself as the introduction. Although the thesis statement does appear in the introductory paragraph (usually as the last sentence), it needs to be framed or led up to by several sentences which encourage the reader's interest in your topic. Think of those sentences which lead up to your thesis as a kind of warmup act for the main event. There are several ways you can warm up your reader.

26e-1
Begin by asking a question which your essay will answer.

Could your home be taken from you? Real-estate taxes could do this very thing if you are on a low, fixed income. People retiring on Social Security are finding that they must give up their homes because of sky-rocketing real-estate taxes. This problem could be solved if real-estate taxes were eliminated in favor of income taxes.

26e-2
Begin with a direct quotation which ties into your topic.

It has often been said that "a fool and his money are soon parted." Although they would never be considered fools, many retirees on low, fixed incomes are finding that they must give up their homes because of

26e
log

sky-rocketing real-estate taxes. People retiring on Social Security need to be made aware of the fact that unless tax laws change, they may be in danger of being "parted" from their homes. However, this problem could be solved if real-estate taxes were eliminated in favor of income taxes.

26e-3
Begin by telling a little story.

Last fall retirees Bill and Diane Logan were forced to sell their home of forty-five years and rent a small apartment. Despite the fact that their house was paid for and their children were raised, their combined retirement incomes could not absorb the cost of their yearly real-estate taxes on their home. People retiring on Social Security need to be. . . .

26e-4
Begin by defining a term.

Homeless can be defined as "having no home or haven." Although we are used to thinking of the homeless as those who live in cardboard boxes and pilfer through dumpsters for food, another group of citizens is joining the ranks of the homeless despite the fact that these citizens have held jobs and owned their own home all their adult lives. I am referring to retirees on low, fixed incomes. . . .

26f
Write an effective conclusion to your paper.

The last paragraph of your essay should serve as your conclusion. Although the content of your conclusion will depend somewhat on your topic, a good conclusion (1) summarizes the points you have used to develop your thesis statement and (2) refers to your thesis statement without using the same wording that appears in the introduction. Because a good conclusion will do at least this much, it should always be at least two sentences long. The following are some suggestions for writing a nicely developed conclusion.

26f-1
Conclude by recommending action the reader can take to solve a problem your essay has explored.

Even though some feel that euthanasia is an inhumane practice, many feel that it is more humane to let people die than to prolong their lives when they are unconscious or in great pain, with no hope for recovery. Perhaps a law should be passed to provide at least terminally ill patients the right to end their lives when they reach a predetermined level of pain or dependency upon machines. After all, perhaps there is indeed a point past which life is not really worth living.

26f-2
Conclude by offering a prediction.

In the future, when our ability to sustain life artificially will be even greater than it already is, what will happen to the terminally ill and those in a coma from which they will never recover? Unless some distinction is made between "being alive" and "quality of life," our hospital beds will be filled with patients who have lain in comas or in insufferable pain for twenty-five years or longer. . . .

26f-3
Conclude by discussing a quotation.

Although my grandmother recently remarked, "I will fight for life with my last breath," when people are terminally ill and in great pain, it is sometimes necessary to help them give up the fight. . . .

26g
Be prepared to write different kinds of papers.

As discussed in **Chapter 24b-2**, the kinds of papers you will be asked to write in a composition class will differ in form and organization because they differ in purpose. For instance, a paper which sets out to explain how to avoid housework will be organized differently and have different criteria from a paper whose purpose is to explain how housework can affect someone's mental and physical health. The following are some models of papers you might have to write as well as their formal outlines and suggestions for writing each particular type of paper.

The Process Paper

A process paper, or paper of instructions, lists the steps followed in performing a job or activity.

 CHECKLIST: Planning a Process Paper

Here are some suggestions for planning a process paper:

1. Pick something that you know how to do.
2. Work through the process in your mind before beginning.
3. List any materials that you might need.
4. Arrange the steps in order. Check to see that you didn't leave out anything important.
5. Give the reasons for steps, when necessary. Include any warnings or cautions that are needed.
6. Avoid making your paper look like a recipe. Include all necessary words when you list steps.

Remove *the* tire from *the* trunk and place *it* nearby.

7. Since you are giving instructions, it is correct and sometimes clearest to use the second person (you) in a process paper.

In the outline and paper which follow, the writer considers the process of babysitting as a series of steps—first, learning about children; next, knowing the particular child; and finally, understanding the responsibilities of the job.

How to Be a Good Babysitter

Thesis statement: To be a good babysitter, you need to do more than stay with children while parents are away.

  I. You should know the characteristics of children from birth to older elementary ages.
  II. You should find out the interests of a particular child.
    A. Is he interested in toys?
    B. Is he interested in books?

III. You should have certain information about the child and his parents.
   A. Does the child have any allergies?
   B. How long will the parents be gone?
   C. What do the parents expect from you?
   D. Do the parents expect you to provide your own transportation?

How to Be a Good Babysitter

Now that families no longer live under the same roof with grandparents, good babysitters are very much in demand. To be a good babysitter, you need to do more than stay with children while parents are away.

First, you should know the characteristics of children from birth to elementary ages. This will enable you to deal psychologically with special situations which may arise. For instance, it is better to love and pay attention to the child who has been harmed by another one than to deal harshly with the one who has dealt the blow. The characteristics of infants and preschool children vary more from year to year than they do in early and older elementary ages. A child two years old shows more changes over a year's time than does a child six years old. The two-year old likes to be with other children but has not learned how to play with other children yet. Early elementary-age children like to please their peers, and older elementary-age children are interested in forming clubs and groups. If you are aware of these interests, you can identify with children on their level.

Next you should try to find out the interests of the particular child you will be taking care of. What are the child's favorite toys, games, and books? If the child has a good imagination and likes the sound of words, you might get out your old Dr. Seuss books, like *The Cat in the Hat* or *Green Eggs and Ham*, before you arrive to babysit. The child's interests are important to him, and by knowing what he likes, you will be able to share in his activities, making sitting an enjoyable pastime for the child and you.

Finally, you should have information about the child and his parents. Find out whether the child is allergic to certain kinds of foods or materials. This is good to know if you need to take a snack or toy to the child. You should also have information about the parents, such as how long they will be gone and whether there are meals to prepare for the child. A babysitter should have an understanding with the par-

ents about what each expects of the other. There should be an understanding regarding transportation, pay, meals, snacks, discipline, and the proper procedure to follow in case of emergency.

In order to be a good babysitter, you should have a genuine concern for children and be interested enough to keep well informed.

A humorous example of a process paper, "How to Avoid Housework," appears on p. **301**.

The Comparison Paper

A comparison paper shows the similarities or differences between two persons, processes, ideas, and so on.

 CHECKLIST: Planning a Comparison Paper

Here are some suggestions for planning a comparison paper:

1. Decide what you are going to compare. Be sure that the two items are similar enough so that there are some grounds for comparison.

2. Decide on what method to use.

   a. Deal with one item in the comparison completely. Then deal with the other.
      EXAMPLE A Comparison of John F. Kennedy and Bill Clinton
      I. John F. Kennedy
         A. His goals
         B. His presidential style
         C. His popularity
      II. Bill Clinton
         A. His goals
         B. His presidential style
         C. His popularity

   b. Or use a point-by-point comparison.
      I. The goals of the two presidents
         A. John F. Kennedy
         B. Bill Clinton
      II. Their presidential styles
         A. John F. Kennedy
         B. Bill Clinton

III. Their popularity
   A. John F. Kennedy
   B. Bill Clinton

3. Be sure to cover each point in the comparison thoroughly. If you deal with popularity, for example, you should discuss the popularity of both men.

4. Decide on a focus. For example, you may choose to emphasize the differences between the two items. In that case, you might comment briefly on the similarities, but you should then go on to show that the differences are more important.

5. Use details to illustrate your points of comparison.

The outline and comparison paper "Life at Sea—Yesterday and Today" appear on pp. **341** and **348**.

The Classification Paper

A classification paper divides one idea or category into groups or types based on some particular principle.

 CHECKLIST: Planning a Classification Paper

Here are some suggestions for planning a classification paper:

1. Decide on the reason or basis for classification. If you classify teachers, for example, are you classifying them on the basis of their classroom experience, their fairness, or their methods of teaching? Don't mix the bases for classification.

CONFUSING TYPES OF TEACHERS	BETTER TYPES OF TEACHERS
I. Teachers who use the lecture method	I. Teachers who use the lecture method
II. Teachers who prefer teaching through discussion	II. Teachers who prefer teaching through discussion
III. Unfair teachers	III. Teachers who use both lecture and discussion

2. Avoid overlapping categories.

OVERLAPPING TYPES OF JUNK FOOD	BETTER TYPES OF JUNK FOOD
I. Food for munching	I. Food for munching
II. Potato chips and pretzels	II. Food for slurping

3. When you classify, or divide something into parts, be sure that you have included all parts. If you classify teachers according to their teaching methods but you have not included all possible methods, you may want to make it clear that you are only considering the main methods, or you may want to narrow the basis or reason for classification. For example, you can classify spectators at a football game on the basis of how they look while they are watching the game.

The following outline and paper classify cashiers on the basis of how they handle groceries.

Supermarket Cashiers

Thesis: Three basic types of cashiers work in supermarkets: "slingers," "zombies," and efficient cashiers.

I. "Slingers" are the cashiers who use your tomatoes to practice their underhand softball pitch.
 A. These cashiers have come to the conclusion that an egg carton protects eggs from any force exerted on the carton.
 B. Canned goods are subjected to even rougher treatment by "slinger" cashiers.
II. "Zombies" are the cashiers who work in slow motion; all their movements seem to have been preprogrammed into them.
 A. "Zombies" give the impression of being robots.
 B. If you are unfortunate enough to have your groceries checked out by a "zombie," you will probably end up spending more time in the checkout line than you spent shopping for your groceries.
III. The best cashiers are the ones who are alert and who think about what they are doing.
 A. When you get home, you will find all your groceries intact.
 B. These are usually the fastest cashiers.

Supermarket Cashiers

Like everyone else, you have undoubtedly spent some of your life in a grocery store. While in the store, you may have noticed that some checkout lines have only two or three people waiting, while others have as many as ten or twelve. Why are the lines so unevenly distributed? The reason is that people prefer one of the three basic types of cashiers: "slingers," "zombies," and efficient cashiers.

"Slingers" are the cashiers who use your tomatoes to practice their underhand softball pitch. These cashiers have come to the conclusion that an egg carton protects eggs from any force exerted on the carton. "Slingers" seem determined to prove this theory by shoving your egg carton as hard as they can toward the low wall at the end of the counter. After your carton of eggs hits the wall, these cashiers are confident that you will be able to look inside the carton and see that none of your eggs has so much as a hairline crack. Indeed, canned goods are subjected to even rougher treatment by "slinger" cashiers. When you get home, you will find that many of the cans you had diligently inspected for dents are so mutilated that there is no way you will be able to use your electric can-opener to open them. "Slingers," as the name implies, sling your groceries with incredible force, using the logic that the harder they throw your groceries, the quicker they will finish with you.

"Zombies" are the cashiers who work in slow motion; all their movements seem to have been preprogrammed into them. "Zombies" appear to be robots because they seem unconscious of the world around them. "Zombies" have usually spent the previous night at a wild party and have no energy left. If you are unfortunate enough to have your groceries checked out by a "zombie," you will probably end up spending more time in the checkout line than you spent shopping.

The best cashiers are the ones who are alert and who think about what they are doing. These cashiers are very efficient. They never squash your tomatoes with your canned goods, and they do not set your gallon jug of milk down on top of your grapes. When you get home, you will find all your groceries in the same condition they were in when you first took them off the shelf. These cashiers are also usually the fastest to check out your groceries. They are the cashiers who have long lines of people waiting at their counters.

All cashiers have their own method of checking out groceries. Some want to get through quickly, others do not want to be aware of what they are doing, and others are very conscientious about what they do and how they do it. You can choose any checkout line you

org

want, but beware of a line with very few people in it. It is likely to lead to a "slinger" or a "zombie."

For another example of a classification paper, see "Types of People at a Shopping Mall" on p. **307**.

The Cause–Effect Paper

In the cause–effect paper you are explaining either why something happened or the effects of something which has happened or will happen.

 CHECKLIST: Planning a Cause–Effect Paper

If you are explaining what has caused something else,

1. State what has happened.
2. Give the reasons the event has happened.
3. Use details and examples as you explain each reason.

An example of such a topic is "Why Are Small Hospitals Closing?"

If you are explaining the effects which something has had or will have on something else,

1. Describe the conditions which have caused or will cause the effects you will explain.
2. Discuss each effect as it relates to what has caused it.
3. Use details and examples as you explain each effect.

An example of such a topic is "What Effects Will Closing Small Hospitals Have on the Community?"

The following outline and paper discuss three reasons that have caused small hospitals to close.

Why Are Small Hospitals Closing?

Thesis: The reasons cited most often for the closing of small hospitals are economic reasons, stricter government regulations, and the nursing shortage.

I. Economic reasons
   A. Operating costs
   B. Higher salaries
II. Stricter government regulations
   A. Diagnosis-related groups (DRGs)
   B. Increased paperwork
III. Nursing shortage
   A. Units improperly staffed
   B. Inadequate patient care

Why Are Small Hospitals Closing?

In the past few years a number of small hospitals across the nation have closed their doors. Why have these hospitals had to close, while others remain open? The reasons cited most often by hospital officials are economic reasons, stricter government regulations, and the nursing shortage.

One of the reasons cited is economics. Increased operating costs such as food, utilities, and supplies are causing hardships for small hospitals. Some of these costs can be passed on to the patients by increasing rates, but there is a limit to what these patients can pay. If a patient's insurance does not cover a good portion of the bill, the hospital may end up absorbing the difference or the hospital may be a long time collecting the money due. Either way the money used for operating costs is greatly affected. Employee salaries are another big item affecting the economics of a hospital. A small hospital still requires many employees if it is to operate safely and efficiently. As inflation causes living costs to increase, employees vie for higher salaries to maintain their standard of living.

Another reason is the stricter government regulations enacted in recent years. Diagnosis-related groups (DRGs) are a big milestone as far as the government is concerned, but are they really as beneficial as they are supposed to be? The hospitals do not think so. These government regulations dictate how long a patient is able to stay in the hospital based on a particular diagnosis. In some cases the patient is not ready to be discharged in the allotted time, and the hospital must absorb the cost of the additional days needed. New Medicare regulations and laws governing insurance companies have increased the paperwork for most hospitals. This means extra work, additional employees, and possible overtime for present employees.

26g
org

The nursing shortage is another reason, generally the main reason, cited by hospital officials for the demise of many hospitals. Smaller hospitals cannot offer the salaries or benefits that most of the larger hospitals can. Most units in the hospital are short-staffed, so the nurses are overworked, and absenteeism runs high. Because of these factors, patient care suffers. Not enough can be accomplished during a particular shift. When patients feel they are not receiving adequate care, they begin to look to other, larger hospitals. With fewer patients, the income of the hospital decreases. No hospital can operate very long with an increase in costs and a decrease in income.

While economics and government regulations have put a strain on many small hospitals and have forced many to close, the nursing shortage seems to be the principal cause. Increased opportunities in other fields have lured many away from nursing. Changes need to be made to make nursing a more attractive career choice.

The Definition Paper

In a definition paper you give the reader or audience a clear idea of what you mean by a particular word.

 ### CHECKLIST: Planning a Definition Paper

The following are suggestions for planning a definition paper:

1. Begin with a clear statement of what you mean by the word. Use a dictionary definition as a start, or define the term in your own words. (See **8a-4** on writing a clear definition.)
2. Say a little about the origin or history of the word, if it will help the reader understand your definition. You may give synonyms for the word.
3. Decide on the method of development.
   a. You can develop the definition by using several examples.
   b. You can develop the definition by using one detailed example. You can define laziness, for example, by showing the characteristics of one particularly lazy person.
   c. You can compare the word with other similar words. Folk rock, for example, could be compared with acid rock or punk rock.
   d. You can define the word by dividing it into parts or types or by showing how it works. A definition of a retractable

ballpoint pen, for example, would probably list and describe the plastic cylinder, the ink reservoir, the metal spring, the ratchet device, and the thrust tube.

In the following example, the writer defines charisma by giving the traditional definition, her own definition, and three examples of what she means by the word.

A Definition of Charisma

Thesis: Charisma is the unusual ability of certain leaders to inspire people to rise above their circumstances by cultivating the strength and courage of the human spirit.

  I. Franklin D. Roosevelt, who lit a flame of hope in the midst of a great depression
  II. John F. Kennedy, who inspired people to ask what they could do for their country.
  III. Martin Luther King, Jr., who touched the conscience of the American people

A Definition of Charisma

My dictionary defines charisma as "a special quality of personal magnetism or charm." I think of the quality in a positive way. My concept of charisma is that it is the unusual ability to inspire people to rise above their circumstances by cultivating the strength and courage of the human spirit.

During his famous fireside chats, Franklin D. Roosevelt lit a flame of new hope in the midst of a great depression when he promised a "new deal." He became president at a time when many workers were unemployed, people had no money for food, and many families had lost their homes because they could not pay the mortgage. As a result, the American people had lost confidence in their ability to control their own destiny and were afraid of what might happen next. In his inaugural address, President Roosevelt called for faith in America's future saying, "The only thing we have to fear is fear itself." After summoning America's courage, he established several work programs designed to provide jobs that would not

26g
org

only put food on the table but also restore personal dignity and self-confidence to the average American worker. Millions of people came to regard Roosevelt as a friend and protector of the common man, and this combination of faith and trust was the key to his success in politics.

John F. Kennedy exhibited this inspiring quality of leadership called charisma when, in his inaugural address, he told Americans, "Ask not what your country can do for you . . . ask what you can do for your country." In this challenging speech, he encouraged Americans to look within themselves for hidden talents that they could develop instead of depending on the government to solve all their problems. His personal charm and enthusiasm were contagious. Because of his belief that average Americans could serve as goodwill ambassadors, the Peace Corps was organized. Vigorously supported by the president, it sent thousands of volunteers abroad to help developing countries raise their standards of living. Although an assassin's bullet snuffed out the promise of a brilliant future, the memory of his personal charisma lives on through the "eternal flame"—an inspirational beacon for all who pause at his grave in Arlington National Cemetery.

In an emotional plea for racial justice, Martin Luther King, Jr., touched the conscience of the American people when he said, "I have a dream that one day this nation will rise up and live out the true meaning of its creed . . . that all men are created equal." By encouraging nonviolent resistance, King urged his followers to work for social, political, and economic equality for Blacks. He cultivated a spirit of black pride and self-respect in the hearts of minority people and called on them to take positive action to improve their position in life. A civil rights movement that began as a bus boycott in Montgomery, Alabama, in 1955 reached a high point in 1963 in Washington, D.C., when more than two hundred thousand people marched from the Washington Monument to the steps of the Lincoln Memorial where they heard Martin Luther King, Jr., deliver his famous speech. Partly as a result of his leadership, Congress passed the Civil Rights Act of 1964 and the Voting Rights Act of 1965. Both pieces of legislation were instrumental in improving the civil and political rights of thousands of people who were previously second-class citizens.

These American leaders were blessed with a rare gift—charisma—that enabled them to draw out the best qualities in the people around them, even during times of great hardship and adversity. They were men of vision and purpose who understood that the true strength of the nation existed in the character and spirit of the average citizens. By nourishing the underlying courage and strength of these citizens, they were able to convince them that they need not be mere victims of circumstance. On the contrary, these leaders held out the promise that it was possible, through self-help and cooperation, to change the course of human events—and they did!

The Persuasion Paper

In a paper of argument or persuasion, a writer states convincing reasons for supporting a particular position. See **261** on presenting ideas logically.

 CHECKLIST: Planning a Persuasion Paper

The following are suggestions for planning a persuasion paper:

1. Be sure you care about the subject you choose.
2. Be sure you choose a subject about which people might argue. If you argue that there is too much crime on the streets, for example, who would disagree with you?
3. Give sound evidence in support of your position. You may use facts or statistics from reliable sources, or you may quote authorities on your subject. You may also use examples or case studies that illustrate the points you are trying to make.
4. You should answer possible arguments of your opponents.
5. It is usually a good idea to save your strongest arguing point for last.

The following outline and paper try to persuade the audience that commercial and private planes should use different airports.

An Argument for Segregated Airports

Thesis: Providing separate airports for large and small aircraft would be safer in terms of relative air speed, wake turbulence, and relative pilot experience.

  I. Air speed
    A. Approach
    B. Landing
  II. Wake turbulence
  III. Pilot experience

An Argument for Segregated Airports

One of the major problems in air safety today is the mixture of large and small aircraft at most of the busy airports. The incompatibility in flight characteristics leads to problems in a number of areas. Although there would be many protests about inconvenience from pilots of small aircraft, providing separate airports for large and small planes would be safer in terms of relative air speed, wake turbulence, and relative pilot experience.

With the present mixture of aircraft at today's busy airports, it is very difficult for the air traffic controllers to sequence the planes on final approach. There is always at least one small aircraft that can fly no faster than 100 knots. Behind him is a large turbojet that can fly no slower than 180 knots. In effect, the small plane has used as much time at the runway as three large turbojets would have used. This overburdens an already busy system. The approach is difficult for the pilot of the small aircraft because he is being urged to keep his speed up to maximum all the way to the runway, leaving him little time to slow down and land.

Wake turbulence is another large problem at many airports. Wake turbulence is caused by the thrust and wingtip vortices generated by large turbojet aircraft. The turbulence from one of these large aircraft can cause control problems for the pilot of another large aircraft. To the pilot of a small plane it can be deadly.

Because of the heavy workload, the instructions issued by the control tower are rapid and concise. The relatively inexperienced pilot of a small plane often has trouble understanding and complying. It is hard for him to ask the tower to repeat an instruction when the radio frequency is kept busy, yet quite often his quick compliance with instructions is needed.

The Aircraft Owners and Pilots Association (A.O.P.A.) is the body which represents the pilots of most small aircraft. This group lobbies heavily to keep the major airports open to small aircraft. In spite of the efforts of the A.O.P.A. it is time to segregate the large and small aircraft. The safety factors far outweigh the inconvenience to the pilot of the small plane.

26h
Write the first draft of your paper with the understanding that it will not be your final draft.

After you have discovered your ideas, sharpened your focus with a good thesis statement, written a formal outline to predict the organization of your paper, and studied models of various types of writing whose differences depend on their purpose, you are ready to begin writing the first draft of your paper. As you express your ideas in complete sentences for the first time, it is important to remember that what you first write may turn into something much different after you have revised your paper. For additional suggestions about how to approach your first draft, see **24d**.

26i
Revise your first draft.

If you work the way most writers do, when you finish your first draft, you will probably have a manuscript with words crossed out, sentences written in the margins, and arrows indicating that phrases or sentences belong somewhere else. Revising the first draft does not mean merely copying the first draft over so that it is neater. Revising means making major changes by adding, taking out, and rearranging material in the first draft. For more specific suggestions about revising, see **24e**.

26j
Edit your revised draft.

After you have revised your draft enough that you are pleased with the quality, quantity, and order of the information, it is time to edit it. It is not time to copy your paper into final form; editing takes place on the revised draft. To edit your paper well, you must look for changes you need to make at the word, sentence, and punctuation levels. For guidelines on effective editing, see **24f**.

26j-1
Try peer review to improve your paper.

26j
edit

If your instructor permits it, peer review (sometimes called peer editing) can help to improve your paper. Peer review involves allowing other students in your class to read and comment on your draft at either the revising or editing stage of the writing process while you read and comment upon theirs. Peer review, usually done in groups of three or four, can be very useful if it is approached systematically, that is, if you and your peers are looking for specific things. However, it is not particularly useful if student comments are limited to "I really liked this paper" or "This paper

Peer Review Sheet

Directions: This sheet may be xeroxed and attached to each essay reviewed within the peer group. After reading an essay, students should write brief comments under each section and initial each comment. These comments will serve both as prompts for discussion within the group and as a record of comments for the writers.

Title of Paper   _____

Author   _____

FORM AND DEVELOPMENT

First Paragraph (Introduction)

1. Do the introductory sentences lead up to the thesis statement in an interesting way? Can you suggest any improvements?

2. Is the thesis well placed and sharply phrased? Can you suggest any improvements?

Developing Paragraphs (Body)

1. Do any paragraphs lack good topic sentences? Which ones? Can you suggest any improvements?

2. Do any paragraphs need more development through examples and illustrations? Which ones? Can you suggest any improvements?

Concluding Paragraph (Conclusion)

Is the conclusion thorough enough? Does it do more than merely restate the thesis? Can you suggest any improvements?

PUNCTUATION, GRAMMAR, AND USAGE

1. Circle and initial any errors in the use of commas, semicolons, apostrophes, periods, and question marks, as well as any other misused punctuation

marks. Discuss the correction of the error with the author of the paper.

2. Circle and initial any errors in grammar (subject/verb agreement errors, errors in verb tense, pronoun errors, and any other grammatical errors). Discuss the correction of the error with the author of the paper.

3. Circle and initial any words whose tone or level of formality is inappropriate for the essay. Discuss with the author of the paper the word or words you would substitute.

was boring" without explanations and suggestions for improvement. The following peer review sheet can help you focus on specific elements of writing as you participate in a peer review group.

26k
Proofread your final draft before turning it in to your instructor.

After you have thoroughly edited your paper, you are ready to prepare the final draft by either copying over the edited, revised version or by making sure your typed or word-processed version reflects all the changes you have meant to make. If you have been working on your paper for a long time, it is sometimes difficult to see your own errors, especially if you are tired. Consequently, it is helpful to proofread your final draft a few hours or even days later when your mind is fresh. See **24h** for proofreading suggestions which will help you to turn in the very best paper you can write.

26l
edit

26l
Use sound logic in developing your ideas.

When you write, it is important to sound logical or reasonable in every statement you make. If you make claims which are false or cannot be proven, your reader might think you are trying to be deceptive or are at least a lazy thinker. When your reader begins to form a negative attitude toward your ability or willingness to think clearly, he or she will no longer take seriously what you have to say. The following are some ways to be sure you are using sound logic.

26l-1
Avoid making generalizations which cannot be supported by evidence.

> Campus parking lots are always poorly planned.

The truth of this statement is almost impossible to prove because we cannot find out if every campus parking lot ever built was poorly planned.

26l-2
Avoid making generalizations about a group of people if the observation is not true of every person in the group.

> All students at the University of Northern Kentucky are snobs.

Even though you may know a few students from the University of Northern Kentucky who are snobs, it is highly unlikely that every student there is a snob. If you insist on making some variation of this kind of judgment in your writing, you must at least qualify your statement by saying *a few, some*, or *many* students at the University of Northern Kentucky are snobs, depending on the truth of the observation.

26l-3
Do not assume that one thing or event necessarily causes or leads to another.

> The campus parking lot is far from the building, so the students are frequently late for class.

Other factors besides the distance of the parking lot from the building cause students to be late to class.

26l-4
Remember that problems frequently have more than two possible solutions.

> The parking lot at our college should either be redesigned or removed.

Other alternatives for solving the parking-lot problem are available, such as reserving small spaces near the building for compact vehicles, changing the exit and entrance signs, and so on. Removing a campus parking lot is not the only alternative to redesigning it.

26l-5
Do not draw an overly obvious conclusion.

> The campus parking lot is not useful for student parking because students do not park there.

If students do not park in the lot provided for that purpose on campus, clearly it is not being used.

26l-6
Avoid appealing to prejudice and emotion.

> Legalized gambling is sure to lead to serious crimes.

The argument against legalized gambling used here seeks support from the reader's emotion rather than from logic. The idea of preventing serious crime is appealing, though the cause suggested in this sentence has not been proven.

26l-7
Do not use unrelated issues as part of your evidence.

> Why should we worry about auditing standards when the whole profession is falling apart?

The sentence contains two separate issues, both of which require careful consideration. Attempting to combine the issues without evidence to support either part of the statement is misleading.

26l-8
Avoid contradictions.

> Although my wife and I do not need to agree on every issue, her opinion should be the same as mine.

The second portion of this sentence clearly contradicts the first portion. Such a statement serves only to confuse or to amuse the reader.

26l

edit

EXERCISE 4

Number your paper from 1 to 11. Beside each number, write the section of the handbook (from **261-1** through **261-8**) which explains the kind of error in logic each sentence has. Be prepared to discuss the lack of logic in each sentence.

1. Night driving takes place after the sun goes down.
2. Most accidents happen at night and are caused by teenaged drivers.
3. Southern California has the worst traffic jams in the world.
4. The price of gasoline is rising rapidly, causing a nationwide decline in tourism.
5. Michelle is an excellent student, so she should be a success in any business venture.
6. Acid rainfall is the world's most serious problem.
7. People are happier today than they were twenty years ago.
8. Cities have two choices: ban firearms or hire more police officers.
9. Either day-care centers must be provided or children will be neglected.
10. Women are too emotional to be good administrators.
11. Although all of my teachers grade fairly, one of them gave me a grade I did not deserve.

EXERCISE 5

Identify and correct any errors in logic in the following paragraph.

Should Women Be Drafted?

Women should not be drafted because they have too many responsibilities. Women should be treated for what they were put on earth for—that is, to bring children into the world. If women were masculine and deserved to fight in war, this would be clear to men. It is difficult to think of a woman being shot down like a dog. Besides, a man can do almost nothing without a woman by his side. Just look at our best presidents; without their wives, some of them would not have been great leaders. If the United States needs women in its wars, women should either be nurses or volunteer their services. Women are gentle and loving, not at all liberated and demanding. A woman should stay at home, take care of the children, keep the house clean, prepare meals, and give support and love to her husband. Going to war would affect her emotionally. She would probably crack up. Since women are weak and fragile, they might betray themselves and their country if they were put under enough pressure.

26m
Although your instructor will often assign a specific topic, here are some topics you could discuss in a full-length paper.

Writing Suggestions: Full-Length Papers

1.   Places often have the power to affect our moods. Choose a place which makes you feel secure and peaceful or one which makes you feel uneasy or upset. Describe the features which have such a powerful effect on you. You may instead describe a place you used to visit in the past.

2.   Have you ever had a day that seemed charmed, when everything you touched turned to gold? Or have you had a day in which nothing you tried worked out? Write about the day everything went right or the day everything went wrong.

3.   Everyone has certain experiences, good or bad, which stand out in memory because of their impact. Write about an experience you learned from or one which in some way was significant to you.

26m
—
edit

4.   An experience that causes intense emotion such as joy or fear is one which we tend to recall. Describe a joyful or frightening experience, and explain its impact on your life.

5.   Have you ever had a very difficult decision or choice to make, one about which you debated quite a while? Write about reaching a decision or making a choice, including the result and whether you feel your decision or choice was the right one.

6. Special times can give us wonderful memories—or sometimes they can be disasters. Describe your best or worst vacation, Christmas, birthday, or any other special day or holiday.

7. Do you remember when you first met a person who became a special friend to you? Did you expect to become friends when you first met the person, or did it take some time or a particular experience to make you become friends? Write a story about how your friendship developed.

8. Imagine yourself winning an award or being recognized for some honor. Describe what type of award or honor it is, and write an acceptance speech in which you acknowledge the person or people who deserve some of the credit for your achievements.

9. Let your imagination go as you write a description of your dream house. Money is no object. If you wish, include a story about how you were able to build the dream house. Include what country or state it is in, the grounds, the house's style, and specific features of the interior as you lead the reader on a tour.

10. Be a movie critic. Choose a film you have seen, from current releases to classics, and write a movie review. Include strengths and weaknesses of plot and acting, any special effects, aspects you particularly liked or disliked, and persons to whom you would recommend this movie.

11. Think of a television show, either current or past, which you loved or hated. Explain your reaction, giving clear reasons for liking or disliking the show. Or use your imagination and explain how it could be improved. As a variation, you could write about a book you have read which influenced your life.

12. The debate about the effect of television on children goes on. Take a position concerning the good or bad effects of television on children and argue your case. Or give examples of the types of programs you feel could be good for children to watch and those you would not let children watch. Mention specific ages where appropriate.

13. Children's toys have certainly changed—but have they changed for the better? Think back to the toys you enjoyed as a child. Do you think today's toys are an improvement? Or do you feel that they don't measure up to that special toy you recall loving so much? Support your opinion with specific examples.

14. Have you noticed how diverse the student population is at your college? Choose one basis for classification, and divide your fellow students into three or four main groups, describing the characteristics and giving examples of each group. Possible methods of grouping include by age, curriculum, study habits, number of courses they are taking, area of the country that they come from, dress, extracurricular activities, food preferences, educational background, and career goals.

15. Have you ever formed an opinion about a person or subject which you later changed completely? Explain your original view and what events or new information caused you to revise it. For instance, have you considered someone a friend who later proved unworthy of your friendship—or discovered a friend in someone you considered merely an acquaintance or even an enemy?

26m
edit

Chapter 27

THE MINI RESEARCH PAPER AND BUSINESS WRITING

Learn to write a mini research paper,
business letters, résumés, memos,
reports, and e-mail.

The Mini Research Paper

Now that you have sharpened your writing skills, you may need to use them for special kinds of writing, beginning with a mini research paper or brief library paper. This paper is not entirely original; rather, it is made up of information from other sources such as books, magazines, and online databases, as well as other information you can find on the Internet. Using this information from other sources, you develop an idea or prove a point. However, your paper is original in the way you select and use your information.

You must carefully record the location, or source, of the information you select to support your ideas or help prove your points because you are using someone else's work. This record, or documentation, appears in parentheses within the body of your own text and in a list of works cited at the end of your paper.

27a
Choose a suitable topic for
a mini research paper.

Although your instructor may supply a list of topics, often you will be asked to choose your own topic. Base your selection on general issues that really interest you or that you already know a little about. If you have trouble choosing a topic, refer to **24a** for suggestions.

EXERCISE 1

Look at a copy of your city's newspaper, published on the date you begin this exercise. List four subjects discussed on the front page, three subjects discussed on the sports page, and three subjects discussed in the entertainment section. Then freewrite, brainstorm, or cluster on three of the ten topics you have collected.

27b
Locate library and online resources.

In the library of your college or university you can access material on your subject through the card catalogue, general indexes to periodicals (like journals, newspapers, and magazines), special indexes (like the *Music Index*), and various online resources which you may be able to access not only in the library but also from your own computer through the library's Web page. A librarian can tell you which resources are available at the library you are using.

27b-1
Use the library's main catalogue to
locate books related to your subject.

Although some libraries may list their holdings on alphabetized cards, most libraries keep their holdings in computer files. You can use either a card catalogue or a computerized catalogue to access works on your topic by either author, title, subject, or keyword. If you are looking for material through a subject search, you should enter a variety of terms related to the subject. For instance, if your subject is early airplanes, you should try not only "airplane," but also the "Wright brothers" and "twentieth-century aviation." You can consult the *Library of Congress Subject Headings* for additional suggestions on conducting a subject search on your topic.

27a
comp

The following is an example of an entry from a computer catalog (brief view):

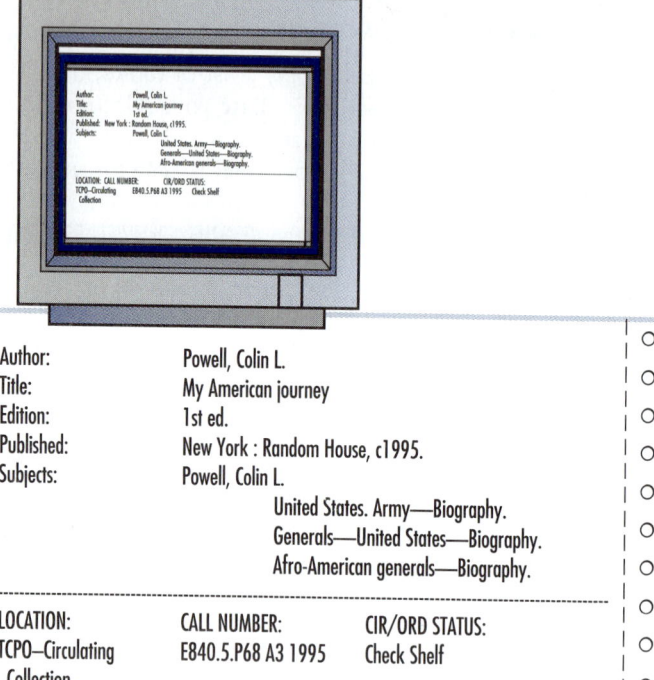

Author: Powell, Colin L.

Title: My American Journey

Edition: 1st ed.

Published: New York : Random House, c1995.

Subjects: Powell, Colin L.

                          United States. Army—Biography.

                          Generals—United States—Biography.

                          Afro-American generals—Biography.

LOCATION: CALL NUMBER: CIR/ORD STATUS:

TCPO—Circulating   E840.5.P68 A3 1995   Check Shelf
  Collection

The following is an entry from a card catalog:

```
E
840.5    Powell, Colin L.
.P68        My American journey / Colin L.
A3       Powell, with Joseph E. Persico. -- 1st
1995     ed. -- New York : Random House, c1995.
            x, 643 p., [ 42 ] p. of plates : ill. ;
         25cm.
            Includes index.
            ISBN 0-679-76511-5


            1. Powell, Colin L. 2. Generals--
         United States--Biography. 3. Afro-
         American generals--Biography. 4.
         United States. Army--Biography. I.
         Persico, Joseph E. II. Title
```

27b-2
Use the library's periodical indexes to locate lists of periodicals related to your topic.

Since not all topics are written about in books, you may find several useful sources by using the library's collection of general and special indexes to periodicals. *Readers' Guide to Periodical Literature* and the *New York Times Index* are excellent general indexes and may be accessed online.

27b-3
Use the library's collection of encyclopedias, biographies, and special dictionaries.

In the reference section or online, your library will have encyclopedias, biographies, and special dictionaries which you might find useful as you begin your research. *Encyclopedia Britannica* and *Encyclopedia Americana* are excellent choices whose entries provide a list of additional sources. Biographies such as *Who's Who, African American Biographies,* and *Dictionary of American Biography* are useful sources. You may also want to consult special dictionaries such as the *Oxford English Dictionary* and *The New Grove Dictionary of Music and Musicians.*

27b-4
Access electronic and online databases in your library.

The library of your college or university will more than likely house CD-ROM or online databases through which you can access information about your topic. CD-ROM databases like *Academic Abstracts* and *ProQuest* can provide not only titles of articles on your subject but also abstracts (summaries) and the full text of the articles. In addition, you will probably be able to access articles about your topic through online databases like *First Search* and *InfoTrac*. The most important skill you can develop when searching these databases is the ability to conduct a variety of keyword searches.

27b
comp

EXERCISE 2

Find one book in the library's main catalogue and one article in *Readers' Guide to Periodical Literature* on each of the following subjects. For each book, write down the author, title, place of publication, publisher, and date of publication. For each article, write down the author, title of the article, name of the periodical, date of publication, and pages on which the article appears.

1. Yoga
2. The Marine Corps
3. Stress

27b-5
Learn to conduct a variety of keyword searches.

Often students fail to find the material they seek because they do not try several different combinations of keywords as they conduct their search. For instance, if you are researching Bob Marley and conduct a search on "music," you are likely to come up with search results containing hundreds of records (titles of articles) which may not prove useful. However, if you narrow your search, you are more likely to find exactly what you need. The way to narrow your search is to use special words in your keywords. These special words—*or, and,* and *not*—are called logical, or Boolean, operators. For instance, if you are searching for information on both Bob Marley and reggae music, use as your keywords "Bob Marley or reggae music." To narrow your search, use, for instance, "Bob Marley and Ziggy Marley," which will produce only the sources mentioning both musical artists. To exclude something about your topic, use, for instance, "Bob Marley not Ziggy Marley."

27b-6
Learn to use the Internet for research.

The Internet can be a valuable resource when you are researching a topic. However, remember that because anyone can post anything on the World Wide Web, not everything you access can automatically be considered a legitimate source. Instead, the Web functions like a huge electronic library in which anyone can place a piece of writing, unscreened by the editors who practice the quality control of a publishing house. When accessing information posted on the Web, use the search engines available to you. There are many search engines available; some of the more common ones are *Infoseek, Lycos, Excite, Yahoo, and AltaVista*. After you direct a search engine to produce material (or "hits") related to your topic, click on the underlined material (called a hyperlink) to access it.

When you begin to access sources through a search engine, you will need to begin with keywords. Consult **27b-5** for help with choosing keywords.

EXERCISE 3

Choosing two search engines available to you, use the Internet to conduct a search using one of the following keywords. First, enter only the keyword. Next, expand your search by entering the keyword, then *or*, and then a term related to the keyword. Finally, limit your search by entering the keyword, then *not*, and then a term related to the keyword.

Shaquille O'Neal	George W. Bush	Al Gore
global warming	the Air Force	ADHD

EXAMPLES Keywords: **Michael Jordan** [Your search will produce all records in which the terms *Michael Jordan* appear.]

Keywords: **Michael Jordan OR Scotty Pippin** [Your search will produce all records in which the terms *Michael Jordan* and *Scotty Pippin* appear.]

Keywords: **Michael Jordan NOT Scotty Pippin** [Your search will produce all records in which the terms *Michael Jordan* appear without the terms *Scotty Pippin*.]

27b-7
Learn which Internet sources are reliable.

27b
comp

Before you begin to use an Internet source in your paper, you should decide whether the source is reliable. (For instance, personal Web pages are usually not considered reliable.) Ask of a potential source the following questions.

1. Is the author qualified to write on the topic? For instance, if the article is on a medical topic, is the author a physician?
2. Does the source contain references to other works respected in the subject's field? For instance, an article on the Irish writer

Seamus Heaney would gain credibility if it referred to an article about him published in *PMLA* (the *Publication of the Modern Language Association*).

3. Was the source written recently or was it updated recently?

4. Does the source reveal attitudes which would be considered biased or prejudiced? For instance, one might read with caution an article about democracy written by a self-proclaimed communist.

5. Would your readers (or your teacher) consider the source reliable?

If you cannot tell if a source is reliable, ask a librarian or your teacher.

27c
Gather the information you will use in your paper.

After you have located enough sources to use in your paper, prepare your sources in such a way that (1) you will have all the information you need for parenthetical citations and a Works Cited list and (2) you can use your notecards and/or photocopies of your material without plagiarizing.

27c-1
Prepare bibliography cards.

Putting all the information you will need for parenthetical citations and a Works Cited list on a bibliography card is a good way to keep track of your sources. If you put on the card all the correct information (in the correct order, with the correct punctuation) you can eventually easily prepare your Works Cited list by alphabetizing the cards by author's last name and copying the information exactly as it is written on your card. The following are some examples of how the cards might look:

Although there are slight variations in bibliographical entries, depending on such things as whether a work has several volumes or a number of authors, the following examples will help you to write entries for many of your sources. For additional help, ask your teacher to direct you to a style manual he or she prefers.

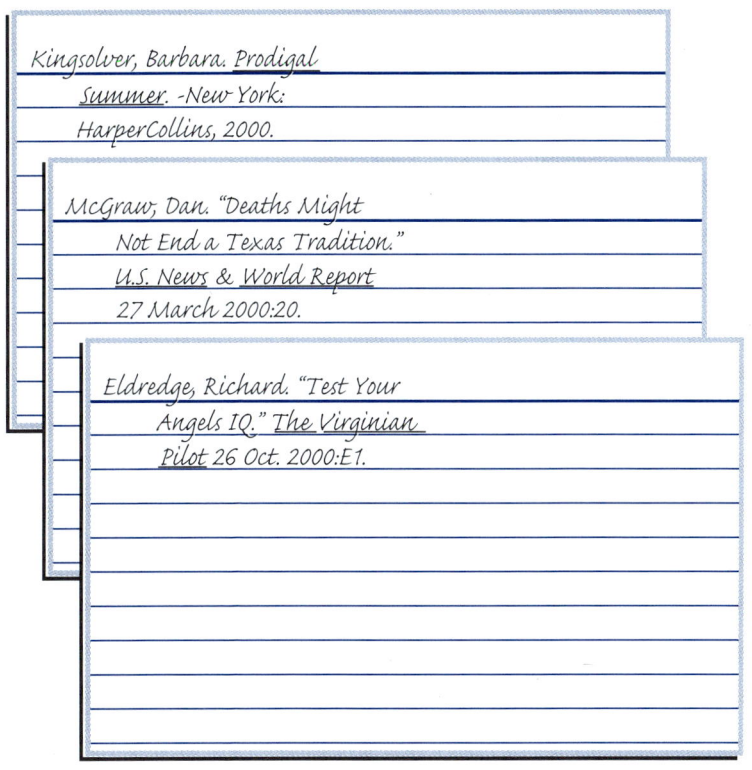

Kingsolver, Barbara. Prodigal
    Summer. -New York:
    HarperCollins, 2000.

McGraw, Dan. "Deaths Might
    Not End a Texas Tradition."
    U.S. News & World Report
    27 March 2000:20.

Eldredge, Richard. "Test Your
    Angels IQ." The Virginian
    Pilot 26 Oct. 2000:E1.

BOOKS: Most book entries include the author, the title of the book, the place of publication, the publisher, and the date of publication.

> Kingsolver, Barbara. *Prodigal Summer.* New York: HarperCollins, 2000.

ARTICLES: Most article entries include the author, title of article, title of publication, date of publication, and page number or numbers. Note that there is no period after the title of the publication.

> McGraw, Dan. "Deaths Might Not End a Texas Tradition." *U.S. News & World Report* 27 March 2000: 29.

27c

comp

DAILY NEWSPAPERS: Most newspaper entries include the author, title of the article, title of the newspaper, date of publication, and section and page numbers.

> Eldredge, Richard. "Test Your Angels IQ." *The Virginian Pilot* 26 Oct. 2000:EI.

ENCYCLOPEDIAS: Most encyclopedia entries include the author, title of article, title of encyclopedia, and date of publication. When you read an article from an encyclopedia, notice that the author's name is usually always at the end.

> Alten, Stanley R. "Phonograph." *World Book.* 1990 ed.

ENTRY FROM AN ELECTRONIC SOURCE: Electronic sources come in many forms (CD-ROM encyclopedias and online magazines, for instance). Also, the correct way to write an electronic entry changes fairly frequently because of the constant creation of new types of sources. The following is an entry for a periodical article accessed through an online service. Notice that you will always include five pieces of information in addition to the author, the article's title, and the publication's title: the date the source was created or updated, the name of the database, the name and address of the library, the date you accessed the source, and the source's electronic address. For additional help with electronic entries, ask your teacher to direct you to a style manual he or she prefers.

> Chenoweth, Karin. "When Hazing Leads to Death: One Campus' Response." *Black Issues in Higher Education* 25 June 1998:20. *Expanded Academic ASAP.* InfoTrac. Tidewater Community Coll. Lib., Portsmouth, VA. 10 April 2000 <http://web6.infotrac.gale-group. com>.

27c-2
Photocopy or print sources.

Instead of making bibliography cards for potential sources, many students prefer to photocopy potential sources (or print a copy if the source is accessed from a computer). If you photocopy or print your sources, make sure that you write on the photocopy or printed copy all the information you will need to create a proper bibliographical entry for the Works Cited list of your final draft.

27d
Avoid plagiarism as you select from your sources the words, phrases, sentences, and ideas you plan to use in your paper.

Plagiarism (using the words or ideas of your sources without parenthetical citations in the sentences in which they are used) is a serious error that could result in a failing grade for your paper. If you plagiarize, you are asking your reader to believe that the exact words and ideas of your source are actually your words and ideas. Plagiarism is, in fact, a kind of cheating; therefore, it is important to understand the various forms of plagiarism and ways you can avoid them. It is also important to understand how to avoid plagiarism before you prepare your notecards because careless copying from sources to notecards can often result in plagiarism.

The following are some common forms of plagiarism:

1. Using three or more words of an author in the exact order they appeared in the source without enclosing them in quotation marks and providing a parenthetical citation in the sentence in which they were used

2. Using even one word from a source without enclosing it in quotation marks if it is an "apt phrase"—that is, a clever, insightful, or original way of saying something

3. Putting into your own words an author's ideas without providing a parenthetical citation

4. Letting another person write any portion of your paper for you, including buying a paper from a service which sells them

EXERCISE 4

27d
comp

The following passage is taken from the essay titled "Life at Sea—Yesterday and Today" in Chapter 26.

Living conditions are another aspect of life at sea which has changed. It has only been in recent years that berthing of sailors aboard ship has even been considered. In early days a man slept wherever he could find a soft plank. In many cases, on warships, men were required to sleep near their battle stations. Men were not allowed to live ashore because of the high desertion rate, but they were allowed to have their wives aboard ship while in port. Many a lad was sired alongside a ship's cannon, giving rise to the old saying, "son of a gun." Today, living conditions are a major morale factor, and sailors enjoy spacious bunks, adequate locker space, and additional recreation areas. In some cases, the crew are lucky enough to have wardrooms to live in.

The following is part of an essay which used the "Life at Sea" essay as a source. Underline the passages which are plagiarized. Then add the necessary quotation marks and parenthetical citations.

Sailors of earlier centuries did not enjoy many of the privileges that modern sailors enjoy. For instance, yesteryear's sailors did not have a proper bed but instead slept wherever they could find a soft plank (Smith 24). In addition, earlier sailors could not live off the ship while they were in port; however, they could bring their wives on the ship if they were in port. One can see that being married was a definite advantage to early sailors. Today, of course, sailors enjoy spacious bunks and additional recreational areas.

27e
Prepare the material you will use in your paper by making notecards or highlighting material you have photocopied or printed.

27e-1
Copy the material you plan to use from your sources onto notecards.

Putting away your sources after you have made your notecards is an excellent way to avoid plagiarism because you will write your paper using only the material on the notecards and not be tempted to copy the words or ideas which surround the selected material. There are three types of notecards you can make: direct quotations, paraphrases, and summaries. Each notecard should identify the author and page number of the source.

The following is a passage from "Types of People at a Shopping Mall," an essay which appears in **24e**. Notice the way the material has been directly quoted, paraphrased, and summarized, depending on the type of notecard.

The first group contains the veteran shoppers. These people usually have a certain gleam in their eyes. This gleam comes from knowing exactly where everything is in the mall and having a mental price list for every item in each store. They know the best times to shop, the good parking spots, and the name of every experienced salesclerk.

Direct Quote

author, page number

People who have shopped for many years sometimes "have a certain gleam in their eyes. This gleam comes from knowing exactly where everything is in the mall and having a mental price list for every item in each store."

Paraphrase

author, page number

Experienced shoppers tend to know how to find everything they want to buy and what each thing costs.

27e
comp

Summary

> *author, page number*
>
> *Experienced shoppers know everything about successful shopping, from what things cost to where to park. They also know every salesclerk by name.*

27e-2
Highlight material you have photocopied or printed.

If you photocopy or print material you plan to use, first make sure that you have added any information you will need for an entry to your Works Cited list. Then highlight material you plan to use, making a mental note not to look at any other material on the page unless you plan to highlight and use it. It is also helpful to make notes in the margins of any ideas that come to you as you study the source.

27f
Plan the development of your paper.

After you have gathered and prepared your sources, it is time to plan the development of your paper. As with any paper, you will need to study the material you have selected until you discover a thesis statement and a plan for organization. For more information on this stage of your mini research paper, refer to **24c**.

27g
Write your paper.

When you have your material before you and an idea of your thesis and organization, it is time to write the first draft of your paper.

You may worry that because you got most of your information from your sources, you will not be able to write very many sentences that do not contain parenthetical citations. This is not true. The following is a list of places in your paper where your own ideas and wording are likely to appear.

INTRODUCTION: You will write several sentences which merely set up your discussion and do not use direct quotations and paraphrases from your sources. (It is possible to refer to a source in your introduction, but it is not necessary.) Likewise, your thesis statement will be an assertion of the main point of the paper and probably will not refer to a source.

TOPIC SENTENCES: In each developing paragraph, you will include a topic sentence which contains the main point the paragraph develops. This sentence will likely not refer to a source.

COMMENTS AFTER EACH REFERENCE TO A SOURCES: You should try not to refer to sources in two or more sentences which follow each other. To do so would make your paper seem like a patchwork quilt of other people's ideas instead of an exploration of your ideas, supported by your sources. Instead, try to follow a sentence which refers to a source with at least one sentence in which you reflect on the ideas of the source. To keep from using too many references to other sources, remember the phrase "Quotation-comment-quotation-comment, etc." Also remember that it is primarily your voice which should dominate your discussion, not the voice of your sources.

CONCLUSION: Although you might want to use one or two sources as you conclude your paper, the conclusion, like the introduction, is an important place for your voice to be heard. Here, you will summarize the points you have made and reflect on your thesis.

27h
bus

27h
Include parenthetical citations.

Each time you refer to one of your sources, you must include a parenthetical citation at the end of the sentence in which the reference occurs. Many students think that adding one parenthetical citation at the end of a paragraph covers all the sentences in that paragraph. This is not true. In fact, to do so would be an act of plagiarism since all the sentences above the one with a citation would appear to contain the student's own words and ideas when, in fact, this is not the case. Therefore, protect yourself by including a parenthetical citation in each sentence which contains material from your sources.

Basically, parenthetical citations include two pieces of information: the author's last name and the page number where the material can be found in the source. If there is no author, use a shortened form of the title of the article. Remember that whatever material you list first within the parentheses will key into the first piece of information for that source's entry in the Works Cited list.

The following is an example of a parenthetical citation.

> One middle-aged American notes that "the ease with which six-year-olds operate computers is astonishing" (Moore 45).

Note that if the author's name is included in the sentence, you need to put only the page number in parentheses.

> Wilroy Moore notes that "the ease with which six-year-olds operate computers is astonishing" (45).

Also note that if there is no author, the first piece of information will be a shortened version of the title of the article. Here, the title of the article is "The Uses of Music in the Twenty-First Century."

> According to one source, "dancing has served as a means of self-expression and communication since the dawn of time" ("The Uses of Music" 32).

27i
Prepare a Works Cited list.

When you put your paper into its final form, you will create a Works Cited list—that is, an alphabetized list of the sources you have cited in your paper. You should not include any source you did not cite in your paper. Refer to **27c-1** for examples of the correct order of information and punctuation for each entry you include.

Note that you do not number your entries. Also note that if an entry has no author, you should alphabetize by the title of that entry's article.

27j
Study the following mini research paper for answers to questions you may have about your paper.

NAME   Willie Davis
COURSE   English 03
INSTRUCTOR   Mrs. Melchor
DATE   April 24, 2000

Dangerous College Traditions

College is a place most kids dream of attending, not just for an education but for the start of their independence. There are many rituals and routines that a college student must follow to become accepted. Most of these rites of passage go back two hundred years or more. The majority of these traditions are safe and fun, but some college traditions are dangerous and deadly.

In 1999, one such tradition at Texas A&M became deadly, killing eleven students and an alumnus. There was a ninety-year-old tradition where logs were stacked end to end and set on fire, thus producing a bonfire. The bonfire collapsed, and a disaster was the result. One source states: "Some of the school's engineering professors warned that the wedding-cake-style pile was a disaster waiting to happen" (McGraw 29). Perhaps if the logs had been stacked on their sides, this disaster could have been avoided. "Still, however harsh the findings," says Dan McGraw, "there is no guarantee the unconventional ritual will die with the students" (29). One can see from this tragedy that it is not always the ritual that is dangerous, but the way it is carried out.

27j
—
rep

Continued

2

Another dangerous college tradition involves hazing. Hazing is the act of harassing pledges during initiations into a group. According to Joe Chidley, hazing can take the form of "sleep deprivation, public nudity and childish pranks or, at worst, extreme drunkenness, gross racial slurs, even beating" (18). Whatever the form, hazing can be mentally or physically dangerous. For instance, there was a case of hazing at Southeast Missouri State University in which a student "died after two weeks of hazing" (Chenoweth 20). The school had to answer many questions. Afterwards, the university changed its rules and began to offer "extensive training with campus administrators and resident advisors" on the problem of hazing (Chenoweth 20). One can see that an act which is meant to increase the bonds within a group can actually have tragic results.

Although disasters have occurred as a result of college rituals, this does not mean that all rituals should come to an end. Instead, rituals should be regulated and supervised so they can be carried out safely. Then the traditions and rituals can continue for at least another two hundred years.

Works Cited

Chenoweth, Karin. "When Hazing Leads to Death: One Campus' Response." *Black Issues in Higher Education* 25 June 1998:20. *Expanded Academic ASAP.* InfoTrac. Tidewater Community Coll. Lib., Portsmouth, VA. 10 April 2000 <http://web6.infotrac.gale group.com>.

Chidley, Joe "Bonding and Brutality: Hazing Survives as a Way of Forging Loyalty in Groups." *Maclean's* 30 Jan. 1995:18. *Expanded Academic ASAP.* InfoTrac. Tidewater Community Coll. Lib., Portsmouth, VA. 10 April 2000 <http://web6.infotrac.galegroup.com>.

McGraw, Dan. "Deaths Might Not End a Texas Tradition." *U.S. News & World Report* 27 March 2000:29.

Business Writing

Business writing is the application of writing skills to correspondence from, to, and within organizations and businesses. Although business writing has many specific purposes, all its forms have some essential elements in common. Since business writing must get ideas across quickly, it should be especially concise, clear, courteous, and correct. Therefore, it is important for the writer to check facts, maintain a professional tone, and avoid errors in format, grammar, spelling, mechanics, punctuation, word usage, and sentence structure. After all, you want the reader to read your correspondence, understand it immediately, and then act on it quickly. This is possible only if you do not have to write follow-up messages to clarify your earlier e-mail, memos, letters, or reports.

The following suggestions will help you with your business writing.

27k
Create clear and correct business letters.

A business letter is written to or from a business and is then placed in an envelope, with correct postage, to be mailed through some type of postal service. Since businesses rely heavily on this type of communication, it is important to learn how to produce excellent letters.

27k-1
Observe standard format guidelines when writing business letters.

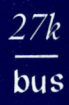

27k
—
bus

You may use several acceptable forms for your business letters, but two of the most common are block and modified block.

Block

HEADING | 4100 Snapdragon Court
Paisley, VA 88888
DATE — June 1, 2000

INSIDE ADDRESS | Mr. James Agee, City Treasurer
Paisley City Hall
888 Woodiss Avenue
Paisley, VA 88888

SALUTATION — Dear Mr. Agee:

During this past weekend, we sold our 1982 Buick for scrap. Please process a refund for the Paisley city sticker for this car and send it to our return address, shown above.

Today I called your office and talked with Mrs. Hernandez, your assistant. I am following her directions by enclosing the sticker that we scraped from the windshield and copies of both sides of the receipt for that sticker.

COMPLIMENTARY CLOSE — Sincerely,

SIGNATURE BLOCK | *David P. Jacobson*
David P. Jacobson

Modified Block

HEADING | 4100 Snapdragon Court
Paisley, VA 88888
DATE — June 1, 2000

INSIDE ADDRESS | Mr. James Agee, City Treasurer
Paisley City Hall
888 Woodiss Avenue
Paisley, VA 88888

SALUTATION — Dear Mr. Agee:

During this past weekend, we sold our 1982 Buick for scrap. Please process a refund for the Paisley city sticker for this car and send it to our return address, shown above.

Today I called your office and talked with Mrs. Hernandez, your assistant. I am following her directions by enclosing the sticker that we scraped from the windshield and copies of both sides of the receipt for that sticker.

COMPLIMENTARY
CLOSE — Sincerely,

SIGNATURE
BLOCK | *David P. Jacobson*
David P. Jacobson

27k
bus

As you can see, the block form aligns all parts at the left margin. Since formatting for this is a little less difficult, its main attraction is the speed with which you can compose such a letter.

The modified block form places the heading, date, complimentary close, and signature block near the center of the page. This more traditional style offers you the possibility of indenting the beginning of each paragraph and achieving a pleasing, balanced look on the page.

27k-2

Use the customary parts of the business letter.

The seven parts of a business letter are labeled in the two samples above:

THE HEADING: Of course, if you are writing your letters on behalf of a company for which you work, you will use their approved letterhead stationery. However, when you are writing personal business letters, create a heading consisting of your complete return address.

THE DATE: If you are using a company's letterhead stationery, place the date two spaces beneath the lowest part of the letterhead. However, when you are writing personal business letters, place it directly below your heading.

THE INSIDE ADDRESS: Identify the person to whom you are addressing your correspondence in the inside address. Include the personal title (Mr., Mrs., Dr., Ms., or whatever is appropriate), the name of the person, his or her professional title, the complete name of the company, and then the address of the company.

THE SALUTATION: Greet the person in the salutation section of your letter. Begin with the word *Dear* and complete your greeting with the personal title and the last name. Use a colon at the end of the greeting.

Dear Mr. Smith:
Dear Miss Smith:
Dear Mrs. Smith:
Dear Ms. Smith:
Dear Dr. Smith:

Note that you may use Miss or Ms. if the person is not married, Mrs. or Ms. if the person is married, and Ms. if you do not know whether the person is married. However, do not use Ms. if you know that a person prefers Miss or Mrs.

If you know only the professional title of the person to whom you are writing and do not know the name, you may use:

Dear Sir or Madam:

For instances when you do not know whether your letter will be read by a group or by an individual, it is now acceptable to use this salutation:

To whom it may concern:

Even though you can leave a specific name of a person out of an inside address and a salutation, make every effort to determine an exact name or names. Sometimes these names are available on the company's Web site or in library reference books listing companies. Taking a little extra time to find a specific, current name will help to ensure that your letter will reach its correct destination quickly.

THE BODY: Single-space the body of your letter, using double-spacing only where separation of the parts requires it and between paragraphs.

Get to your main point quickly, in the first paragraph, and include concise information. You do not want to lose the attention of your reader. It will help if you remember that the reader of your letter has piles of correspondence to sort through. You will want your letter to be one that he or she reads and responds to with swift, appropriate action. To ensure that will happen, you must use a professional, tactful approach with polite, clear wording and short paragraphs.

Make sure that the details you include are correct. Use accurate dates, names, numbers, and so on, and present this information in an organized manner. After you present the main point and requested action, your letter type should determine your method of organization. In the case of a complaint letter, for instance, you can supply the details of your problem in chronological order.

27k
bus

THE COMPLIMENTARY CLOSE: End your letter courteously with a complimentary close. Select from one of the most common expressions, capitalize the first word only, and end with a comma.

> Sincerely,
> Cordially,
> Very truly yours,
> Respectfully yours,

THE SIGNATURE BLOCK: Create a signature block by leaving four blank spaces after the complimentary close and then typing your full legal name. In the blank space created, neatly sign your name by hand.

27k-3
Add other letter parts as they are needed.

Especially when you are writing on behalf of a company for which you work, you may need additional parts.

THE SUBJECT LINE: Sometimes you will want to identify the subject of your letter immediately so that someone can act efficiently on the matter. Do this by using a subject line. The subject line usually appears two spaces under the salutation, even with the left margin.

> Subject: Order #7800, computer disks

REFERENCE INITIALS: You may want to show that you have prepared a letter for someone else. Indicate this by placing two sets of initials two spaces below the signature block and even with the left margin. The initials of the person who wrote the letter should appear first, and your initials should appear second.

> CDK/dt

ENCLOSURE NOTATION: If you want to show that you have enclosed something with your letter, indicate this two lines below the reference initials.

> Enclosure: Résumé

COPY NOTATION: If you are sending copies to other people, add a copy notation two lines below the enclosure notation.

> cc: Sally French

If you leave out any of the four optional parts, place the ones you do choose to use in the order listed above.

After following these format rules, arrange your letter so that it looks attractive on the page. That may require that you leave more or less space than recommended between some parts such as the heading and the inside address, but your letter should still present your ideas and information in an acceptable business form.

27k-4
Select the paper, fold your letter correctly, and prepare the envelope properly.

Because you want to make a good impression and you have taken great care to use business letter format, you must also follow a few final details. Use standard 8½-by-11 paper. After you prepare and print the letter, divide it into thirds by first folding the bottom third up, and then folding the top third down. It should then fit neatly into a No. 10 business envelope.

In the top left corner of the envelope, place your return address. Near the center of the envelope, write the inside address. Information in both address areas should match your letter's addresses. The U.S. Postal Service requires the following format. Note that the state's abbreviation is capitalized.

Mr. James Agee, City Treasurer
Paisley City Hall
888 Woodiss Avenue
Paisley, VA 55555

27k-5
Learn to write three common types of letters.

LETTER OF REQUEST: When you want to ask someone to do something or you need information, write a letter of request. Follow the basic rules for business letter writing. Remember to include accurate and complete details so that the person receiving your letter can act promptly.

One example of a request letter is presented earlier in this chapter. David P. Jacobson requested in his concise letter that

27k
—
bus

James Agee, Paisley City Treasurer, send a refund for an automobile city sticker. Notice that David Jacobson is following the directions given to him in an earlier phone conversation. Chances are great that his request will be processed.

LETTER OF COMPLAINT: You may be angry, or maybe just a little annoyed, about something that a company did or did not do. However, it is important that you maintain a professional, businesslike tone in your letters. Be direct and provide accurate information. If possible, wait until you have calmed down enough to be able to present your case clearly. Perhaps a company continues to send you the wrong printer cartridges, even after repeated reordering attempts. Maybe an employee was rude to you in a store. Regardless of what prompts you to communicate your dismay to a company, be firm but polite. This approach is more likely to produce the results you want.

The following letter is an example of a complaint letter. Notice the firm but respectful attitude.

4100 Snapdragon Court
Paisley, VA 88888
October 15, 2000

Mr. John Jones, Supervisor
Customer Service Department
Eat-Right Food Stores
1 Potato Lane
Rolling Fields, NC 77777

Dear Mr. Jones:

My husband and I have shopped exclusively in your food stores in our area for the past ten years. However, recently I have been unhappy with some issues regarding your stores. I know that you will want to know my concerns so that you can begin to achieve and maintain the high quality of service and merchandise your company once offered.

Early last year, I began to notice that your meat department was stocking pork products with more waste than usual. Also, I am afraid to buy chicken parts because the odor indicates that the products have been in the case too long.

Too often, I have to spend ten minutes or more just finding a carton of eggs that has not been damaged. I have mentioned this problem to the store manager twice recently, but I still find many discolored, cracked, and sticky eggs in each carton.

Your produce is also suffering from this new lack of concern. Oranges are often piled high in the cases, causing the bottom ones to become moldy and soft. Lettuce is wilted and brown almost as soon as it is displayed. In addition, your produce variety is not as good as it once was.

Finally, your store employees are showing a complete lack of regard for customers. I do not even expect friendliness; I just request common courtesy and respect. On one recent occasion, I tried to present my senior citizen discount card before the cashier rang up my order. She indicated that I would not need to present this card. However, when she finished my order, she expressed surprise at the fact that one item would have been offered at a lower price with my discount card. She then told me I would have to go to the manager's office to get a refund because she did not have time to ring up my order again. Her exact words were, "It's only 25 cents."

Although I usually shop in the store closest to my home, it does not seem to matter which of your stores I try. What is happening? Are you trying to open in too many new locations at once? I wish to continue to shop at Eat-Right, but I will not do so much longer.

Respectfully,

Virginia K. Jacobson

Virginia K. Jacobson

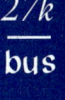

The letter is longer than the first one presented in this chapter, but consider the points covered. Mrs. Jacobson had a wide range of concerns and she covered each in a clear, organized way. Notice that she also mentioned that the company once offered pleasant shopping experiences for a long-time customer. She also communicated her firm belief that the customer service department would want to know of her concerns and that they would correct the problems. Do you think that her letter will get a positive response and achieve speedy corrections of the problems?

LETTER OF APPLICATION AND RÉSUMÉ: A letter of application for a job is one of the most important letters you will write. It is necessary, then, for you to understand that it is mainly useful as a cover letter to draw your reader's attention to your enclosed résumé. It should have three main parts. The first paragraph tells why you are writing and shows that you know something about the company for which you want to work. The second paragraph focuses on skills that you possess and that you feel may be useful in this particular job. The third paragraph asks for an interview and makes it easy for the reader to reach you. You may include a home phone number and a time when it is easy to reach you.

300 Cardinal Lane
Portsmouth, VA 23703
June 1, 2001

Mr. Melvin Olmbard, Manager
Human Resources Office
The Virginian-Pilot
150 West Brambleton Avenue
Norfolk, VA 23510

Dear Mr. Olmbard:

Your recent ad in the Career Connection section of *The Virginian-Pilot Online* indicated that you are searching for a competent programmer. My enclosed résumé should assure you that I am well qualified for this position. I know that *The Virginian-Pilot* is well respected in the state, and I feel that my expertise in my field will add much to your organization.

As you can see by my résumé, I recently received a Bachelor of Science in Information Systems at Old Dominion University. While pursuing my education I gained not only the knowledge presented in the classroom, but also the ability to troubleshoot computer problems and upgrade systems. Since you are currently looking for someone to lead your technicians through a series of upgrades, you will find my skills in dealing with people useful. I gained these skills in organizations on the campuses and in the community. In addition, I have held other positions which required me to guide coworkers in projects using Java and C++.

May I meet with you for an interview soon? I can be reached by telephone after 5:00 each evening at (757)555-1111.

Sincerely,

Roberta Chen

Roberta Chen

Today's technology requires that you be familiar with three types of résumé: the conventional printed copy, the scannable copy, and a version that can be electronically submitted. It is also important that you know which companies require or allow which types. However, the information submitted in all three types is about the same. Therefore, we will focus on one type only—the conventional printed copy—which you can modify to meet the requests of any individual company.

Begin the summary of your education with your current or most recent experience. Do not include anything before high school.

Describe your work experience specifically, starting with your current or most recent position.

Get permission to use as references at least one fairly recent employer or supervisor and one fairly recent instructor. Keep a word-processed list of your references and their addresses and phone numbers on a separate page so that you can supply them during an interview or upon request.

The following is a résumé for Roberta Chen, the young lady who wrote the letter of application.

27k
—
bus

ROBERTA CHEN
300 Cardinal Lane
Portsmouth, Virginia 23703
Phone: (757)555-1111

OBJECTIVE
To obtain a position of computer programmer that will allow me to use my educational background and computer skills.

EDUCATION

August 1997 to May 2001•	BS in information systems Old Dominion University (Norfolk, Virginia) Coordinated student volunteers for Habitat for Humanity
August 1994 to May 1997	AS in Business Administration Tidewater Community College (Portsmouth, Virginia) • President, Student Government Association, 1996–1997
September 1990 to June 1994	Diploma Churchland Senior High School (Portsmouth, Virginia)

EXPERIENCE

May 2001 to present	Assistant Manager/USFL Computers (Portsmouth, Virginia) • Supervise team of technicians • Specialize in data recovery • Assemble new computers according to customer wishes • Troubleshoot software and hardware problems • Accomplish maintenance and upgrades
June 1997 to May 2001	Head Sales Associate/Software Unlimited (Virginia Beach, Virginia) • Managed sales staff of 20 • Accessed customer needs and matched those needs to appropriate software
June 1994 to May 1997	English Computer Lab Assistant Tidewater Community College (Portsmouth Campus) • Helped students in two labs with on-the-spot computer assistance • Determined daily status of all equipment • Kept records of output and software and hardware requirements • Monitored and ordered supplies and components

SPECIAL SKILLS AND ACHIEVEMENTS

• Fluent in Java, C, C++, Visual Basic
• Certified in Microsoft (12/97), UNIX (2/01), Novell (4/01)
• Designer and installer of LANs/WANs

EXERCISE 5

Revise the following letter, correcting any errors that you see. Use the modified block format.

Apt. 3d
709 Cherokee Road
Portsmouth, Va., 23701.

August 2, 2000

Mr. James Wilson
Advertising Mgr.
Hadley Gifts

New York, N. Y., 10021

Gentlemen,

It has come to my attention that your illustrious firm stocks Reek-No-More cologne in 2-ounce bottles. I have long admired this scent and would like to order some for my cousin. Please send it by return mail and bill it to me at my present address. I would also like to know if you can identify the scent on the piece of cloth that I am enclosing.

Your prompt attention to this matter will certainly not go unappreciated.

Most Respectfully, I
remain

Janet Dawson
encl—one piece of
perfumed cloth

27k
bus

EXERCISE 6

Choose one of the following:

1. Write a letter to accompany an item you are returning to the seller because it is unsatisfactory for some reason.
2. Write a letter to an insurance company, asking for a review of a claim that was denied.
3. Write a letter to the placement office of your college, requesting that your file be sent to a prospective employer.

271
Observe current guidelines when writing memos.

A memo (memorandum) is a short letter sent to co-workers. Because it is used for written communication within businesses, a memo usually includes information about meetings, changes in procedure, announcements of changes in personnel, and so on.

Many companies now provide forms for memos. However, you can easily format one yourself. The following example shows one possibility:

MEMO

TO:
FROM:
DATE:
SUBJECT:

After double-spacing, begin the body immediately below the heading. Do not include a salutation or a complimentary close. Single-space within each paragraph, and double-space between paragraphs. Indent each paragraph if you wish. You may include reference initials, enclosure notations, and copy notations, using normal letter format. Finally, sign your initials next to your name on the *From* line.

As with any business correspondence, keep this communication brief, accurate, and precise. Give some thought to your subject line so that your reader can tell immediately what the memo is about. As always, remember that your co-workers will receive large amounts of correspondence each week. You will want those co-workers to read your message immediately and to understand you without a need for follow-up communication. Your well-worded memos will save everyone time and effort.

Study the following sample memos.

Memo 1

TO: Robert Kean, Manager of Materials
FROM: James Smith, Buyer   *J.S.*
DATE: March 3, 2000
SUBJECT: Meeting with parts supplier

My recent meeting with Hal Johnson, salesman for Consolidated Metals, was not productive. He told me that his company finds it necessary to increase its prices on size 24 bolts by $3.39 a gross and on size 49 screws by $2.89 a gross. In addition, he cannot guarantee immediate delivery.

I have set up appointments with two other suppliers for tomorrow afternoon. Perhaps I will have better luck then.

Memo 2

TO: All Department Heads
FROM: Charles Sims   *C.S.*
DATE: October 3, 2000
SUBJECT: Staff development

In a management meeting on July 15, I asked you to compile a list of various seminars, institutes, and lectures in your fields which staff members could attend in order to upgrade their skills. This list was to include brief descriptions of each activity, costs, names of employees who might attend, and your assessment of the plan. This information was due September 15.

So far I have received only three lists. I understand that you are busy and that you may have delegated this task. However, I am faced with the need to supply cost figures to our accountant by October 15 so that money can be budgeted for this project.

If you have not already done so, please send me this information before October 10.

CS/hm

cc: Randolph Howard, Chairman of the Board
      Elizabeth Holland, Accountant

EXERCISE 7

Write a memo using the following information: You are employed in the stockroom at Atlas Appliance Store, Sacramento, California. Write a memo informing your supervisor that the stockroom is out of the following freezer parts: retainers (56912-A), gaskets (777503-B), hinges (91256), and box switches (4847337). Include the date of your last inventory. Add any information you need to write a complete memo. Suggest the action that should be taken.

27m
Write accurate and attractive reports.

Most of us, at some time in our lives, must write reports. Reports serve a variety of purposes. They may show buying habits of a company's best customers over the past three years. They may supply information that is legally required by organizations such as the Internal Revenue Service. They may prove to a boss that an employee is progressing nicely in college courses for which the company is paying.

Reports written for employees within an organization (internal), and reports written for those outside the organization (external), supply essential information. They may be submitted by e-mail or by hard copy. However, in either case, you should organize the information so that it can be easily read and understood. Check your facts and do not include any unnecessary information. The idea is to get your information across with speed and accuracy.

One type of internal report that can be submitted either electronically or by hard copy provides the minutes of a meeting.

A sample follows. Notice the format the secretary used to present his information. Bold, centering, and white space help to create a report which is pleasing to the eye.

MINUTES
STUDENT GOVERNMENT ASSOCIATION
SEPTEMBER 19, 2000

Present: Glenda Allen, George Cutbert, Debra Gallo, John Tyler, Minnie Vargas, and Robert Zena

Absent: Marge Denver and Al Monroe

President Glenda Allen called the meeting to order at 4:00 P.M.

Glenda Allen reported on progress made in planning the Fall Fest for October. ABC Catering will provide and serve fried chicken, potato salad, green beans, roll and butter, soft drink, and cake at $4.00 per serving. She is still in the process of interviewing disc jockeys for the karaoke area. However, she has already reserved a cotton candy machine and a popcorn maker for the occasion.

John Tyler added that there is a need to get more students, staff members, and faculty members to attend the event this year. He offered to arrange for information to be placed on the campus electronic bulletin board. He and his committee will also make and distribute posters throughout the school.

Robert Zena reported that his committee is busily planning a blood drive for January.

Open discussion followed about the list of events for which the SGA will provide discount tickets this school year. Recommendations included plays, the opera, ice skating, a ski trip, bowling, and a visit to a museum in Richmond.

Debra Gallo offered to contact the appropriate people about arranging for the tickets for these events.

Submitted by

George Cutbert, Acting Secretary

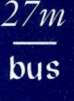

27m

bus

EXERCISE 8

Complete the following exercises.

1. Several employees in your office are consistently late for work. Their excuses relate to conditions in the parking lot. Your supervisor has asked you to investigate their claims and submit a report within two weeks. Write the report, supplying necessary dates, additional information, and your recommendation.
2. Your company is considering opening a day-care center for children of employees. You are charged with locating and investigating any such centers sponsored by three other companies. Write a complete report, including your recommendation.

27n
Write courteous, brief, and error-free e-mail.

E-mail is a wonderful invention. Whether you are writing to your friends, those at a company's Web site, your co-workers, or other business associates, e-mail offers you speed and ease of communication.

Always answer another's message to you promptly when possible. In fact, it is best if you answer as soon as you finish reading it. This saves you time and effort, not only because you will not have to open the message again, but also because the ideas are fresh in your mind. Often, however, you will need to look up information before you answer. Or sometimes, the person has written something that has irritated you. In these two cases, you should wait a while before answering, to either allow time to do a little research or time to help you avoid an emotional answer.

Furthermore, just because it is e-mail, some people have the idea that the relative informality it offers also opens the door for sloppy and careless correspondence. This is not true. Courtesy, a simple, direct style, careful spelling, and correct grammar are as important with this type of business writing as they are with any other.

THE ADDRESS: Get into the habit of adding to your software's address book the e-mail addresses of those you contact frequently. Most programs offer a very simple way to do this. With practice, you will actually save yourself time. Usually, when you are beginning to write an e-mail message, you should just start typing the person's name in the address block. If that address is in your file, the formatted name and address will appear quickly in the space. This feature enables you to proceed promptly. If you learn to do this, you will not have to waste your time searching for an old message from the person before you can press *Reply* and write back.

THE SUBJECT LINE: Always fill in the subject block. It may turn out to be the most important part of your e-mail because it is one of the first things the person to whom you are writing sees. If the subject block is blank, or if it contains a subject which is not specific enough or is misleading, the person may not even read your message. Worse yet, the recipient may delete the message because he or she is too busy to figure out what you mean.

Give some thought to the purpose of your message and then add a subject line that will get your reader's attention. For instance, if you are writing to ask your supervisor if you can attend training sessions offered out of state next month, do not just write *trip*. That, of course, is too general. Instead, write *Myrtle Beach Training*.

If you are corresponding with someone with a series of replies, it is better to come up with a fresh subject line instead of using the same one a second time. Multiple messages with the same subject line can cause confusion.

THE GREETING: Use a greeting in all of your e-mail messages. It shows courtesy and lets your reader know that you are writing this message to him or her and not to a group. As with any correspondence, however, let the occasion and the relationship you have with your reader determine the formality of your greeting. You may use *Hi, Brian*, or *Dear Dr. Callahan*, depending on the situation and whether you are writing this at your work station or from your home computer.

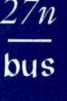

27n
bus

THE BODY: Organize your ideas and be as brief as possible. Keep in mind that your message will be read from a screen, so be considerate of your reader. Begin with the most important details first, and do not include anything unnecessary. Try to restrict your message to the length of one screen. Sometimes this is not possible. Nevertheless, if you cover the essential information in the first couple paragraphs, the person who receives your message can stop reading before the end and still get the main ideas.

As with any correspondence, be courteous. Never use offensive language. Also, select simple, direct words so that your reader can easily and quickly understand your intent. Do not ramble.

Do not use an unusual font or italic or bold type unless you know for sure that the reader has software and hardware that can recognize those features. If not, the reader may receive a garbled message or one that he or she cannot even open.

Avoid making pictures from punctuation marks, like :-) or :-(or ;-) or :/. Also limit your use of popular e-mail acronyms like *tnx* for *thanks*. Furthermore, do not use all capitals because in e-mail messages this is like shouting.

Finally, remember to proofread carefully. Why write messages if they do not say what you want them to say? In addition, careless misspellings and word, sentence, and grammar errors may give the reader the idea that you do not think he or she is worth the effort it would take you to correct these problems. Show your respect with all of your correspondence, even if your message contains bad news or indicates that you are unhappy about something.

THE CLOSING AND SIGNATURE: Include a closing, even if you wish to use an informal one like *Thank you*. Use a more formal one like *Respectfully* if you wish. End it with a comma. Then skip a line or two and type your name. Depending on the situation, you may use only your first name, your first and last name, or both names and a title. This makes your message more personal and shows courtesy.

 Caution: Remember that you are not anonymous when you write e-mail messages. Your correspondence can be tracked. It also can be forwarded, and you will be revealed as the originator of the message. Therefore, whether you are writing to a friend or fellow worker or supervisor, adjust your tone so that you do not embarrass yourself or your reader.

EXERCISE 9

You want to ask a co-worker to attend a luncheon conference with you. You are willing to drive even though the event is forty miles away. Make up details, and compose an e-mail message.

Then, respond to this same e-mail as if you are the person who has received the message.

 CHECKLIST: Writing Effective Business Correspondence

Ask yourself these questions:

1. Have I followed format directions?
2. Is my correspondence   Concise?
                           Clear?
                           Correct?
                           Courteous?

27a
comp

Chapter 28

ESL REFERENCE GUIDE

Review basic ESL concerns.

If English is your second language, you will find that many sections in this handbook will be of help to you; the ESL index lists these sections. There are also special areas, however, where writers who have studied English in ESL classes or who have had classes in English before coming to this country may need some additional assistance. This chapter is meant to help these writers.

28a
Use the correct articles when and where they are needed.

You may find that you still have questions at times about when to use articles (*a*, *an*, and *the*). Here are some guidelines.

28a-1
Use *a* (or *an*) before a singular count noun that you have not mentioned before; use *the* before a count noun that you have already mentioned.

A count noun is (simply), a noun that can be counted (a boy, a tree, an idea, a house, etc.). If you have mentioned the noun (boy, tree, idea, house, etc.), use *the* because the reader already knows what particular boy, tree, idea, or house you mean.

I saw *a* boy crossing Main Street.

[*A* boy suggests a single boy, but the reader doesn't know who he is.]

I saw *the* boy crossing Main Street.

[*The* boy means that the reader already knows what boy you mean.]

An idea occurred to me this morning.

[You haven't told the reader what the idea is.]

The idea occurred to me this morning.

[You have already identified or described the idea to your reader.]

28a-2

Do not use *a* or *an* with any noncount noun.

A noncount noun is a noun that cannot be divided without adding a word or an expression like *some, any, more, a box of, a piece of,* or *a pound of.*

Here are some common noncount nouns:

ABSTRACT WORDS	FOOD OR DRINK	OTHER COMMON NONCOUNT NOUNS
ability	bread	chemistry (and other school subjects)
advice	butter	
courage	flour	furniture
friendship	lettuce	homework
happiness	milk	money
honesty	rice	surgery
interference	sugar	traffic
truthfulness	wine	weather
wisdom		work

WRONG	a flour
RIGHT	flour OR a pound of flour
WRONG	a bread
RIGHT	bread OR a loaf of bread
WRONG	a happiness
RIGHT	some happiness

28a

Some nouns can be either count or noncount, depending on what you mean to say.

> COUNT   I picked out *a* chicken for dinner. [Just one chicken.]
>
> NONCOUNT   We had chicken for dinner. [Chicken is the name of the dish; you don't know how many chickens were eaten.]

If you have some doubt about whether the noun you are using is count or noncount, it is wise to consult an ESL dictionary.

28a-3
Use *the* with a noun in certain cases.

You usually use *the* with a noun

when the noun is a specific person, place, or thing

> I found *the* letter that I wanted.

when you have already referred to the noun

> I wanted an answer and soon got *the* answer I wanted.

when a superlative (the most, the best, the worst, the lowest, etc.) precedes the noun

> Annette is *the* youngest child in our family.

when a group of words (a phrase or clause) identifies the noun clearly.

> *The* life of a student is not always easy. [*Of a student* tells what kind of life you mean.]

when the noun you use is one of a kind

> I saw *the* Coliseum when I was in Rome.

28a-4
Do not use *a, an,* or *the* before a plural noun when you are making a general statement.

> SPECIFIC   I sat with the children next door.
> GENERAL   Children are in need of guidance.

SPECIFIC   I chopped the onions that were on the cutting board.
GENERAL   Teenagers often avoid eating onions before going on dates.

28b
Put cumulative adjectives in the proper order.

Adjectives can appear before nouns.

the happy child
the marble floor

They can also appear after linking verbs.

The child is happy.
The floor seems clean.

NOTE: See **4c** for help in recognizing and using adjectives with linking verbs.

Most adjectives appear before the nouns they are describing, and sometimes you will want to put two or three adjectives before a noun. These are called cumulative adjectives. There is a certain order that you need to follow when you use more than one adjective before a noun:

1. an article or a noun marker (a, an, the, his, their, Mary's, most, several, some, etc.)
2. an opinion word (lovely, simple, ugly, wild, wonderful, etc.)
3. a word that gives a physical description of size, shape, age, or color (large, short, square, old, young, blue, red, etc.)
4. an adjective of nationality or religion (Mexican, Thai, Catholic, Muslim, etc.)
5. a kind of material (cotton, gold, plastic, wood, etc.)
6. a noun used as an adjective (study room, bedroom lamp, etc.)

28b

The following are some cumulative adjectives that precede nouns in a logical order:

a lonely old man
Ely's red leather jacket
some large German knives
the diligent house sitter

Notice that in these examples there are no more than three adjectives before any noun. More than three would seem awkward to most readers.

28c
Do not omit the subject or verb of a clause or sentence or the word there *when it introduces the subject.*

Chapter **22** tells you to be careful not to omit little words like short verbs (is, was, etc.), prepositions (to, for, etc.), or short pronouns (it, she, etc.). Native speakers of English can often correct these errors through careful proofreading. You may find, however, that you sometimes omit words because such an omission is permitted in your native language, and you are not sure whether you need them when writing English. Here are some reminders about omissions that do not occur in English.

28c-1
Do not omit the verb of a sentence or other clause.

In English the verb of a sentence is necessary.

> WRONG   My friend here at last.
> RIGHT   My friend *is* here at last.

For practice recognizing and correcting this omission, see **22b**.

28c-2
Do not omit the subject of a sentence or another clause.

In English the subject always appears, except in commands or requests where the subject is *you* (understood).

> **Close the door.** [*You* is understood to be the subject.]

Include the subject in all other cases.

> WRONG   Want to see you next week.
> RIGHT   *I* want to see you next week.

28c-3
Do not omit *there* when it introduces the subject.

In **1b-3** you learned that *there* is sometimes used to introduce the subject of a sentence or clause. It is a necessary part of the sentence.

> WRONG   Are many reasons for my decision.
>
> RIGHT   *There* are many reasons for my decision.

28d
Be alert for certain problems with the use of verbs.

One of the biggest hurdles for any student for whom English is a second language is the verb. This is also a hurdle for native speakers of English. In fact, you may have noticed that Chapter 7, which is about verbs, is the longest in this book. The following sections already offer help on problems that both native and non-native speakers encounter in the use of verbs:

6a	subject–verb agreement
7a–7c	regular and irregular past and past participle forms
7d	present participles
7e	the verb *be*
7f	fixed form helpers (will, do, can, etc.)
7h–7i	verb tenses
7j	infinitives

There are, however, verb problems that may be troublesome for you but not for native speakers of English. This section offers help in those areas.

28d

28d-1
Know when to use the progressive (*-ing*) form of the verb.

Sections **7d** and **7h** tell you that the progressive (*-ing*) form suggests that action is continuing, but how do you know when you can use this form? The decision depends on whether you are using an action or a nonaction verb. A nonaction verb expresses a state, not an activity. The following are some common nonaction verbs:

appear or disappear	forget or remember	own	smell
be	hear	prefer	sound
belong	know	recognize	taste
consist	like or dislike	require	think
contain	love or hate	resemble	understand
desire	mean	see	want
feel	need	seem	wish

With some exceptions, you cannot use a nonaction verb in the progressive (-*ing*) form. You need to use the simple form of the verb.

WRONG	I was wanting a new car.
RIGHT	I *wanted* a new car.
WRONG	I am loving strawberry shortcake.
RIGHT	I *love* strawberry shortcake.
WRONG	That box will be containing the tools that you need.
RIGHT	That box will *contain* the tools that you need.

Since there are certain nonaction verbs that do sometimes use the progressive form, keep a list of these exceptions.

EXAMPLES   I am *thinking* of you.

Adele is *seeing* a therapist about her problems.

28d-2
Use transitive and intransitive verbs correctly.

Transitive verbs take direct objects; intransitive verbs do not.

TRANSITIVE	I bought a sweater.
INTRANSITIVE	I fell.

It is incorrect to use a direct object after a transitive verb.

WRONG	I fell the floor.
RIGHT	I fell on the floor.

A dictionary tells whether a verb is transitive or intransitive.

28d-3
Use the passive correctly.

Section **7e-3** tells you that a verb can be active (something is happening or someone is doing something) or passive (something is happening to someone or something).

| ACTIVE | We set the table. |
| PASSIVE | The table was set. |

Only transitive verbs (verbs that take direct objects) can appear in the passive.

WRONG	A terrible thing was happened. [*Happened* is intransitive; do not use the passive.]
RIGHT	A terrible thing happened.
RIGHT	The doctor examined the patient. [*Examined* is transitive; you can use the passive.]
RIGHT	The patient was examined.

28d-4
Know how to use two-word verbs.

Two-word verbs are verbs followed by prepositions or particles. Such a combination influences the meaning of the verb. For example, you can say

Give back the letter. [Let me have the letter that I had before.]
Give up the struggle. [Don't struggle any more.]
Give in to pressure. [Surrender to pressure.]
Don't give away the answer. [Don't let anyone know the answer.]

The particle of a transitive verb (a verb that takes a direct object) can appear right after the verb or be separated from the verb.

I *put on* my new dress.   OR   I *put* my new dress *on.*

If the direct object of a two-word verb is a noun, the particle may follow the verb,

I *cut up* the vegetables.

or it may be separated from the verb.

I *cut* the vegetables *up.*

28d

If the direct object is a pronoun, the particle must be separated from the verb.

> I *cut* them *up*.

The particle used with an intransitive verb (one that cannot take a direct object) must come immediately after the verb.

> I *came across* his name in my address book.

A complete list of two-word verbs would be very long; however, here are some common two-word verbs:

ask about	ask out	bring up	burn down (or up)
call off	clean up	come across	cut up
do over	drop in	drop off	drop out
fill up	give away	give back	give in
give up	go out	grow up	hand in
hang on	hang up	help out	look into
look over	look up	pick out	pick up
point out	put away	put back	put off (or put on)
quiet down	run across	run into	speak to
speak with	speak up	stay away	stay up
take off	take out	think of	think over
throw away	throw out	try on	turn down
turn on	wake up	watch out	(or turn up)
(or turn off)			wear out

An ESL dictionary gives the meanings of two-word verbs and tells you whether they are separable. You should soon begin to make your own list of these verbs as you see them in the books, magazines, and newspapers you read.

28d-5
Recognize verbs that are followed by gerunds and verbs that are followed by infinitives.

Section 7j deals with some of the problems students have using gerunds and infinitives. It tells you that a word ending in *-ing* can be a noun (gerund) when it names a person or thing.

> Too much noise can damage a person's *hearing*.

Section **7j** also tells you that an infinitive is a verb form with no ending. It is usually preceded by *to*.

I want *to learn* several languages.

You may find, however, that when you want to use a gerund or an infinitive after a main verb you are not sure which form to use.

My brother really needs (to get? getting?) a haircut.

In this case you need the infinitive: My brother really *needs to get* a haircut.

The best way to be really confident that you know which form to use is to start making a list of verbs that are followed by gerunds, verbs that are followed by infinitives, and verbs that can be followed by either form. Here is the beginning of such a list:

VERBS FOLLOWED BY GERUNDS BUT NOT BY INFINITIVES

admit	deny	imagine	practice
appreciate	discuss	mention	quit
avoid	enjoy	mind	resist
consider	escape	miss	risk
delay	finish	postpone	suggest

EXAMPLES   My mother *appreciated receiving* a note from Alicia.
I always *avoid doing* things that I dislike.

VERBS FOLLOWED BY INFINITIVES BUT NOT BY GERUNDS

agree	expect	mean	pretend	wait
appear	have	need	promise	want
ask	hope	offer	refuse	wish
decide	intend	plan	seem	force

EXAMPLES   A friend *offered to help* me with an assignment.
The Lees *hope to drive* to Los Angeles today.

28d

Some verbs require a noun or pronoun before the infinitive. This noun or pronoun tells the reader who is receiving the action of the verb.

VERBS THAT REQUIRE A NOUN OR PRONOUN BEFORE THE INFINITIVE

advise	cause	encourage	instruct	remind
allow	command	force	invite	require
ask	convince	have	persuade	tell

EXAMPLES I asked *Charlie to go* to the game with me.
          Remind *them to bring* along some heavy clothing.

There are also some verbs that can be followed by either a gerund or an infinitive, such as *begin, continue, start, love,* and *hate.* You may want to use them to start your list.

Begin writing your paper.   OR   *Begin to write* your paper.

EXERCISE

Underline the correct item in parentheses.

1. I sometimes get (advice, an advice) from people whether I expect (getting, to get) it or not.
2. A small car is often (a, the) best choice if someone needs (saving, to save) money.
3. (An ugly brown dog, A brown ugly dog) was digging up my yard.
4. (Are decorations, There are decorations) on (the Indian wool, the wool Indian) rug.
5. The money (was disappearing, disappeared) from (the black wooden, the wooden black) box yesterday.
6. I often make (mistakes, the mistakes) in my work; then I (do over it, do it over).
7. I (ran across his name, ran his name across) in the Cleveland telephone directory.

INDEX

ESL INDEX